Christopher Washburne

Sounding Salsa

Performing Latin Music in New York City

TEMPLE UNIVERSITY PRESS
Philadelphia

All attempts were made to locate the people in the photographs published in this book. If you believe you may be one of them, please contact the publisher at Temple University Press, 1601 N. Broad Street, Philadelphia, PA 19122. The publisher will be sure to include appropriate acknowledgment in subsequent editions of this book.

Temple University Press
1601 North Broad Street
Philadelphia PA 19122
www.temple.edu/tempress

Published 2008
Printed in the United States of America

♾ The paper used in this publication meets the requirements of the American National Standard for Information Sciences—Permanence of Paper for Printed Library Materials, ANSI Z39.48-1992

Library of Congress Cataloging-in-Publication Data

Washburne, Christopher, 1963–
Sounding salsa : performing Latin music in New York City / Christopher Washburne.
p. cm.
Includes bibliographical references (p.) and index.
ISBN-13: 978-1-59213-315-4 (cloth : alk. paper)
ISBN-10: 1-59213-315-0 (cloth : alk. paper)
ISBN-13: 978-1-59213-316-1 (pbk. : alk. paper)
ISBN-10: 1-59213-316-9 (pbk. : alk. paper)
1. Salsa (Music)—New York State—New York—History and criticism. 2. Salsa (Music)—New York State—New York—Social aspects. I. Title.
ML3535.5.W37 2008
781.64089'6807471—dc22 2007045407

2 4 6 8 9 7 5 3 1

For Maiken, August, and Isa

and in memory of Tito Puente, Ray Barretto,

Celia Cruz, Pete "El Conde" Rodríguez,

and Hector Lavoe.

Contents

Acknowledgments

This project stems from my research and performance in the New York salsa scene over the last eighteen years. Throughout that time I was greatly assisted by many fellow musicians, academic colleagues, mentors, professors, students, and friends, so numerous that it would require many pages to include all of their names. So I would like to collectively express my sincerest gratitude to all of the people whose support was vital in this project. There are some folks, however, who played a more prominent role and deserve special mention. With pleasure, I would like to acknowledge them at this time.

I must begin by expressing my deepest gratitude to five bandleaders who have passed away during the researching and writing of this project and with whom I had the honor of sharing the stage. I dedicate this book to the memory of Tito Puente, Ray Barretto, Celia Cruz, Pete "El Conde" Rodríguez, and Hector Lavoe. Playing and recording with Tito's band was a dream come true. His musicianship and professionalism never have been surpassed on the salsa scene. I learned more from him than from any other bandleader. His contribution to American music has been represented poorly in scholarly literature, and I only can hope that this will be rectified one day soon. Ray Barretto's musicality and jazz sensibility was truly unique and innovative in salsa. His encouragement during all those late-night hangs was so valuable to my musical growth. The electrifying experience of sharing the stage with Celia Cruz was exhilarating. Her performance technique, panache, and respectful demureness were such an inspiration. It was in Pete "El Conde" Rodríguez's band that I learned how to really play salsa. He was so encouraging and supportive. His vocal improvisations and refined performance style gave me the fundamental tools to excel in salsa performance. Hector Lavoe's unrelenting wit and swing will forever reverberate in my music. I miss them all dearly.

I would like to acknowledge some of the other bandleaders with whom I worked regularly during the writing of this book. Playing and recording for Eddie Palmieri was my biggest thrill. It was Eddie Palmieri's white album and Barry Rogers's trombone sounds that inspired my love for salsa. Eddie's spirit and inexorable left-handed grooves have made an indelible mark on my spirit. I thank him deeply for hiring me in his band. I am so grateful to Marc Anthony, La India, Tito Nieves, Ray Sepulveda, Raulín Rosendo, Sergio George, Johnny Rivera, Larry Harlow, Domingo Quiñones, Orlando "Watusi" Castillo, and Isidro Infante for the opportunity of sharing in their musical worlds.

This book centers on the experiences and lives of salsa musicians. Key to my research have been those musicians with whom I performed and hung out night after night, and who were willing to share their musical lives with me. I want to express my sincerest thanks to my good friends and fellow *salseros* Bobby Allende, Tony Barrero, Jimmy Bosch, Gil Colón, Hector Colón, Wilson "Chembo" Corniel, Barry Danielian, Jose Davila, George Delgado, Angel Fernandez, Bob Franceschini, Ricky Gonzalez, Oscar Hernandez, Ite Jeréz, Lewis Kahn, Angel "Cookie" Lebron, Eddie Montalvo, Pablo "Chino" Nuñez, Barry Olsen, Orlando Peña, Marc Quiñones, Rubén Rodríguez, Barry Rogers, Chris Rogers, Danny Rojo, Willie Ruíz, Bobby Sanabria, Claudette Sierra, John Silipote, Abiúd Troche, and Ray Vega. Their insights and feedback have been so integral to my work. I want to especially thank Leopoldo Pineda for giving me my first big break in the New York salsa scene. It was an honor to be asked to fill in for such a master trombonist. And I want to express my special thanks to John Walsh, who has been such a good friend and colleague and repeatedly has given so much. His contribution to this work has been invaluable.

Throughout my education I have been blessed with the opportunity of working with a number of teachers who have inspired deeper understanding and encouraged me to pursue my musical dreams. I want to thank Ran Blake, Richard Davis, William Richardson, John Swallow, and Les Thimmeg. I owe special thanks to Steven Cornelius, whose research, consultation, and encouragement over the years have been beneficial in so many ways and initially inspired my ethnomusicological research. Peter Manuel has been an inspirational teacher, mentor, and good friend over the years. His enthusiasm for Latin music ultimately convinced me to pursue ethnomusicological research on salsa. His incisive and thoughtful editorial style greatly enhanced this book. I so appreciate his patience and continued belief in my work.

Much of this work stems from my dissertation research, and I would like to acknowledge the valuable contributions of the committee members in that process. I would especially like to acknowledge the diligent work of my sponsor, Daniel Ferguson, whose patience and thoroughness enhanced this project in many ways. As a member of my committee, Dieter Christensen's support, guidance, and editorial comments were invaluable. And my other committee members, Linda Buckley-Green and Francisco Rivera-Batiz, provided insightful guidance. Aaron Fox deserves special mention here, as he not only served on the committee, but he also has been the most generous colleague and friend. His research in particular has been inspirational for me, and I so value his unwavering support over the years. I thank him for all of his constructive feedback and for always being there with encouraging words.

My colleagues at Columbia University continually have given their generous support and encouragement. In particular, I would like to thank Ian Bent, Deborah Bradley-Kramer, Susan Boynton, David Cohen, Joe Dubiel, Steven Feld, Walter Frisch, Brad Garton, Guiseppe Gerbino, Farah Griffin, Ellie Hisama, Jonathan Kramer, Fred Lerdahl, George Lewis, Robert O'Meally, Jeff Milarsky, Elaine Sisman, and Tim Taylor. And I would like to thank Kay Shelemay and Ingrid Monson for their support during my visiting semester at Harvard. It is so valuable to be working in an environment with such esteemed and inspiring colleagues.

Many parts of this book have benefited significantly from the feedback I received from the graduate and undergraduates students I taught over the years. There are too many to thank individually, so I will collectively thank them all for the great dialoguing. I have learned so much from them. I would like to individually thank four students who worked as my research assistants on this project—Matt Sakakeeny, Ryan Skinner, Brian Karl, and Simon Calle—whose diligent efforts greatly enhanced this work.

I want to thank Janet Francendese and everyone at Temple University Press for all their support and patience. And I thank the four anonymous reviewers for generously giving their time and constructive feedback. Several of my esteemed colleagues generously read earlier drafts of this work and gave constructive feedback. I am so grateful for their efforts and assistance. I thank especially Ellen Gray, Steve Loza, Jairo Moreno, and Ana Maria Ochoa.

I gratefully acknowledge the Sinfonia Foundation and the Mellon Foundation for their financial assistance in this research. Their support enabled my travel to Puerto Rico and Cuba. I thank Ramon Rodríguez, director of the Harbor Conservatory for the Performing Arts at the Boys and Girls Harbor School, for allowing access to their wonderful archives.

I am most grateful to the special people in my life who have been there for me unrelentingly throughout the long researching and writing process. First and foremost, I would like to thank my parents, Marv and Ellen Mell, for their love and constant support and for being my number-one fans; my nymph muse, Maiken, for her inspiration, love, and impeccable editorial skills; Dr. Zide for saving my life as well as my playing career with his brilliant cutting style; and to my two biggest joys of all, August and Isa.

Introduction

Salsa in New York

August 1992. Hector Lavoe is putting together a new band, making a comeback after a self-imposed hiatus during which he fought for his life, tried to beat addiction, and, as we would find out later, battled AIDS.[1] A rehearsal is scheduled for 7 P.M. in the basement of the Boys and Girls Harbor School ("Boys Harbor"), located in El Barrio (Spanish Harlem) on the corner of East 104th Street and 5th Avenue, a favorite spot for salsa bands to work out new arrangements. Why? Cheap rates, an out-of-the-way place that fans don't know about, and a location in the most historically significant neighborhood for Latin music in New York City. In fact, just blocks from Boys Harbor is where it all began back in the 1930s: Machito, Tito Puente, Eddie and Charlie Palmieri, everyone lived there. Most salsa musicians do not live in the neighborhood anymore, although many teach Latin music to kids and novices at the Harbor's after-school program, one of the few places where 15 bucks will get you a lesson with Tito Puente's *bongocero*.

Rehearsal begins just shy of 8 P.M. It was delayed while several musicians copped in the neighborhood. Copped what? Blow, *perico*, cocaine. Other musicians just straggled in late with no explanation, but no real need: No one complains about the late start. It's par for the course. Regardless of their tardiness, everyone who enters the room makes his rounds greeting everyone else. No one is left out. Acquaintances shake hands, friends embrace, everyone touches. It would be rude not to. The atmosphere is formal, yet casual. In contrast to the strict dress codes for performances (coordinated formal attire, typically), the preferred rehearsal garb is cutoff jeans (with freshly ironed creases), new white Nikes, T-shirts, baseball caps, and jerseys with such names as "Guillen" and "Martinez" emblazoned on the back (without accents). Spanish, English, and Spanglish are spoken simultaneously. Code switching is the norm. ("Oyeme . . . let's take it from the top . . . arriba! Vamonos . . . one . . . two . . . a one, two, three, four.") Everyone there understands at least part of it.

Dented metal folding chairs, music stands, and open instrument cases, all illuminated in a bright fluorescent glow, litter the small subterranean rehearsal space. A few framed Fania All-Stars concert posters from the 1970s hang on the wall; from them, such icons as Willie Colón, Ruben Blades, Ray Barretto, Johnny Pacheco, and even a young Hector Lavoe gaze out from the past, overseeing the next generation of *salseros*.

A much-older-looking Lavoe arrives around 8:30 P.M. with an entourage of family, friends, and amateur musicians/dealers. Though he can hardly walk and is strung out and weak, when he grabs the mike his slurred speech sculpts crafty witticisms and the inventive irony for which he is famous and so loved. His real name is Hector Juan Perez; *Lavoe* is a derivation of *La Voz* (translated as "The Voice," but really meaning "The Voice of the People," or, better yet, "Through Him the People Are Given a Voice"). He sings "Oye mi gente . . ." ("Listen, my people . . .").

The sound system is deafening within that small space where walls, windows, and doors can do little to contain the music. The sheer volume is transgressive as it penetrates the cinder block, crossing boundaries and bleeding into the street. With cowbells ringing, maracas shaking, hands and sticks beating congas, bongos, and timbales, *coristas* (chorus singers) harmonizing 1970s anthems of Puerto Rican pride crowd around three microphones. Piano and bass amps are pushed just short of distortion (sometimes just past), trumpet and trombone players reach deep into their diaphragms to compete, dynamic marking . . . BLAST!

The twelve musicians—all male, several Puerto Rican and Nuyorican,[2] a Dominican, a Colombian, and myself (an Anglo), twenty- and thirtysomethings, some new to the city, others born and raised there, some of the best musicians on the scene—blast off, relishing in the old and outdated style of *salsa dura* (hard), not that new commercial *monga* (limp) shit everyone now plays. Improvisation, *sabor* (flavor), fire, *filin* (feeling), Latino pride, and *clave* are the keys in which these canonized classics are written, played, and remade.

Both the weather and the aesthetic are hot. No air-conditioning relieves this stifling New York summer evening. The pulsating rhythms coming from the instruments and the speakers provide the only air movement. The neighborhood children, most of whom live just around the corner in the public housing projects that dominate the East Harlem cityscape, up past their bedtimes (hard to sleep in this heat!), crowd around the barred and sidewalk-level windows to listen and dance to the music their parents were raised on, sounds that emanate from below as the musicians sweat.

At 10:15 P.M., *conguero* Eddie Montalvo gets up from his drums to rap about a musical passage with Gil "Pulpo" (Octopus) Colón, Lavoe's longtime pianist. The door of the rehearsal room swings open, and a young Dominican hit man—whom many of us recognize because he always sits at the same table near the stage at Fuego Fuego (Fire Fire), a club at 157th Street and Broadway owned by C., a Dominican dealer who got busted with fifteen kilos in his trunk, they say—bursts into the room, brandishing a large gun. Pointing the gun at the empty chair behind the congas, he asks, "Where's Eddie Montalvo?" Stunned, but not too stunned, we collectively band together: No one responds. We are a band, even more so now. Montalvo remains silently concealed behind Colón. The gunman orders all of us to line up against the wall as he threateningly points his gun at each of us. In a last ditch effort to lure out Montalvo, the hit man throws the conga drums out into the hall. No one moves. After a pause, he yells, "This is from Ramon!" and fires the gun twice into the ceiling before fleeing. As the bullets ricochet above our heads, I crouch next to trumpeter Ray Vega, praying. The music is silenced. The children are no longer at the window. Everyone splits before the police come. This incident is a matter that will be handled internally, in a manly fashion, *mano a mano*.

The trouble was fueled by an incident that occurred one month earlier, when veteran musician Montalvo took a stand against common salsa business practices (this is not usually done). Ramon, an established bandleader, hired Montalvo for a gig in Philly. Montalvo, along with the other band members, arrived in Philadelphia, a two-hour commute from New York, and waited several hours for Ramon's arrival. Ramon never showed up (this sometimes happens). The irate club owner sent the band back to New York without pay (this occasionally happens). Ramon never gave an explanation for his absence, nor did he respond to messages Montalvo left demanding payment for the canceled gig. The evening of Lavoe's rehearsal, as Montalvo arrived at Boys Harbor, Ramon, coincidentally, just arrived to rehearse his new band, since several musicians had quit after the Philly incident. Words were exchanged. Tempers flared. No resolution. When Ramon refused the request for compensation, Montalvo resolved to make Ramon pay in other ways (this is unusual). Montalvo then ventured out to the street and vandalized Ramon's Mercedes by breaking all of the head- and taillights (this is really unusual). Montalvo returned to Lavoe's rehearsal and began to play. Ramon sent the hit man in retaliation (this is *extremely* unusual).

The following week I received a message on my answering machine from Ramon. "I'm sorry that you were there last week, Chris, because it didn't have anything to do with you. I want you to know that Eddie and I have worked it out. Everything is cool now. And I hope you are not scared of me and will still play with my band because I have lots of gigs coming up." Several percussionists had banded together and gone to Ramon's house in New Jersey to threaten the safety of his family if anything happened to Montalvo. Therefore, it was "worked out." "Everything was cool," then. I played for Ramon only once more, just so I could tell him face to face, man to man, how stupid he had been. I saved the tape from my answering machine, too. I still have it.

This incident became one of the most popular "salsa stories" among musicians and has been disseminated throughout the salsa community ever since the night it happened, told, retold, and remade. I continue that tradition. Ramon's lack of judgment, his endangerment of twelve musicians, and his decision to hire someone to inflict bodily harm on or even to kill Montalvo was condemned by the entire salsa community. However, club owners still hired him. And Ramon continued to perform regularly with his band, some of whom were present at the ill-fated Lavoe rehearsal. Really.

Violence, community, drugs, cultural identity, exploitation, interculturality, and, above all, such beautiful music. Salsa allures me, yet I am troubled at times by the difficult conditions that my friends and fellow musicians endure to be salsa musicians. I needed to make sense of it all. That night in August 1992, I came home and began writing about salsa in New York.

I have written this book from the perspective of musicians.[3] Not all salsa musicians, but professional salseros who live in New York City and work in the highest echelons of the industry, doing the majority of the recording and performing with the most famous bands. Their/our/my perspective is captured by a photo taken in 1998 at a street festival on East 107th Street and 3rd Avenue, in the heart of El Barrio, not far from Boys Harbor.

Shot from the trombonist's position at the back of the stage looking outward, just behind the music clipped to the stand, the photo shows a perspective against the grain, gazing in the opposite direction of the thousands of onlookers, but following the trajectory of the sound. The police barricades read DO NOT CROSS, but the traffic lights are green. Oh, how the sounds, images, and sung ideas disregard those prohibitive fixtures and flow freely between the audience and the musicians. The band, though elevated on the stage, remains firmly grounded, tied to the community, rooted to the people . . . "peopleness." No possibility of containment, yet bounded in some ways by the music's rich cultural history. Geographically, culturally, ethnically, and racially . . . the community transcends the authoritatively imposed order

Figure I.1 Domingo Quiñones singing at a street festival in Spanish Harlem in 1998. *(Photograph by Miguel de Casenave.)*

while simultaneously being shaped by place, class, race, ethnicity, nationality, and cultural affiliations in complicated ways.

The photo's vantage point frames singer Domingo Quiñones—who is Puerto Rican but lives in New York City from time to time—as he stands centered and draped in the Puerto Rican flag while singing *soneos* (improvised lyrics) about his love for Puerto Rico, positioned between a conga drum (an instrument that symbolizes salsa's African ancestry and more recent Cuban genealogy) and timbales (double-headed tunable drums derived from the European timpani, acknowledging a colonial past that remains so present). Beyond the stage, the audience, awash in red, white, and blue (just one star and five stripes on these flags, even though the flag-wavers all carry U.S. passports, acknowledge the colonial present), sings along with the *coros*, whose repetitions serve as mantras for cultural pride ("Que cante mi gente," meaning "Let my people sing").[4] No guns fire today, just *orgullo profundo* (profound pride). This perspective shows the music looking out from the inside, where Puerto Rico is centered; awnings declaring AMERICAN and SAVERAMA (which is even more American!) frame the margins. The hegemonic American culture is temporarily relegated to the margins in this place, El Barrio.

Embodying several different layers of subjectivity, my dual roles as scholar and performer create an ongoing dynamic of alternating perspectives: At some points, my position as observer is one of identity, merging with the object of scientific investigation (I am playing that music seen in the foreground of the photo); at other points in my analysis, I strategically exploit my ability to retain a critical distance by assuming an observing participant role, introducing an alien terminology, a degree of otherness in the relation between my own discourse and the observed field. I step back, set my trombone aside, grab my camera, and take a photo.

From this inside-out perspective, I conduct an analytical and interpretive ethnographic journey into New York salsa of the 1990s. Using salsa musicians, performance events, and the salsa scene as the objects of study, I focus on processes embedded in performance events, music structure, and discursive practices in an effort to explore relationships among broader cultural issues. In particular, I examine how musicians navigate their everyday lives, grappling with the intercultural tensions and commercial pressures that are so pronounced on the salsa scene. I discuss their attitudes, working environment, education, difficulties they face, and how they conduct their business. I also explore the organizational structures, recording processes, rehearsals, and gigging of salsa bands. I pay particular attention to how bands create a sense of community, privilege *la gente* (the people) over artistic and commercial concerns, and incite cultural pride during performance events. I also examine how violence, the illicit drug trade, and issues of gender inform sound structure, salsa aesthetics, and performance practice. I conclude this study with a discussion of salsa style in the 1990s, focusing on how certain structural principles involved in music-making (e.g., clave) and the intercultural dynamics of Puerto Rico and New York inform performance practice and guide stylistic change, respectively.

From my perspective, the 1990s was a remarkably vibrant and pivotal era in salsa music history, marked by a second generation of salseros who coopted the music of their parents, reinventing and transforming the salsa scene with sounds and expressions that better represented their own experiences as Latino[5] youth growing up in New York City. This generation experienced a further expansion of the salsa industry into the global arena that resulted in the establishment of a number of significant centers of production outside of New York City. These developments introduced an overt commercialism to the music, expanded audiences, and heightened the stakes in the debates over cultural ownership, all of which prompted significant changes in style and performance practice. Regardless, I argue that the fundamental processes at work in the 1960s and 1970s, when salsa emerged as an identifiable Latin popular dance music genre, remained remarkably centered in these newer forms. As such, at the core of salsa music-making and performance lie the tensions involved in the dynamics of intercultural exchange, so fundamental to the cultural milieu of New York City and, more recently, throughout the "globalized" salsa communities, where diverse people collide and collude in their navigations of their everyday lives.[6] Through salsa, tensions of ethnic and national differences play out in fascinating ways as the music serves as an arena for contestations concerning ownership, authenticity, and representation.

At the same time, by embracing the cultural heterogeneity so fundamental in its production, salseros forge a counter-hegemonic space where diverse communities are brought together through performative constructions of *Latinidad* and a consciously constructed pan-Latino ethnic identity. Salsa events agilely function as communal glue, even though they remain highly contested spaces. I find the term "counter-hegemonic" more useful than "subaltern" in the case of salsa because it emphasizes the idea of an alternative power structure (Rowe and Schelling 1991). It better represents the position of El Barrio (the place from which salsa emerged) in relation to the rest of New York City, how the salsa community negotiates and grapples with the social disparities so endemic in this relationship, and the creation of an emergent transgressive space where marginalized communities take center stage and hegemonic forces are kept at bay (see Figure I.1, above). Indeed, the role of place is central in shaping performance practice and aesthetics. The everyday social issues faced by residents of El Barrio, and the barrios of the South Bronx and Brooklyn—such as violence, the illicit drug trade, and economic and political marginalization—remain significant factors in how salsa in New York sounds, how it is performed, and how it is produced. But these factors are not based solely upon bounded physical locations; rather, they extend beyond into the realms of the psychical, cultural, historical, and social. I am guided here by the writings of Ed Casey, who urges a conception of place as an "open system," fleshlike and porous, something that we continually have to discover and invent new forms of understanding (Casey 1996). For salseros, El Barrio remains emergent; they rely upon a variety of strategic conceptions of that place to serve as tools in forging an alternative social milieu that unites the disparate groups and diverse communities living in those spaces.

Figure I.2 Mural entitled "Nuestra Barrio" on a building facade in Spanish Harlem, 1998. Included on this triptych are portraits of Puerto Rican composer Rafael Hernández and salsa singer Marc Anthony, depicting music, and specifically salsa, as significant symbols associated with *El Barrio*. *(Photograph by Christopher Washburne.)*

Indeed, salsa's alterity has been fundamental from its inception. Salsa emerged in New York in the 1960s in the aftermath of the Cuban embargo, in the shadows of rock and roll, and at the forefront of political and racial strife in the United States—especially for Latino communities, which adopted the rhetoric and stances of the civil rights movement. Salsa initially served as what Jorge Duany calls "the unmistakable voice of the Puerto Rican barrio," being marketed as alternative, representative, and voice-giving to an unheard and disenfranchised people (Duany 1984: 198). Though historically salsa was "bounded" by the confines of the barrios in New York City and played and produced mainly by Puerto Rican New Yorkers (Nuyoricans), over time its popularity transcended those original city blocks as Latino populations grew, more Latino enclaves formed in other cities in the United States, and the music began appealing to a growing international market.[7] Partially out of a need to appease this expanding market and the reality of who was making and consuming the music, as well as from a shift in the political landscape (at least publicly) from divisive nationalistic politics toward the establishment of coalitions among various Latin American and Caribbean nations in the United

States (*la raza latina*), salsa producers soon began fashioning the music as something much more multivocal—"Nuestra cosa latina" ("Our Latin Thing").[8]

Throughout these changes, however, salsa as symbolic cultural expression never became divorced from its barrio roots. Instead, as a cultural construct, El Barrio underwent a conceptual shift, emerging more as a symbol of shared experience based on real or imagined common linguistic (Spanish), cultural (Latino), historical (colonization), and geographic bonds (Caribbean and Latin America) rather than the boundaries of a particular neighborhood. Reminiscent of Arjun Appadurai's ideas concerning the contemporary world as one in which "groups are no longer tightly territorialized, spatially bounded, historically unselfconscious, or culturally homogenous," salsa and the groups that associated themselves with the music were "deterritorialized" through travel, immigration, commerce, and communication (Appadurai 1991: 191, 193). Similarly, conceptions of El Barrio also became deterritorialized, morphing into a metabarrio of sorts, an imagined international shared space of commonalities based upon experiences of immigration, discrimination, language differences, and culture clashes that suspended the locally inflected specificities and, instead, embraced broader postcolonial, sociopolitical trends. Salsa was the music at the forefront of these trends for Latinos living in New York City.

As such, I conceive of salsa as an "inter-Latino" and "trans-Caribbean" music, regardless of the fact that it emerged from the cultural climate of New York City, owes much of its stylistic particularities to African American expressions (jazz and R&B in particular) and Cuban music practices as performed in New York in the 1940s and 1950s, and has maintained a vibrant presence on the musical landscape in the United States for more than forty years (ignored by most scholars of American music, I might add). These labels assert social difference and reflect the cultural resistance that is so essential to salsa performance. As Hernando Calvo-Ospina points out, even though salsa is a mass-mediated and -produced popular music, it strongly resists assimilation in the English-speaking hegemonic U.S. culture, retaining a perspective of alterity despite its dependence on U.S. economic structures (Calvo-Ospina 1995: 56). Salsa subverts and colludes with the mainstream, depending on an imagined conventional U.S. culture that it sets out to resist. It operates in a shadow economy, at times appearing to be aligned with mainstream cultural constructs, and at other times remaining on the margins, unseen, often heard but not recognized when souped-up Toyotas with tinted windows and open hatchbacks cruise down Broadway with sound systems blasting. As the cowbells dopplerize past, those who cannot recognize the myriad meanings and associations of those clave-inflected rhythms are nonetheless forced into a sonic space of difference. Street conversations are

Figure I.3 Bicycle revelers in Spanish Harlem celebrating during the Puerto Rican Day Parade. *(Photograph by Christopher Washburne.)*

quelled temporarily, if only for moments until the sounds subside. Varying degrees of misunderstanding accompany a microcosm of cultural mixing. The reaction to those rhythms ranges from annoyance to engagement, at times creating a momentary and spontaneous concrete dance floor. Salsa opens an alternative space.

Because Puerto Ricans and Nuyoricans primarily drive those Toyotas, playing, producing, and consuming the music in New York, many mark salsa as something essentially Puerto Rican. Indeed, Puerto Ricans and Nuyoricans often use salsa to incite nationalistic pride. New York's Puerto Rican Day Parade, which features numerous salsa bands, provides just one example among many of how salsa is engaged for nationalistic purposes. Experiencing the parade, one cannot avoid noticing what Frances Aparicio labels the "*gran familia puertorriqueña,*" which is the "central political, cultural, and social rhetoric on the island" that aims to purport an emblematized image of a "unified, homogeneous, and harmonic society devoid of racial and social conflict" (Aparicio 1998: 5). This unified public image politically empowers the Puerto Rican community within a larger New York City context. However, it does not reflect the divisive and disparate groups found within the island and within the Nuyorican community. Associating salsa solely with a monolithic assertion of Puerto Rican and

Nuyorican culture without interrogating the intracultural dynamics involved in such an association is problematic, to say the least. Moreover, not accounting for the broader intercultural transethnic, transracial, transgeographic, and transnational dynamics fundamental to the music's production misses an important, large part of the picture. The heteroglossia of the intercultural dialectics involved in salsa music-making and production makes it so pliable to serve simultaneously as Puerto Rican, Cuban, Colombian, Venezuelan, and New York music. Salsa can and does represent a multitude of diverse perspectives and richly signifies a diverse set of perspectives. What is obvious from the wide range of discursive interpretations related to the music is that a prismatic study of salsa is essential to attend to its multifarious uses, the wide-ranging claims of ownership, and the myriad ways that the music is central to cultural and personal expressivity.

Marking salsa as something "inter-Latino" and "trans-Caribbean" assists in this venture and suggests an alternative genealogy: that of the Caribbean. The Caribbean, in this case, is not solely a geographic location, but also a conceptual framing that is marked by migration, immigration, movement, and flow. As Puerto Rican bandleader and pianist Papo Lucca observes, "[Salsa] is a more contemporary treatment of the Caribbean music that originated in Cuba . . . it's a movement that has transcended all national affiliations to become a musical phenomenon of the entire Caribbean."[9] Antonio Benítez-Rojo is particularly helpful here; he writes, "To refer to the culture of the Caribbean as geography—other than to call it a meta-archipelago—is a debilitating and scarcely productive project" (Benítez-Rojo 1996: 24). Rather, his postmodern reading interprets the Caribbean at large as sharing tropisms that are girded by migration, travel, and search for fluvial and marine routes. They transcend borders and are emplaced in multiple ways. For Benítez-Rojo, the Caribbean is an island bridge that extends globally and is difficult to pin down geographically: "There is an island that repeats itself until transforming into a meta-archipelago and reaching the most widely separated trans-historical frontiers of the globe" (Benítez-Rojo 1996: 24). At the core of these ideas is a ruptured history that, according to Aimé Césaire, all Caribbean people share: "Throughout their history, people in the Caribbean . . . have suffered a great deal. . . . What we have suffered from the most, more than any other people, is really alienation, in other words, the lack of knowledge of oneself. . . . The Antillean being is a human being who is deprived of his own self, of his history, of his traditions, of his beliefs . . . he is an abandoned being" (Sephocle 1992: 360). Jorge Duany adds the important point that, during colonial times, both European and African cultures in the Caribbean were "equally uprooted, in the process of adapting to an alien environment . . . incapable of fully reproducing their ancestral lifestyles in the colonial setting" (Duany

1984: 188). I examine salsa in light of these postcolonial conditions fully reverberant with alienation, hardship, homeland, uprootedness, diaspora, cultural pride, and displacement. It is from this metacontextual backdrop that I enter the salsa stages of New York City in the 1990s. As the processes of the colonial past repeat, salsa musicians must grapple with and navigate through multilayered complexities that often create extremely difficult working conditions in which to make beautiful music. These conditions inform their sonic expressions in elusive and subtle ways. The study of these conditions and their correlative musical expressions are the subject of this book.

Salsa History

> "To search for the first moment in either time or space is to incur shipwreck on the shoals of Pure Reason."[10]
>
> —Ed Casey

I now turn to the historical backdrop from which I conducted my fieldwork. My aim is not to construct a comprehensive historical narrative here, but rather to highlight significant moments and trends that are particularly salient to the development of New York salsa in the 1990s.[11]

Salsa's emergence was contingent upon the vibrant Latino immigrant communities that settled in East Harlem in the first half of the twentieth century. By the late 1920s, Spanish Harlem was established as the center for Latin music production, performance, and business in New York City. In fact, salsa's emergence began just around the corner from Boys Harbor. In 1927, on Madison Avenue, between 113th and 114th streets, Victoria Hernández opened Almacenes Hernández, the first Puerto Rican–owned record store, which soon became a record label, booking agency, and management company for Latino musicians. In 1930, her brother, Rafael Hernández, wrote "Lamento Borincano" ("Puerto Rican Lament"), the unofficial national anthem of Puerto Rico, in a neighborhood restaurant. Throughout the 1930s, Gabriel Oller's Tatay's Spanish Music Center on Fifth Avenue and East 110th Street was the preferred meeting place for Latino musicians. It was the first stop for those "fresh off the boat" who were looking for work. In the mid-1920s, the Golden Casino, on East 111th Street and 5th Avenue, and the Park Palace Caterer's Hall, located on the corner of 110th Street and 5th Avenue, were the first places in the city to host Latin dances. Many of the most influential musicians and bandleaders lived in this community. Longtime residents Frank "Machito" Grillo and Tito Puente now have streets named in their honor. Machito Square is the stretch of East 111th Street between Third and Lexington Avenues, and Tito Puente Way extends the entire length

Figure I.4 Machito Square in *El Barrio.* *(Photograph by Christopher Washburne.)*

of East 110th Street. Charlie and Eddie Palmieri lived on East 112th Street and Madison Avenue. And the list goes on and on.

The residents of East Harlem in the early part of the twentieth century included people from a variety of Latin American countries, but Puerto Ricans represented by far the largest numbers due to that island's unique relationship with the United States. In 1898, Puerto Rico was ceded to the United States as a result of the Spanish-American War, beginning a long and complex relationship of intercultural exchange. As the new colonial power, the United States quickly established regular travel and trade routes upon which an immigration wave soon followed. Within the United States, the Puerto Rican population grew rapidly, especially after the United States began granting citizenship to Puerto Ricans in 1917, and later in the aftermath of the collapse of the coffee industry in 1930. In 1910, it was estimated that 5,000 Puerto Ricans were living in the United States; by 1930, the number had grown to 45,000. A second, even larger immigration wave began after World War II, facilitated by Puerto Rico's acquisition of its commonwealth status in 1952. By 1960, there were 600,000 Puerto Ricans living in the United States (U.S. Census of 1960), and by 1980, it was believed that one million Puerto Ricans were living in New York City alone. As these numbers grew, so did the demand for music.

The burgeoning community in East Harlem, which eventually spread to the other boroughs (the Bronx, especially), did not exist in isolation, but, rather, was engaged in various ways with the surrounding cultural milieu, in particular with the African American communities living in close proximity.

Figure I.5 Tito Puente Way in *El Barrio*. *(Photograph by Christopher Washburne.)*

Ruth Glasser has examined how Puerto Ricans became caught up in the rigidly biracialized North American society, and like African Americans, faced increasing segregation and discrimination. She writes, "their musical development in New York City music must be understood within the context of opportunities for black artists" (Glasser 1995: 66–67). Confronted with many of the same prejudices and difficulties as black musicians, many early-immigrant musicians were forced to either pass for white or black, working in whichever scene would accept them. In response to these difficult conditions, many allied themselves with African American social movements, playing a role (though often ignored) in the racial formation of the United States. J. Lorand Matory importantly observes that "the Harlem Renaissance of the 1920s and the Black Power Movement of the 1960s extensively involved Afro-Caribbean immigrants in the reformulation of African-American collective identity" (Matory 1999: 42). This affiliation would be a significant factor in the emergence of salsa in the 1960s.

Regardless of the large number of Puerto Ricans living in New York City throughout the 1930s, '40s, and '50s, Cuban styles (*son*, rumba, conga, *guaracha*, mambo, and cha-cha) dominated. Many factors contributed to the popularity of Cuban music in the United States, including Cuba's economic dominance in the Caribbean, its close proximity to the United States, and a vibrant sheet music industry. By the 1920s, the Cuban son had evolved into a cohesive set of commercial popular styles, and, starting in 1930, RCA Victor began an aggressive campaign to monopolize the recording industry in Cuba and internationalize its popular appeal (Manuel 1991b: 104).[12] U.S.-based record companies RCA Victor, Columbia, and Decca dominated Latin music throughout the 1940s, capitalizing on the music's exotic appeal to white audiences. These white-owned and -operated majors tended to limit diversity in style, producing music about which the executives knew almost nothing. However, the recording strike in 1942–44 by the American Federation of Musicians (AFM, the musician's union) and the dispute in 1941 between the royalty collection agencies—the American Society of Composers, Authors and Producers (ASCAP), and Broadcast Music, Inc. (BMI) that led to the banishment of all ASCAP-associated composers from radio airplay—prompted an upsurge in "alternative" music production that served niche markets in more innovative ways. Since Latin music was not covered under the auspices of these agencies, producers of Latin music were not affected by the strike, and, thus, benefited by the emergence of a number of small independent labels that were dedicated solely to Latin music production; these included SMC, Tico, Alegre, TR, Montuno, Coco, and Salsoul, among others. These companies supported a wide range of experimentation, and the 1950s proved to be one of the most fertile eras for Latin music performance in New York. In particular, blendings of African American and Latin music styles spawned striking and imaginative Latin jazz mixings and innovative approaches to the mambo, cha-cha, and, later, *pachanga* and *boogaloo* genres, all of which provided the foundation for the development of salsa. This designation to a niche market remained commonplace until the late 1990s, relegating Latin music productions to the domain of small independent labels. Excluded from the mainstream music industry in New York, the business of Latin music would remain separate and distinct, and often a different set of structures and unique ways of doing business were established that operated independently from the mainstream.

In the 1960s, the social landscape of the New York Latin music scene changed dramatically. First, the cessation of diplomatic relations between the United States and Cuba in 1962 and the subsequent economic and travel restrictions greatly reduced the influence of Cuban music styles, opening new opportunities for other Latino communities. Second, the dominance of rock and roll led to a decline in Latin music's popularity, especially among English-speaking youth. On the one hand, this situation caused economic difficulties for Latin musicians as performance opportunities dwindled; on the other hand, it prompted a new wave of experimentation as musicians sought to develop a new sound that would capture the next generation of audiences. Third, the civil rights movement profoundly changed the political climate within the barrios as many Latinos adopted similar modes of protest and organization (Lyndon Johnson passed the Civil Rights Act in 1964). Fourth, by this time Latino populations in New York had grown large enough to support a music scene that was separate from the English-speaking mainstream. Indeed, in 1961, WADO was the first radio station to adopt an all-Spanish-language format.

Young musicians reacted to these developments by seeking a new sound that would capture the sentiments of the street and speak to Latino youth living in the New York barrios. Rejecting the assimilation goals of immigrant communities of the past (i.e., that of their parents), which sought economic prosperity and a modicum of acceptance into mainstream Anglo American culture, these new artists turned to their own culture for inspiration and support. With American racial conflicts coming to the political forefront and frustration growing from continual prejudicial obstacles barring Puerto Ricans and other Latinos from attaining upward mobility, a shift toward a more pluralistic stance began. The Young Lords, a New York–based militant and activist Puerto Rican organization, reacted by calling for Latinos to be proud of their heritage and to view it as a strength rather than a hindrance. Their activism is credited for creating a new sense of pride of being Latino. El Barrio became a "cauldron of militant assertiveness and artistic creativity" (Manuel 1995: 73). These changes in the political climate were concurrent with the advent of salsa and were intrinsically tied to its emergence as a music style. As Roberta Singer writes, "The large and powerful Latino identity movements of the late 1960s and early 1970s, with their focus not only on social and economic justice but on seeking their roots of their own cultures, brought about a renewed interest in traditional music forms on the part of younger New York Puerto Ricans" (Singer 1983: 139). The music originating from the New York barrios then became more culturally introspective (i.e., made for and by Latinos), incorporated a wider range of traditional music from the Caribbean, and often included politically charged lyrics. Using the Cuban son as the foundation and building upon the Latin and jazz mixings of the mambo and the Latin soul, and rock mixings of boogaloo, the next generation of Latin musicians in New York City developed a new style that had, at its core, an aesthetic of high energy and an unrelentingly hard-driving sound that was viewed as uniquely of the New York barrios. This new sound would eventually be referred to as *salsa dura* (hard salsa).

The establishment of Fania Records in 1964 must be understood against the backdrop of the Cuban embargo, the wane of Latin music markets, the political fervor of the times, and the emergence of this new style of music. This seminal record company, founded by Dominican flautist and bandleader Johnny Pacheco and his Italian American lawyer, Jerry Masucci, had as its main objective the revitalization of the Latin music scene by transforming music emerging from New York's barrios into a commercially viable commodity. Their efforts resulted in salsa becoming an international phenomenon, with the music being widely associated, especially with respect to barrio culture in New York City, with Latino essence in a way that is analogous to the word "soul" as a description for black American essence (Baron 1977: 217). Pacheco commented, "Blacks had Motown, the Whites or Anglos had their own sound, and here we come with a different sound for Latin music" (Contreras 2006).

A dispute with Pacheco's former record company precipitated the formation of Fania Records. In 1960, Pacheco had signed with Al Santiago's Alegre Records and quickly became a partner, assisting in productions and bringing new artists to the label. In a dispute over royalty payments, Pacheco left Alegre in 1964. Together with Masucci, his divorce lawyer at the time, he borrowed $3,000 to record his next album, *Cañonazo* (LP 325), with his group Pacheco y su Charanga. The recording included a composition by Cuban composer Rolando Bolaños entitled "Fania Funché." According to Pacheco, that is where the record company's name originated: "The word is catchy not only for Latinos but for Anglos as well, we wanted to reach all markets" (Padura-Fuentes 2003: 58). However, there is some contention concerning the true meaning of *Fania*. Cesar Miguel Rondón simply states that it is a female name (Rondón 1980: 48). Pacheco claimed that it meant "family" in an unspecified African language (Contreras 2006). Larry Harlow claims that there was a café in Havana named Fanía where he and Masucci used to hang out in the late 1950s. And musicians involved with the record company in its earliest days believe that Fania was the name of a drug-smuggling ring operating in Mexico, although the connection between Masucci and that outfit is unclear and based on hearsay.

Pacheco and Masucci started by selling records out of Pacheco's old Mercedes trunk and realized they were on to something when more than 100,000 units of their first record sold. They then started signing a slew of other artists; the first included Bobby Valentín, Larry Harlow, Willie Colón, Hector Lavoe, and Ismael Miranda. The rhetoric of "family" was central to Fania, even though Masucci and Pacheco employed ruthless business tactics that included underpaying musicians, buying up all of the competition (other small labels), securing radio airtime through elaborate payola schemes, and establishing a monopoly of club bookings in New York, often through the use of heavy-handed tactics. Regardless, Pacheco stated that his philosophy with Fania artists was to "respect the rights of musicians and make them feel like they were a part of a family" (Padura-Fuentes 2003: 58). The establishment of the Fania All-Stars in 1971, a group consisting of bandleaders signed to Fania and highly regarded musicians who regularly recorded with them, enabled the label to showcase all of their talent while portraying a unified family of salseros. This notion of family extended beyond the musicians and was marketed to the communities to which they targeted their sales. This strategy capitalized on the newfound cultural pride being incited within Latino neighborhoods, as well as the calls for a unified Latino consciousness by new political movements. Fania deliberately constructed salsa as an exclusively Latino cultural expression, a discourse that reverberated through the barrios and swiftly transformed the fledgling company into an economic powerhouse. Though still considered an independent label compared to the majors, by the mid-1970s Fania accounted for 70 to 80 percent of all salsa record sales.[13] Singer Ruben Blades pointed out that there were both positive and negative aspects to Fania's monopoly: "Masucci was clever enough to understand the potential of the music and he made it big . . . he facilitated the talent's opportunity, but he ended up keeping all of their money . . . if it hadn't been for Jerry Masucci and Fania, the impact of salsa music would never have occurred . . . he ripped off everybody . . . but there was nowhere else to go. Fania was the only game in town" (Polin 1996: 6).

In order to accomplish such success, Fania needed to distance postrevolutionary Latin music in New York from Cuba, both as an economic necessity due to the U.S. government-imposed sanctions and because it conveniently opened a space for others to stake their claim of ownership. Even though much of the repertoire recorded by the label was composed by Cuban composers, Fania began substituting the initials D. R. (meaning *derechos reservados*, or "rights reserved") for the composers' names in the record liner notes. In this way, the prolific Cuban contribution was obscured, distanced, and denied. Without documentation of publishing and composition rights, ensuring that royalty payments were properly distributed was difficult (Fania was notorious for not paying royalties). Fania further promulgated an anti-Cuban stance in its 1971 release of *Nuestra Cosa Latina* (*Our Latin Thing*), a promotional film in which live concert scenes from the Cheetah dance club in New York were spliced with a montage of street scenes of New York's barrios, visually positing salsa as inherently of those streets. Their later films went further by including montages of Africa and African musicians. The obvious suggestion was that this barrio expression was intrinsically tied to "Mother Africa," which conveniently played into the popular pan-Africanist discourse of the day; it also assisted in the erasure of the Cuban influence, the route many of those African roots took in order to proliferate in the New York barrios. Additionally, Fania passed over many Cuban artists with established careers in New York City, refusing to sign the likes of Arsenio Rodríguez, for instance. This omission is particularly significant considering that Rodríguez continued to perform regularly during the initial rise of Fania, and, as David García (2006) has pointed out, his performance practice, arranging style, and compositions heavily influenced Fania's early productions. Recognition only came after his death in 1970, when Larry Harlow recorded his *Tribute to Arsenio* album (SLP 00404). For Fania, omitting Cuba in salsa opened the music up for greater pan–Latin American identification and, eventually, greater record sales and profits.

Marketing this new music was a central concern for Fania. Prior to the 1970s, Latin music either fell under the marketing rubric of tropical, which covered a wide range of music, or it was listed in a genre-specific way (mambo, cha-cha, etc.). Fania wanted a new appellative that would differentiate the music from its antecedents, especially from Cuban styles. Salsa, literally meaning "sauce," would prove to be the catchy marketing label they sought, serving as an umbrella term for diverse musical performances and productions. Though popularized by Fania, this culinary metaphor was not foreign to Latin music performance and had played a role as a performative exclamation and aesthetic trope for quite some time. Cuban musicians in the first half of the twentieth century used the phrase *"Toca con salsa!"* as a bandstand interjection, meaning "swing it" or "play it with feeling." The title of Cuban composer Ignacio Piñeiro's famous son "Echale Salsita" ("Put a Little Sauce in It"), written in 1933 and performed by the Septeto Nacional, aptly captures this type of usage.

The word "salsa," however, reemerged more prominently in the 1960s in several ways. In 1962, Joe Cuba's release *Steppin' Out* included a composition by Jimmy Sabater entitled "Salsa y Bembé" (Seeco Records 9292). Sabater later claimed that he was using the word to label the music, although the lyrics suggest that it was more of a call to the dancers to "spice things up a bit" (Salazar 2002: 255). In 1963, Charlie Palmieri recorded an album called *Salsa Na' Ma'* ("Salsa, Nothing More") for Alegre Records. The lyrics of the title track suggest that "salsa" was the name of a new dance. However, Santiago's liner notes use the term more in the traditional sense, writing that Palmieri's band "possesses that all important 'sauce' necessary for satisfying that most demanding of musical tastes. It is for this reason that the album . . . is titled *Salsa Na' Ma*'" (Salazar 2002: 255–256). According to Max Salazar, Cal Tjader's album *Soul Sauce* (Salsa del Alma), released in 1964, started a trend among Latinos living on the West Coast to use "salsa" as a label for Tjader's "groovy" Latin jazz mixtures (Salazar 2002: 256). Most likely, though, salsa as a generic label stems from Venezuelan disc jockey Phidias Danilo Escalona, who launched a show in 1966 entitled *"La Hora del Sabor, la Salsa y el Bembé"* ("The Hour of Flavor, Salsa, and Party"), playing a variety of modern Cuban dance music, most of which was produced in New York City. Salsa was soon adopted by audiences in Carácas to refer to Latin music coming from New York in the 1960s, which included bands playing pachanga, guaracha, boogaloo, cha-cha, and mambo, specifically.

It was not until the early 1970s in New York that salsa became widely accepted as a generic marker. At that time, numerous song titles and albums were produced that included the word "salsa"; promoter Ralph Mercado launched an advertising campaign in which he called the Cheetah club "the home of salsa"; radio disc jockey Polito Vega began announcing his WBNX show as "100 percent salsa"; and Izzy Sanabria, publisher of *Latin New York* magazine, began systematically writing articles about salsa (he also claimed that he coined the term while emceeing a Fania All-Stars concert). Finally, Fania's release of Larry Harlow's *Salsa,* recorded in 1973, and its subsequent success left no doubt as to the name of this new music. In fact, in 1973, Fania also released its second promotional film, simply titled *Salsa.* Pacheco commented: "The word 'salsa' came about when we started traveling in Europe with Fania and I realized that, except in Spain, no one knew anything about Cuban music. After all, what we were doing was taking Cuban music and adding more progressive chords, emphasizing rhythms, and highlighting certain aspects, but without changing its essence. And since the word . . . has always been associated with the music, it seemed logical to call it that. Likewise, since in Fania we had Dominicans, Puerto Ricans, Cubans, Anglos, Italians, and Jews, that is, a diverse group of condiments that would make good sauce" (Padura-Fuentes 2003: 58–59). Indeed, this diversity involved in salsa production in New York would prove to be key to the music's wide appeal that crossed ethnic, racial, and national boundaries.

However, it is important to note that a minority of traditionally minded musicians, some of whom were performing Latin music prior to the founding of Fania Records, continued to reject this commercial label. For instance, in 1978, bandleader Tito Puente remarked, "This is not a musical terminology at all. The music that I am playing today, which I have been playing for the last 20 years or more, if they want to call it salsa or matzoh ball soup, the name doesn't make any difference to me" (Blum 1978: 144). Throughout his career, from the bandstand and in interviews, he continually reiterated this perspective, reminding everyone that "salsa comes in a bottle and is something you eat," and what he played was "Cuban music." Bandleader Eddie Palmieri added, "We must eliminate that [salsa]. It's Afro-Caribbean music" (Birnbaum 1994: 17). And bandleader Mario Bauzá asked, "Who said salsa exists?" (Padura-Fuentes 2003: 23). Regardless of these objections, salsa has been widely accepted as a generic marker since the 1970s, stylistically binding a diverse collection of produced recordings and performance practices, unifying the positioning of recordings in stores and on websites, dictating radio programming, and designing marketing campaigns.[14]

During the 1970s, Fania controlled most aspects of the salsa business and performance scene in New York City. In fact, the practices it developed in that decade remained the models for future generations of salseros and producers. The Fania All-Stars became an essential marketing tool and disseminating vehicle. By sending only one band on tour to back up a number of its singers, Fania was able to reduce touring costs and to produce concerts throughout Latin America, the Caribbean, Europe, and Africa. These salsa ambassadors internationalized the music and greatly expanded markets. Their growing popularity through the promotional films, record releases, and touring enabled them to play for larger and larger crowds. Eventually, Fania started booking them in large stadiums, including Yankee Stadium in August 1973, with 44,000 people in attendance, and, for their Puerto Rican debut, the Roberto Clemente Coliseum in August 1974.[15] Each of these concerts was filmed, recorded, and later commercially released, maximizing their economic potential. Fania's promotional efforts paid off as its success became noticed by the larger mainstream music industry. In February 1973, *Billboard* started reporting the top Latin music LPs for the first time. In the June 12, 1976, issue, it included a twenty-four-page supplement entitled "The Salsa Explosion," announcing this new genre to the non-Latino market. In March 1975, salsa was programmed for the first time on Don Kirshner's *Rock Concert*, a popular television program on NBC. Due to a performance by Eddie Palmieri at Avery Fisher Hall at Lincoln Center, *Time* magazine published an article on May 5, 1975, introducing the music to its readership. And, most significantly, in 1975 a new category, "Latin Record of the Year," was implemented at the Grammy Awards. Eddie Palmieri won for his *Sun of Latin Music* album (Coco CLP-109XX).

Fania's early success was due in part to its ability to capitalize on salsa's resistant tendencies through its connection to the culture of El Barrio. Salsa became emblematic of that culture and, by extension, Puerto Rican culture at large. This connection remained strong throughout the 1990s. As Marisol Berrios-Miranda observes, "For Puerto Ricans, for whom identification with a wider community of Latinos is a source of strength and resistance to U.S. domination, salsa provides an exuberant experience of pride, independence, and solidarity" (Berrios-Miranda 2000: 20). However, as salsa's international markets grew, Fania moved the music away from being associated solely with Nuyorican barrio life, an experience that did not necessarily translate crossculturally. Subsequently it initiated a push to "Latinize" (i.e., market the music as representative of a shared common Latino experience both in New York and abroad) in order to appeal to a broader Spanish-speaking audience. These efforts proved successful because, once again, they paralleled political movements of the 1970s that sought empowerment through coalition-building among Latino groups, thereby establishing a "pan-Latino identity." Panamanian vocalist Ruben Blades was key in Fania's efforts since he was the first lyricist and singer to bring a broader Latin American perspective to salsa, as well as a penchant for writing political songs that resonated across nationalistic and ethnic lines.

Fania's success in this pan–Latin America venture, though, was double-edged. As Keith Negus (1999) points out, salsa helped unify Latin American cultural expression in the 1970s and provided many Latino musicians great performance opportunities and recognition, but, at the same time, it limited the proliferation of other localized styles that did not fit into the salsa rubric. In order for a cohesive pan-identity to be constructed, the interplay of cultural and national difference had to be set aside and temporarily suspended.[16] As Aparicio points out, this played into the larger "tendencies of the mainstream to conflate all Latin(o) popular music as one homogeneous, tropicalized cultural expression" (Aparicio 1998: 116). This conflation was convenient for Fania, which planned to cross over to even larger English-speaking audiences, a goal that it would never realize due, in part, to the vitality of those local scenes that it had penetrated.

In fact, its resounding success in Latin America was the beginning of the end for Fania. Salsa's popularity spawned many localized scenes, where outposts of salsa production were established throughout the Caribbean and Latin America that would eventually compete for market share and decentralize the salsa industry. A number of influential Colombian, Venezuelan, Dominican, and Puerto Rican bands emerged in the late 1970s. These local productions co-opted this barrio-inflected expression and made it their own, as each was imbued with local sounds, particularities, and experience, which in turn captured local audiences. Claims of ownership began to cut a broad cultural swath. For instance, in salsa's first historical monograph, Venezuelan writer Rondón states, "Salsa is a music that we legitimately consider ours" (Rondón 1980: 6). Colombians, Puerto Ricans, Cubans, Dominicans, and Nuyoricans made similar claims.

As these localized and innovative music scenes grew, Fania seemed to lose its experimental edge, and, instead, relied upon time-tested formulas for its later productions. Unable to change with the times and capture the next generation of listeners (who were more inclined to listen to pop, rock, and more locally inflected music), by 1979 Fania's sales had dropped substantially. Adding to this decline was the general financial slump in Latin music markets stemming from currency problems in various Latin American nations. Further, this decline coincided with imminent financial problems for Fania that stemmed from the strident greed of its business practices. Many musicians, promoters, composers, and producers that Fania had underpaid for years began a forceful campaign to collect and share in the profits from the salsa boom. Masucci responded in 1979 by ceasing further productions and, in 1980, he sold the company to a group of South American investors. Masucci immigrated to Argentina to pursue other business interests, although he ended up with the label in the end, and his family still owns it today.[17]

The demise of Fania set the stage for the emergence of a new salsa sound that would predominate through the end of the twentieth century; however, it would take a few years for the industry to rebuild. Fania's decade-long monopoly caused a real vacuum when it left. Other companies, promoters, or producers just did not possess the infrastructure, economic means, or artistic vision to replace the label. A few small companies made attempts to reignite interest in salsa, but with only limited success. SAR, formed by three entrepreneurs (Sergio Bofill, Adriano Garcia, and Roberto Torres), focused on older Cuban styles; the TH record label promoted older stars like Oscar D'Leon and Willie Rosario. The growing popularity of merengue further contributed to salsa's decline, sparked by the influx of Dominican immigrants to New York and Puerto Rico in the early 1980s. Such singers as Wilfrido Vargas and Johnny Ventura, with their flashy staging; humorous, light, and often overtly sexual lyrics; and easy merengue dance steps appealed to younger generations of Latinos. Many salsa clubs in the United States and Puerto Rico began programming merengue bands instead of salsa acts. In addition, the rise in popularity of North American pop music, rock, and urban dance styles (e.g., rap) among Latino youth was a factor. This was especially true for second- and third-generation Latinos living in the United States who associated salsa with their parent's generation.

Emerging from the vacuum left by Fania in the 1980s were two interdependent and closely aligned centers of salsa production in New York and in Puerto Rico. Both adopted a similar approach to salsa production that significantly changed the music's stylistic direction and aesthetic. Proponents in both locations were concerned with rejuvenating the salsa scene and providing a new marketable product. Taking note of the popularity of rock and pop music among Latino youth in both places, salsa producers turned to those styles for direction and influence. New York–based arranger and percussionist Louie Ramírez and Puerto Rican producer Isidro Infante (who had relocated to New York in 1976) are widely credited with the introduction of the new salsa sound of the 1980s. Ramírez, an arranger who regularly worked on Fania productions, was the first to experiment with combining salsa rhythms and familiar rock tunes. In 1978, he recorded two Beatles' songs, "Something" and "Because," arranged in a salsa format. Both songs were not particularly successful in terms of sales, but they sparked the interest of Joni Figueras, a representative of K-tel Records (a mail-order company and subsidiary of CBS Records that built its sales through late-night television commercials). Figueras contacted Ramírez in 1982 and proposed a project that would capitalize on the widespread popularity of romantic songs used in *telenovelas* (soap-opera-like miniseries) and hit *baladas* (ballads) from South America, Spain, and Mexico, sung by the likes of Julio Iglesias and Roberto and Raphael Carlos. Inspired by the Beatles' remakes, Figueras suggested recording remakes of these widely known songs featuring young salsa singers. In 1982 and 1983, Ramírez teamed up with arranger Infante and they co-produced two recordings for K-tel Records, known as *Noche Caliente* (commercially available as *Lo Mejor De Noche Caliente, Volume 1 and* 2; Caiman 2888 and 2889). The album featured up-and-coming salsa singers José Alberto, Tito Allen, Johnny Rivera, and Ray De La Paz. The arrangements, written by Ramírez, Infante, and Marty Sheller, toned down the "hot" or hard-driving sound that dominated the recordings associated with Fania. Instead, these new productions featured a milder and more tranquil sound, with a slick and highly polished, pop-influenced studio production. Tempos were slower, percussion and brass parts were executed in comparatively subdued fashion, and vocals were sung in a smooth, "crooning" style. The lyrics centered on topics of love, replacing the politically charged lyrics of Blades, Lavoe, and their contemporaries.

K-tel promoted these releases by assembling a pickup band led by Ramírez and Infante and sending them on a promotional tour throughout Latin America. Sales began to soar thanks to K-tel's late-night TV commercials and supermarket promotions, much to the surprise of its originators. Infante commented, "Everyone involved in the *Noche Caliente* recordings had all been working for Fania, and we had no idea at the time how influential these records would be. It was just another project for us. I was playing for Machito at the time and out of the country on tour for a few months when the first record came out. When I got back everything had changed. Everyone was copying us" (I. Infante, pers. comm.). This new stylistic approach reached beyond New York City, appealing to a wide demographic of Latinos throughout Latin America, the Caribbean, and in other U.S. cities. And, like the popularity of the original material (*baladas*), it cut across national, ethnic, racial, and class divisions. In some ways, *Noche Caliente* surpassed the pan-Latin appeal for which Fania had been striving. The commercial success of these releases established a subgenre of salsa that would eventually become known as *salsa romántica*. In 1983, capitalizing on their success, Ramírez partnered with Ray De La Paz to launch the first salsa band that played with this new aesthetic exclusively.[18]

Producers in Puerto Rico were quick to follow, adopting this new approach, albeit with their own locally inflected sound. Infante commented: "If you listen to our *Noche Caliente* records you can still hear instrumental solos, danceable tempos, and high-energy coros. We even used Pacheco on coro and all the musicians from the Fania All-Stars to record. We still left some of the Fania sound in there. But in Puerto Rico, it was very different. It is a tropical island, a more laid-back lifestyle, and their version of the music was slower, focused on the lyrics, and had no solos" (I. Infante, pers. comm.). Producer Bobby Valentín's work with singers Ubaldo Rodríguez and Tito Rojas, Tommy Olivencia's productions with vocalists Paquito Guzman and Frankie Ruíz, and Julio Caesar Delgado's productions for Eddie Santiago and Lalo Rodríguez were central in establishing a distinct Puerto Rican sound. In order to distinguish the Puerto Rican sound from the productions in New York, the labels *salsa erótica* and *salsa sensual* were preferred. Eventually, though, salsa romántica was used for both productions in Puerto Rico and in New York. A second wave of producers—such names as Humberto Ramírez, Cuto Soto, and Ramón Sánchez—sustained this Puerto Rican sound throughout the late 1980s and into the 1990s by working with a new crop of singers that included Luis Enrique, Jerry Rivera, Domingo Quiñones, and Rey Ruíz.

This new approach to salsa deemphasized images of barrio life, reduced calls for Latino unity, and avoided political lyrics; hence, it aligned with the sociopolitical environment of the Reagan era, where political activism and global awareness were largely pacified (at least in the United States). Moreover, borrowing from pop music, a salsa artist's physical and sexual image became increasingly more important than his or her musical prowess. Record companies sought young, predominantly white or light-skinned male singers with sex appeal. Many middle-aged and well-established singers, such as Pete "El Conde" Rodríguez and Adalberto Santiago, found themselves without recording contracts.[19] The words used to distinguish this style—sensual, erótica, and romántica—reflected both the content of lyrics as well as images used to market these artists. Singer "Giro" López commented: "Salsa used to have a nasty image, with its sexuality and rough performers, but my salsa is romantic, soothing, pretty . . . sort of like a rhythmic *bolero*, and that's today's salsa, which has changed a lot from the original style. Salsa used to be all about the timbales and bongó, but now it's about sweet and elegant words, and the girls like it much more than the earlier, macho salsa" (Manuel 1995: 91).[20]

The proliferation of the new sound was further facilitated by the start of RMM Records in 1987, a company founded by Ralph Mercado, a concert promoter and talent manager turned entrepreneur. Mercado first approached the musicians involved in *Noche Caliente* to help launch his company, relying on the formulas they borrowed from pop music in which the bands were formed and arrangements written with the sole purpose of featuring star singers as bandleaders. Mercado hired Ramírez and Infante to produce and arrange his first production, which featured José Alberto. From the beginning, though, it was apparent that Mercado had a different goal than just reproducing romántica copies. Coming of age in the salsa business during the heyday of Fania, Mercado retained his love for the older, hard-swinging styles, but he also knew that the music he produced had to evolve and appeal to younger generations to enjoy any longevity. So his productions, though firmly rooted in the romántica style, often included unique blends of older styles or other types of music, such as soul, R&B, and hip-hop. The turning point for his company came in 1989 with his first production for Tito Nieves. Nieves and Ramírez had a falling out during the initial sessions that resulted in Ramírez's quitting. Infante was unavailable to step in and recommended a young Nuyorican pianist, Sergio George. George took over the production, inflecting it with a blend of romántica, pop, and soul that took full advantage of Nieves's versatile vocal abilities. The overwhelming popularity of that release, *The Classic* (Sony 80707), propelled the team of Mercado and George to a dominant position in the New York salsa scene. Mirroring the Masucci and Pacheco relationship, George was hired as producer and arranger for Mercado's productions and eventually was promoted to a full-time position in charge of A&R (Artists and Repertoire).

Figure I.6 Ralph Mercado (Right) and DJ Ricky (Left) backstage at the Latin Quarter in New York, 2005. *(Photograph by Christopher Washburne.)*

Figure I.7 Sergio George at his home studio, Teaneck, New Jersey, 2002. *(Photograph by Enid Farber.)*

Well-schooled in Masucci's business practices, with whom he collaborated while running the Cheetah club, Mercado modeled RMM on Fania: RMM quickly absorbed all of the competition, signed almost every major salsero, and established control over radio airplay and club bookings. By the early 1990s, RMM Records had effectively filled the void left by Fania's dissolution to become the largest and most influential Latin music record company and concert promoter in the salsa business. In 1994, they even started the RMM All-Stars, modeled on the Fania All-Stars, consisting of studio musicians who regularly worked on RMM productions.[21] RMM began producing large-scale concerts at venues like Madison Square Garden and Carnegie Hall, where Mercado had his All-Star band back up the singers signed to his company. This group also toured regularly in Latin America, Europe, and around the United States. These concerts were often filmed, recorded, and later released commercially. Their most notable video was filmed during a live concert at the Miami Arena and was released as *Combinación Perfecta* (*The Perfect Combination*).[22] These tours and commercial releases served as highly effective promotional campaigns for Mercado's roster, bolstering the careers of his mainstay artists, including José "El Canario" Alberto, Tito Nieves, Tony Vega, Ray Sepulveda, Domingo Quiñones, Johnny Rivera, Oscar D'Leon, and Ray De La Paz. Further, Mercado did not forsake the older salseros he had been working with since the 1970s and signed them to his label as well. Such singers as Cheo Feliciano, Celia Cruz, Pete "El Conde" Rodríguez, and bandleader Tito Puente all had their careers reinvigorated. The RMM All-Stars concerts featured a unique generational mix ranging from performances by septuagenarian Cruz to twentysomething newcomer Marc Anthony. Mercado commented, "The '90s belonged to RMM the way the 1970s were Fania's. RMM created a second wave of an explosion" (Navarro 2001). By the mid-1990s, Mercado had fifty-five employees and distribution deals in forty-two cities around the world, and his offices occupied a chic 9,000-square-foot SoHo loft.

George's ability to recognize and adapt to changes in the salsa audience as second- and third-generation Latinos living in the United States came of age contributed to his success. Many had grown up in the suburbs of New Jersey and Long Island, far removed from the barrio where George was raised. Some did not speak Spanish or know how to dance. He reached out to this audience by having many of his artists sing cuts in English on each of their recordings. The most successful song was Nieves's version of Taylor Dayne's "I'll Always Love You," a top-forty hit from 1987. In addition, he sought new talent that shared this younger generation's experiences and musical sensibilities. La India and Marc Anthony are two artists who are credited with bringing younger audiences to salsa in the late 1990s. Both were known for their work in the underground dance music scene in New York, but they had no experience in salsa and they did not speak Spanish fluently. George combined their styles of house music, soul, and salsa to change the direction of salsa once again. George explained: "I am not interested in crossover. I want my market expanded to include reggae/rap/salsa. I want to bridge the gap in the Latino market between Colombians, Mexicans, and Puerto Ricans, not crossing over to the Anglo market. If we unify the Spanish-speaking market, stay true to the art and music, people will buy it" (S. George, pers. comm.). And they did.

Their preponderant role and commercial strength contributed to the success and dominance of George's pop-oriented style of New York salsa throughout the 1990s; however, Mercado also supported a separate group of arrangers and studio musicians in Puerto Rico that produced milder forms of romántica,

Figure I.8 Marc Anthony backstage before his salsa debut in Madison Square Garden, 1994. *(Photograph by Enid Farber.)*

thereby promulgating these two distinct scenes. This Puerto Rican–based group would eventually prove very influential in the late 1990s. As with Fania, however, the growing success and dominance of just one company was double-edged. Opportunity for other voices and alternative approaches, save for these two scenes Mercado supported, was nearly nonexistent. One struggling salsa artist complained, "If you are not signed with Ralph [Mercado], you are nowhere. He's got the market locked up. You can't get on his Madison Square Garden concerts, the other companies don't have the same record distribution capabilities, and forget about radio airplay" (Anon., pers. comm.). Mercado's monopoly on all aspects of the business allowed him to dictate how business was conducted, and his choices often involved questionable practices that contributed to the continued marginalization of salsa within the music industry at large. For instance, since Mercado did not properly report sales figures, traditional indicators used by the recording industry (e.g., Nielsen SoundScans that track commercial sales) could not be applied. The Recording Industry Association of America (RIAA) did not even establish a separate report for salsa that distinguished it from other tropical genres until 1997. Further, many of the smaller mom-and-pop record stores where salsa was primarily sold, both in the United States and in Puerto Rico, did not report their figures. According to Keith Negus, salsa held 4 to 7 percent of the market share of the recording industry in the 1990s, but only 1 percent was reported (Negus 1999: 141).

As RMM grew, major record labels slowly began to recognize the economic potential of the Latino market for salsa. Mercado partnered with Sony and BMG in the mid-1990s, greatly expanding his distribution and business opportunities. However, Mercado's expansion into the legitimate business world would lead to the eventual demise of RMM. George stated, "When I started with Ralph [Mercado], everything was informal. We came to terms over a handshake, there were no contracts. But when we started to work with Sony and other companies, we had to change how we did business" S. George, pers. comm.). Most transactions between RMM and musicians had been in cash and remained unreported. Changing how RMM did business meant paying taxes, royalties, residuals, and reporting sales figures. As the company began transforming and legitimatizing their business practices, the changes sparked the scrutiny of the Internal Revenue Service. In the mid-1990s, RMM and a number of its artists were audited. As proper sales reports were published, artists, producers, and composers began to realize the amount of royalties that they rightfully deserved but had never received. George was one of the first to demand better compensation. When Mercado refused, George left in 1996 to form his own record and production company, Sir George Records, where he experimented further with hip-hop, rap, reggae, and salsa mixtures. *DLG* (Dark Latin Grooves) was his first highly influential project. (Isidro Infante was hired as his replacement at RMM). Some artists began seeking relationships with other companies who were willing to offer better deals. For instance, in 1999, Marc Anthony threatened to sue Mercado and expose his questionable business practices in order to terminate his contract with RMM and sign with Sony Records. Mercado was forced to let him go, settling out of court. In 2000, La India sued Mercado for $500,000 in unpaid royalties. However, it was another lawsuit that same year that closed his company for good. Songwriter Glenn Monroig in Puerto Rico brought the suit, claiming that RMM had used one of his songs in several recordings and in a documentary without obtaining permission, and that he had never been paid royalties for that use. The federal jury in Puerto Rico awarded Monroig $7.7 million in damages, forcing Mercado to seek Chapter 11 bankruptcy protection in November 2000. As part of that settlement, Mercado was banned from the record business for several years. In 2001, the Universal Music Group acquired RMM Records for $16 million. Mercado remains in the salsa business as a promoter and club owner, but the absence of RMM records created another vacuum in the salsa scene, the effects of which still linger as of the writing of this book. Performance opportunities remain limited in New York, with only a few clubs programming salsa with any regularity; no new company has emerged to fill this void.

This book focuses on the RMM era, investigating how its business practices and stylistic dominance impacted the performance practice and sound of salsa in the 1990s. The dominant discourse in salsa scholarship frames salsa romántica as something distinct from salsa dura. Such scholars as Peter Manuel, Jorge Duany, and Cesar Rondón have criticized, in differing ways, RMM's preference for a depoliticized, commercialized, pop-music approach. For them, salsa romántica productions lack the authenticity, creativity, and artistic integrity so fundamental to the Fania era. My analysis goes against this scholarly trend. Though romántica differs substantially from salsa dura, both in terms of lyric content and sound aesthetic, its performance practice remains firmly grounded in the tropes and strategies developed in the 1970s, where Latinidad, pan-Latino identity construction, and self-empowerment remain firmly centered in performance. The same social struggles remain, but they are couched in a new era and generation. Indeed, Mercado and George achieved their success by their ability to keep the music "in the family" and "of the people," despite its overt commercialism. Live performances were key in this venture. The subdued sounds heard on their recordings rarely matched the performance practice of live shows, where grittier, pride-inducing aesthetics were privileged. The ethnographic perspective put forth in the following pages, its view from the "trenches," examines just how these ideas were sustained on the New York salsa scene.

Fieldwork

> "[T]o ignore the encounter not only denies the power of such factors as personality, social location in the community, intimacy of contact, and luck (not to mention theoretical orientation and self-conscious methodology) to shape fieldwork and its product but also perpetuates the conventional fictions of objectivity and omniscience that mark the ethnographic genre."[23]
>
> —Lila Abu-Lughod

In the 1990s, salsa was performed, produced, listened to, consumed, and danced to throughout the world. Its global reach and the cultural complexities involved in its creation required some limitation in the scope of this fieldwork-based project. I focused primarily on the salsa scene in New York City, the place that was central to the emergence of the music as a distinct genre and that served as the epicenter of salsa performance, production, and promotion throughout the 1990s. Most major salsa performers, producers, composers, and arrangers either resided in or regularly performed in the New York metropolitan area. The majority of record companies, record distributors, and concert promoters had offices in Manhattan. A significant number of recordings were made either in the city or nearby. In addition, the premier salsa performance venues that featured the most famous bands were located in Manhattan. These top-level bands, and the musicians who performed and recorded with them, served as my focus in this study. I studied people who self-identified and were recognized in their communities as "salsa musicians." All were professional musicians for whom salsa was the central monetary and artistic focus of their musical careers.[24]

My decision to study this particular group reflected my own personal performance experience. Those musicians with whom I consulted, interviewed, observed, "hung out," and researched were the same individuals with whom I had been performing for the last eighteen years. I played with everyone whose voice is represented in this book. I had intimate working and personal relationships with many. To use the conventional anthropological term "consultants" to label their role in my research thus seems inadequate. Rather, the salseros involved in this project included fellow musicians, bandleaders, music directors, record producers, concert promoters, radio disc jockeys, club deejays, and academic colleagues, most of whom I considered to be my friends. Aaron Fox (1995) prefers the term "interlocutors," in order to emphasize the roles of speech, silence, dialogue, and their importance in the research process. Reflecting my own experience, this term acknowledges the central role of interchange, the sharing of ideas, observations, perceptions, and conceptions of the music and the scene in the development of the perspective put forth in the following pages. Several groups with whom I performed on a regular basis played a more pronounced role in this research. Indeed, I viewed the musicians who played in the bands of Tito Puente, Eddie Palmieri, Ray Sepulveda, Tito Nieves, Marc Anthony, La India, and RMM All-Stars as my collaborators.

Participation through performance served as my principal means of collecting data. As a musician participant, I was privy to many aspects of both the music and social conditions that other scholars in this field either have not seen or have chosen to ignore. I focused upon these uncharted waters and wrote about the parts of the New York salsa scene with which I was most intimately acquainted. This level of close intimacy provided unique opportunities for insightful observation; however, it presented problems, too, especially when attempting to distance myself for the sake of objective analysis and interpretation. As I spent more time on the salsa scene, it became increasingly

Figure I.9 Tito Puente and Christopher Washburne performing at SOBs in New York, 1998. *(Photograph by Maiken Derno.)*

difficult to distinguish between "fieldwork," "gigging," and "just hanging." These modes of being were inseparable and this blurred and multivalent position felt like the most natural course to take in my fieldwork. But where does ethnography begin and real life end? Aaron Fox relates about his own work, "Fieldwork, music making, friendship, and writing have grown together into a dense thicket of stories in which knowledge, memory, emotion, and practice are simply inseparable. Making an analytic, scholarly path through this thicket is a tricky, though pleasurable business" (Fox 1995: 64). Indeed, the very act of engaging my interlocutors in ongoing dialogues concerning the issues examined in this project contributed to my navigation through this "tricky thicket." Consequently, their criticisms and feedback played an integral part in forming the observations and conclusions put forth in this book. John Blacking continually stressed the importance of musical performance as a research tool (1973), though he added that an "ethnography of performance must include as many perceptions as possible of what is happening when music is played or sung, and what are the relationships between the sounds produced and the attendant social and cultural process" (Blacking 1977: 2). As such, my aim was to maintain a level of multivocality, presenting diverse perspectives and allowing the voices of my friends to be heard.

As a white musician born and raised in rural Ohio, steeped in rock and roll, and schooled in jazz and classical music, I had little exposure to Latin music and culture before I began performing with salsa bands in Boston in the late 1980s while attending the New England Conservatory. I played my first salsa gig as a complete outsider. I had never heard salsa (except for brief moments when blasting car stereos passed me while driving through Boston's Latino neighborhoods); I had only met a few Latino musicians; I had never visited a Caribbean, South, or Central American country; and I did not speak Spanish. I was sent as a last-minute substitute player for Jim Messbauer, a white, North American trombonist. When I asked how to play salsa, Messbauer responded, "Just show up on time. Smile a lot and have a good time. And most importantly, play really LOUD. They are going to love you!" Armed with this scant but essential advice, I possessed just enough insider information to be hired as a regular member of the group by the end of the evening's performance. After moving to New York City in the summer of 1989, I began performing in the "salsa scene" almost exclusively, playing four to seven nights a week. Since I worked as a freelance trombonist, performing with various groups at one time, I had the opportunity to play in a number of diverse contexts, including rehearsals, clubs and discos, private parties, festivals, on television, and on music videos. In addition, I toured extensively with salsa bands throughout Central and South America, the Caribbean, Europe, and the United States. Further, I participated in a number of Latin music recordings during my research.[25]

In total, my acceptance into the salsa scene was rather swift, attesting to a sincere openness of the Latino community in New York City for cultural interchange. This is something for which I am most grateful, but I am equally troubled by the lack of reciprocation (Latino musicians continually have difficulties breaking into the New York's jazz scene, for instance). My acceptance was not unprecedented, though. Latin bands in New York typically included white horn players, a practice that was established in the 1940s during the mambo era. The large horn sections required a number of skilled players, more than any one community could support. In fact, arguably the most influential salsa trombonist was Eddie Palmieri's longtime collaborator Barry Rogers, who was of Jewish descent and born and raised in Brooklyn. Because of his influence, white trombonists represent the most common participants of non-Latinos in salsa bands. Their participation and influence on the salsa scene is indicative of its intercultural nature, but it also calls into question the simple binary drawn between cultural insiders and outsiders, still widely discussed in the social sciences today. My own experience was much more fluid and multi-layered instead of being a simple shift from "out-ness" to "in-ness." As my competency level in playing salsa increased, and as I learned how to navigate the cultural cues and behaviors of the scene, I became more deeply entrenched and many more performance opportunities arose. However, my background and physical appearance (6 feet 3 inches tall, and of fair complexion), continually marked me as an outsider. Even after I appeared on numerous recordings and videos and performed with the busiest salsa groups, the issue of my insider/outsider status continued to play a role in my interactions with Latino musicians, especially when making new acquaintances. Such questions as "Why do you play our music?" or "You prefer playing jazz, right?" were not atypical. On a few isolated occasions I received jealous remarks, such as "Why did they hire you, a white boy, instead of me?" But for the most part, salsa musicians readily accepted my participation after I conveyed my respect for and knowledge of the music. Further, some fluency in Latino social expectations and my willingness to exhibit acceptable behavioral skills also expedited my cultural acceptance. I found that such displays of cultural competence were not singular affairs, required only in the case of each new acquaintance, but rather were continual processes in which I often was made to feel that I must re-prove my sincerity and respect for musicians with whom I had performed for a significant number of years. In contrast, I did not notice the same level of recurring critical examination of Latino musicians. At times, the challenges caused by the harsher standards that I was held to, which emphasized my "otherness," spawned my own ambivalent feelings about the scene. I desired to be treated as just any other salsa musician. However, the objective distance I needed as a researcher conducting fieldwork did set me apart from the other participants. The process of stepping back from the scene, analyzing, and interpreting cultural data was most likely not a process in which other salseros were routinely engaged. Ultimately, I chose to use these heightened critical standards as inspiration to foster deeper levels of examination and analysis and to strive for higher levels of artistic competence in performance. When my last name was transformed from "Washburne" to "Whiteboy" by several Puerto Rican musicians and the nickname "Chris Whiteboy" began to be used with some frequency, I did not interpret it as an exclusionary gesture. Instead, I came to realize that for these musicians, it was a reflection of their need to assert their Puerto Rican status and cultural ownership of the music. At the same time, it served as an endearing appellative for a colleague who shared their love for salsa and their desire to make great music. I felt fortunate to be included as a participant in such a dynamic scene.

In this way, I straddled various complex positions within the salsa scene simultaneously. I found that other musicians I worked with, no matter what their cultural affiliations, also were positioned in multivalent ways. These positions remained in constant flux.[26] I, however, came to view such multipositionality as a strength for conducting fieldwork. As Renato Rosaldo points out, we must recognize that a researcher's "multiplex personal identities," which are constituted by the sum of researcher's various identities, enable multiple sources of knowledge and perspectives for social analysis. Each offers unique ways of approaching various circumstances encountered in the field (Rosaldo 1989: 168–195). I tried to incorporate such an approach in the following pages, often drawing upon personal interactions for insight and analysis.

Engaging in fieldwork also served as the means by which I endured some difficult real-life experiences. When performance conditions became dangerous, exploitative, or degrading, my position as participant-observer was arduous. At times, I only found solace in the knowledge that these situations provided provocative and racy insight; at other times, I hoped that, through publication and documentation, I could possibly precipitate change and improve the situation for future salseros. For instance, during a performance with Ruben Blades in Venezuela in 1995, a gunfight erupted in front of the stage. Witnessing such violence as the band played on was disturbing and painful. As a performer, I deeply questioned my motives for placing myself in such close proximity to danger. Simultaneously, I was awed and inspired as Blades used his music to douse the fires and bridle the audience's aggression by singing of his love for his deceased parents. Witnessing the transformation from social chaos to literally tearful cell-phone calls home, and a general feeling of brotherly and sisterly love, was invaluable to me as a researcher. E. P. Thompson observed, "One way to discover unspoken norms is often to examine the untypical episode or situation . . . a sudden breach of deference enables us to better understand the deferential habits which have been broken . . . even a highly untypical ritual may thus provide a valuable window onto norms" (Thompson 1977: 251–252). After witnessing this incident, the insight gained into family structures, cultural role models, psychological effects of music, relationships between audiences and performers, and relationships between violence and music was monumental. It was in this way that I took advantage of my position as researcher, performer, and participant-observer to access diverse resources and experiences that ultimately served to enhance scholarly knowledge of the field, hoping to strike a balance between performance-oriented data acquisition and pre- and post-performance interpretive analysis.

In Chapter One, I focus on salsa bands working in New York City in the 1990s, exploring their organizational structures and highlighting several features of the scene within which the bands performed. The chapter is organized to mirror the steps involved in the formation, preparation, and performance of bands, exploring issues associated with each formative step. The discussion then progresses to address specific topics involved in performance practice, providing insight into a variety of cultural structures, relationships, and processes within the salsa community. Professional salsa bands work in a highly structured performance environment; however, much of their performance practice involves the concealment of those structures and the blurring of boundaries associated with staged performance. Underlying this trend is a drive to construct the music as "people's music," regardless of its overt commerciality. Bandleaders accomplish this through performative strategies that promote collective participation and inclusiveness. Through the use of blurring and boundary-crossing techniques, salsa performers are able to maintain a connectedness to the urban barrio culture from where salsa emerged, which in turn invites a wide range of personal and cultural identifications.

In Chapter Two, I focus my ethnographic study on salsa musicians. I explore their attitudes, working environment, education, and business practices. In particular, I discuss how they navigate through a variety of conflicting agendas involved in salsa performance. Salsa, as cultural expression, straddles various identificatory positions simultaneously (i.e., embracing cultural pluralism, signifying disparate cultural particularities, and erasing cultural difference). Salsa musicians work, create, perform, and live on the front lines of contentious battles concerning ownership, nationality, and ethnicity. Performing salsa demands the mastery of an intricate array of social strategies to contend with these concerns, all the while balancing issues of personal artistic expression and economics. I examine the fluid negotiations that musicians must engage to navigate this challenging terrain.

After completing the ethnographic mapping of bands and musicians, I adopt a more pointed and issue-oriented approach, turning to three relatively underexplored areas in salsa research: violence, the illicit drug trade, and the role of gender. New York salsa has long been associated with urban street life, a life that violence commonly permeates. This violence stems from various societal factors, including poverty, unemployment, lack of education, the illegal drug trade, and gang activity, among others. Since much of New York's salsa performance takes place in locations where violent acts are typically experienced (night clubs and after hours in dangerous neighborhoods), and the salsa business's infrastructure often is tied economically to the illicit drug trade, makers and consumers are frequently exposed to violent acts or are participants in those acts. In Chapter Three, I explore the role these experiences play in how the music sounds and is performed. My contention is that the violence inherent in the scene manifests itself in sound, and tropes of violence inform performance practice.

In Chapter Four, I explore the dynamic relationship between salsa and the illicit drug trade. The emergence of salsa in the late 1960s and early 1970s coincided with the establishment of an internationally organized narcotics trading industry for cocaine. The pervasiveness of cocaine, the impact of its physical and psychological effects on the body, and its associated business practices on the salsa scene over the last thirty-five years have fundamentally informed salsa aesthetics, sound structure, and performance practice. Through a historical perspective, this chapter shows how salsa has been shaped by complex economic forces, illicit activity, and identity politics.

In Chapter Five, the fluidity of identity construction is interrogated through the performances of salsa singer La India. This chapter focuses on India's ambiguous manipulation of her stage selves, caught in the negotiations between the effect of stereotypical notions of masculinity and performative excess, and it offers a critical rereading of certain controversial and violent events in the singer's career. India is reconsidered for her radically gendered performance practice within a male-dominated music industry, as her presence on the salsa scene transcends the simplistic male-female binary that fails to articulate the multiple modes of gendered subjectivity. I argue that India's musical innovation and her nontraditional stage image had a profound effect on the salsa scene in the 1990s. Her pioneering efforts led the way for a number of other female singers/bandleaders to follow, and they collectively forged a space for female voices and perspectives to be represented in a significant way for the first time in this traditionally male-dominated domain.

Finally, in Chapter Six, I focus upon issues involving music style, demonstrating how cultural factors are intrinsically tied to, reflected in, and affect the sonic qualities of the music. This chapter provides the musical scaffolding from which I conduct my ethnographic research.[27] Through an analysis of various elements of salsa's sound structure, I explore how salsa's rich intercultural production reverberates sonically in ways that play out larger cultural processes microcosmically. I contend that the fundamental intercultural history of the music imbues it with a wide range of interpretation and inscription, making it pliable to serve as ethnic code, nationalistic pride, and essence for a wide variety of peoples. Specifically, the discussion explores elements of salsa's sound structure by examining performance practices associated with the predominant style of the late 1980s and 1990s—salsa romántica. The role of clave in salsa performance, as well as the relationship between New York and Puerto Rico, will be central to this discussion.

1

Salsa Bands and the Performance of Pueble

In the song "El Cantante," Hector Lavoe delivers words that sound autobiographical although the song was written by Ruben Blades. He begins with, "Yo soy el cantante" ("I am the singer"), and continues this personal sketch by stating that people pay to hear him sing and that he is popular everywhere he goes. He concludes this boastful opening quatrain with the following modest and quite revealing line: "Pero cuando el show se acaba soy otro humano cualquiera" ("But when the show is over, I am just a regular guy"). The sentiment of these lines aptly captures the fundamental operative modes of salsa performance—economics and artistry girded by a firm connection with *gente*, *plebe*, and *familia* (people, common folk, and family). I shall borrow the umbrella term *pueble,* coined by Mayra Santos-Febres, to refer to these three terms collectively. She writes that ". . . *puertoricanness* is not the dominant signifier in salsa. Pueble, that is, peopleness, is . . . therefore . . . a tradition that is larger than national and broader than ethnic" (Santos-Febres 1997: 179). Pueble is a dominant force behind how salsa is staged, dictating not only performance practice, but informing much of the discourse around the music and the musicians who make it. The key to understanding the role of pueble is to first acknowledge the centrality of the *barrio* as the cultural milieu and "place" from which the music emerged. The barrio represents an environment that involves the processes of cultural mixing and the dynamic power relations that are fundamental to salsa performance. Comments made by Willie Colón, the archetypal salsa persona emerging from El Barrio, are particularly enlightening in this respect:

> Latinos are a minority living in the context of discrimination, and only in the barrio are they able to reproduce their original environment . . . an expression of a little piece of their homeland . . . and in that environment all things Latin American are valued . . . I think that in those spiritual necessities and the lack of communication beyond the borders of the barrio, we can find the profound psychological and cultural factors that give rise to salsa . . . where it emerges as a manifestation of cultural resistance . . . Salsa emerges as something of our own. (Padura-Fuentes 2003: 29)

Notice how Colón, who is Nuyorican, avoids particularities of national affiliations and instead only refers to a broad and vague grouping, "Latin Americans." Though Puerto Ricans and Nuyoricans have accounted for the majority living within the borders of Spanish Harlem throughout the twentieth century, it is not necessarily that particular barrio to which he refers. Reflecting a strategic positioning rooted in both political and economic considerations, his "little piece of homeland" extends beyond the confines of East Harlem and should be read as multisited, or, as Mayra Santos-Febres encourages, as a "translocal" phenomenon rather than a multinational one. In this way, salsa and the barrio "cuts across national boundaries to create a community of urban locations linked by transportation, communication technologies, and the international market economy" (Santos-Febres 1997: 180). Furthermore, this reading reflects the pliability of how salsa is actually sounded within identity politics that simultaneously assert a particular group's essence and yet consistently transcend those asserted boundaries of nation and ethnicity, market economies, and folk traditions. Pueble, as common denominator, facilitates such fluid affiliations.[1]

This chapter is an ethnographic study of salsa bands, examining their organizational structures, recording processes, rehearsals, and gigging. I explore how pueble undergirds these structures and processes, as well as informs performance practice. Using the salsa band as a microcosm, I aim to provide insight into a variety of broader cultural relationships that play themselves out within the salsa community. As Mark Slobin writes, "the small performing group encompasses the full range of communal enterprise, from the mundane commercial life of the hired band through the transcendent fellowship of song, including links to local and intercultural industry, diasporic and intercultural contact networks, cross-subcultural rapport, and a sweeping sense of history which can bridge centuries or can almost instantaneously invent a tradition" (Slobin 1992: 80).

Using pueble as a theoretical lens intrinsically ties my discussion to the politics of identity. Identity, as an object of and framing for ethnomusicological exploration, has dominated studies of salsa and Puerto Rican music in New York. The title of Roberta Singer's (1982) pioneering dissertation on salsa, "My Music Is Who I Am and What I Do: Latin Popular Music and Identity in New York City," reflects this discourse, as does Ruth Glasser's (1995) insightful monograph *My Music Is My Flag: Puerto Rican Musicians and Their New York Communities, 1917–1940*. I do not wish to revisit identity as a productive force in a similarly comprehensive way; this has been done, and done well, by the two authors mentioned, among others. My interests lie elsewhere. However, avoiding the subject of identity would ignore a significant force that is consciously acted upon and acted out in some manner on almost every salsa gig. Rather, I acknowledge the question of identity in salsa performance, but with a more bounded and limited focus. In my approach, pueble is in the foreground, and I examine its role in how salsa bands navigate identity politics in their performances.

Pueble, as operative mode, has consistently played a role throughout the history of Latin music in New York City, but it was not until the advent of salsa that it became central in performance. Prior to the emergence of salsa, Latin music performance styles, though tied to El Barrio in many ways, often consciously catered to a demographic not associated with barrio life. For instance, the Palladium became a place "to be seen" by the New York jet set, especially on Wednesday nights, with such actors as Marlon Brando and Sammy Davis Jr. making frequent appearances. Likewise, the thriving Catskill Mountains resort scene of the 1950s and 1960s, which often employed mambo bands from New York City, catered mostly to Jewish and Italian American clientele. According to Cesar Miguel Rondón, the orchestras of Machito, Tito Puente, and Tito Rodríguez played for the predominantly white affluent set of New York society in order to establish more prestige, developing performance styles that easily translated across cultural boundaries. In particular, Jewish audiences were large, and their interest in Latin culture grew because the music was presented as a cosmopolitan and refined music of the city, not as a product exclusively belonging to El Barrio (Rondón 1980: 30). Comments made by Puente illustrate the conscious staging of ethnicity and nation in such performance settings, where balancing agendas of cultural pride and economics were required: "I have always had a big, large English-speaking audience . . . [but] wherever I go, I represent more or less, the Puerto Rican people . . . Wherever I go, I travel, they ask me, 'What are you?' [and] I say 'I'm Puerto Rican.' But I am international, too. I play for all kinds of people, and they dance to my music and I have all kinds of following, so I don't want to tag myself" (Loza 1999: 224–225).

But for the next generation of musicians associated with the emergence of salsa, a much different stance was adopted. In part, this stance was due to the broader effects of the civil rights movement among Latinos. In the late 1960s and into the 1970s, salsa was seen as an effective cultural and political tool for Latino activists struggling for equality through social, economic, and political recognition. Consequently, marketing strategies for Latin music production in New York City changed dramatically, becoming more culturally introspective. As Latinos became the primary targeted demographic for this music, the lyrics adopted an overtly political bent, and performance practices changed from the glitzy mambo-era showiness to a more grassroots aesthetic. The fundamental difference was pueble. As Rondón points out, there was a change in character of the new generation of Latin musicians in the 1970s; they presented themselves as "common folk" coming directly from the street and moved on and off the stage without "pretense or poses" (Rondón 1980: 32). The superstar images employed in the pop music world were not adopted; instead, artists were marketed as having rooted connections to the people. These musicians looked and dressed like the audience they were singing to and for. El Barrio provided authentic credentials for young artists and, as they sang about their own barrio experiences, they became the voice of the people in the process. Of course, this positioning did not in any way remove the music from its commercial ties. U.S.-based record companies began to recognize that Latino populations in the United States and abroad represented substantial markets with significant capital. Indeed, Fania Records spearheaded the marketing of such strategically employed "authenticity." Fania producers pushed to establish broader pan-Latino identity markers in the music, catering to an emergent pan-Latino consciousness and moving salsa away from being primarily associated with Puerto Ricans in New York. This push was where the barrio as a multisited and translocal phenomenon became central. Salsa artists were able to adeptly harbor the intensity of the New York City barrio experience while effectively divorcing it from its geographic specificities. Diverse communities and ethnicities became unified into *la gran raza latina* (the grand Latino race), later referred to as "pan-*Latinismo*," a politically motivated empowerment strategy adopted throughout Latin America. Salsa artists and record companies quickly captured this sentiment and were able to capitalize on the political fervor of the day, and, ultimately, played a significant political role in that process. The gente (people) of salsa then became global, greatly expanding audiences, markets, and sales, as well as simultaneously serving seemingly contradictory agendas: the market and grassroots politics. As Keith Negus writes, "salsa has become a marketing category within a set of business practices that often represent a stark contrast to some of its political meanings and cultural associations" (Negus 1999: 132).

This perceived conflict between pueble and economics has prompted such scholars as Negus, as well as Santos-Febres and Felix Padilla, to frame salsa in terms of this inherent tension. Febres focuses on the participatory elements of the music, writing that salsa relies on "two mutually excluding modes of access (direct participation and indirect consumption) . . . [a] contradictory coexistence of salsa in both market and participatory economies" (Santos-Febres 1997: 177). Padilla posits salsa at the nexus of dominant and resistant forces that are played out between record companies and individual musicians. For him, salsa "represents a contested terrain marked by the recording industry's structural contradictions as well as by socially conscious informed musician resistance" (Padilla 1990: 87). I agree that salsa does harbor such contradictions and tensions at its core, but we must avoid reducing these dynamics into either/or binaries. Reducing the complexities inherent in the dynamic relations of economics, business, art, politics, ethnicity, and sound structure misses the opaqueness of the everyday experiences of musicians and industry people alike. Aren't some record company executives interested in resistance, especially those associated with small independent labels? Aren't musicians complicit in how market pressures and economic factors shape sound structure and performance practice? Salsa is a commercial music and has been so since its inception, as are the many music styles from which salsa is derived (jazz, *son*, soul, etc.). Each facet involved in the production and signification of the music informs the other and must be seen in such a dialectical light rather than within tight dichotomies of oppositional forces. It is precisely this irreducible complexity that opens salsa to diverse signification and interpretation, and this complexity is what I explore in this chapter.

Even as salsa became less overtly politicized and its commercial concerns were accentuated with the advent of the *romántica* style throughout the 1980s and 1990s, pueble remained (and continues to be) a significant force in salsa performance, despite other stylistic changes that have emerged over time. The predomination of pueble partly is due to the cultural hybridity involved in salsa production, as well as the relationship of El Barrio to New York City. Homi Bhabha (1996) and Stuart Hall (2003b), among others, have used "hybridity" to reference "in-between sites of enunciation" in a cultural minoritization context where new cultural forms emerge and hold potential for resignification due to their inherent unsettledness. Hybridity aptly captures the space of salsa production that straddles a variety of identificatory positions simultaneously. Marginalized communities, like those found in El Barrio, seek empowerment through the cultural capital that is produced by way of the movement of sounds and images across prior impenetrable boundaries (like those Willie Colón alludes to above). As Hall writes, "contemporary migration intrudes directly into, disturbs, challenges, and subverts metropolitan cultural space" (Hall 2003b: 196). But these new arrivals are doubly inscribed as they remain tied to their cultures of origins, "which are themselves deeply enmeshed in the system of global power in profoundly subaltern ways. And they are recruited into subaltern positions in the division of labor and cultures of belongingness in the metropolitan spaces . . . And inevitably, in the disrupted flows of everyday life, they participate in the wider cultural life, transforming it and themselves simultaneously in the process" (Hall 2003b: 197). This results in a type of globalization from below. Pueble serves as the unifying force of such minoritarian resistance, builds coalitions, and creates inclusive empowerment contact zones in the "salsascape" (Appadurai 1991).[2] Salsa bands provide the soundtracks for such zones, and their performances serve to frame the spaces where such sentiments are built and felt. And, as I later discuss, the inner group dynamics of bands play out the tensions caused by these unifications that seek to erase, or at the very least attenuate, deeply held cultural divisions.

New York Salsa Bands

I shall first map out a generalized ethnographic description of salsa bands in order to provide the backdrop for further exploration of pueble. I have organized the following material to mirror the steps involved in the formation, preparation, and performance of salsa bands, exploring issues associated with each formative step along the way.

In the New York salsa scene, there are several types of bands: amateur bands, professional cover bands, and professional original bands. Amateur bands consist of either student or nonprofessional musicians who gather to jam together in informal settings, such as someone's basement or a rented rehearsal space, playing either original music or transcribed arrangements from professional bands. They rarely, if at all, perform publicly or for paid engagements. Professional cover bands employ professional and semiprofessional musicians performing the repertoire of professional original bands (they play the hits that are regularly heard on the radio). They perform for paying audiences at private parties, weddings, smaller clubs (known as the "*cuchifrito* circuit," a name derived from the fried food sold at these neighborhood restaurants/discos), and festivals that cannot afford the more famous groups. Professional original bands are comprised of professional musicians who play for paying audiences at clubs, private parties, festivals, and concerts. They differ from cover bands because their repertoire consists mainly of original material, their musicians have attained a high level of competency in salsa performance practice, they enjoy at least a modicum of commercial success (record sales, prestigious bookings, and music video and radio airplay), and they subsequently can charge much higher performance fees. These professional original bands are the primary focus of this book.

How Salsa Bands Form

Salsa bands typically are formed in several ways. Splintering, the most frequent method, became popular during the 1970s and was fueled by musicians, managers, club owners, and booking agents eager to cash in on the Fania-era salsa boom. Typically, after attaining some popularity, bands splinter into two separate groups, with the lead singer departing to form his own band while the original group continues to perform with a new vocalist. This trend toward splintering has continued; examples include Ruben Blades and Hector Lavoe leaving Willie Colón, Ray De La Paz splitting from Louie Ramírez, Pete "El Conde" Rodríguez leaving Johnny Pacheco, Adalberto Santiago splitting from Ray Barretto, Tito Nieves and Johnny Rivera separating from Conjunto Clásico, and Ray Sepulveda leaving Johnny Zumont, among others. The financial benefits and the advantages to having sole artistic control of a salsa band are the most significant motivating factors for this trend. Furthermore, starting as a sideman or lead singer with an established band provides a modicum of recognition among salsa audiences for the new bandleader, allows time for artistic maturation (learning how to front a band and developing one's own style), and gives essential experience concerning the machinations of leading a band. As Johnny Rivera said, "It was with Clásico that I learned how to sing. Their songs are really high and strong and I had to figure out how to make my voice last. Sometimes we would have two or three gigs a night, playing night after night like that" (J. Rivera, pers. comm.).

Another formative trend that became more prominent throughout the 1990s, borrowed from popular music practices, is when a producer or record company "discovers" a singer. Once a new talent is found, the producer or company grooms and prepares him or her to become a commercially viable product. In this case, a band forms around the new singer. Producers' choices are often young, good-looking performers who have little or no professional performing experience. One example is Huey Dunbar, the lead singer for the Dark Latin Grooves (DLG) band. Sergio George discovered Dunbar at an amateur talent contest. George recalls, "When I first heard Huey sing, he was 17 years old. I knew at once he had potential and I signed him immediately. But we didn't record right away because he wasn't ready. He had no experience. So I had him sing background vocals with La India for six months before I had him record with DLG. Then I had him dye his hair and start wearing hipper clothes. I want DLG to look almost cartoon-ish. I want them larger than life. You know, it's a gimmick. It's what people remember" (S. George, pers. comm.). At other times, producers "rediscovered" singers who had careers in music styles other than salsa. Examples include Marc Anthony and La India, both of whom recorded house music tracks for producer Little Louie Vega before embarking on salsa careers. Vega, along with George, combined their dance music experience with salsa to produce a new salsa sound in the mid-1990s.

A third way bands are formed is through the cooperative effort of several of the group's members, who agree to share leadership and financial responsibilities. Often these groups start out as amateur or cover bands and slowly develop their own repertoires along the way, working their way up to more prestigious gigging opportunities. A handful of bands in the New York scene have been formed in this way; one example is the group Palenque, which was started by three members of the band.

Once a bandleader or producer has decided to launch a new professional band, the following organizational steps are taken. New York salsa group structure is fairly uniform and the following schemata are applicable to most bands. First, a commercial recording must be produced. This is followed by the formation of a band, the performing unit, which prepares for public performance through a series of rehearsals. Once the band is deemed fit for its debut performance, venues are sought and performances are arranged. For each of these steps a social and business infrastructure, a collection of individuals with clearly defined roles, must be in place.

The Recording Process

The commerciality of salsa is no more evident than in the fact that producing a recording is the primary concern and initial step to forming a professional band.[3] It is through radio airplay and spins by dance club deejays of a commercially available recording that a band's popularity grows. This in turn generates performance opportunities and record sales that support a second recording and a sustained career. Music videos also have been playing an increasingly larger role in providing audience exposure. One radio hit, though, is enough to establish a new group within the scene and can generate a regular working schedule. Subsequent recordings also need to receive airplay to maintain audience interest and demand. Reciprocally, more club performances provide exposure and can create greater listener radio requests for the band's songs. Much of the salsa scene is driven by economic factors, and the dynamics of live performance are tied to the salsa business structure. Salsa bands must perform to perpetuate their careers. Regular performance schedules help to maintain consistent group membership, optimize the group's cohesiveness, raise performance competency levels, and maintain and build audiences.

In order to stimulate this reciprocating relationship between airplay, record sales, and club bookings, record companies and bandleaders lobby both radio programmers and club deejays. Bandleader Johnny Rivera remarks, "The way this business is, you can have the greatest record in the world, but if you don't got the radio thing together, you don't got shit! They have to play your record on the radio. That's the bottom line" (J. Rivera, pers. comm.). Ralph Mercado routinely frequented New York City clubs, visiting deejay booths to ensure that music on his label was played between the live music sets. At other times, his employees patronized clubs for similar purposes. At Club Broadway in 1994, one of his employees said to the manager, "Ralph lets you book his bands for a good price, and tonight between the sets I didn't hear any RMM artists played. That's not right." The manager responded, "I'll have a talk with the deejay and take care of it." Mercado's artists exclusively were played the rest of the evening. The level of influence record companies and promoters exert over the dissemination networks and media outlets for salsa ring true to the observations of Jacques Attali, who writes, "Everywhere we look, the monopolization of the broadcast of messages, the control of noise, and the institutionalization of the silence of others assure the durability of power" (Attali 1985: 8). Indeed the business of salsa remains centralized and insularly powerful, with only a handful of entrepreneurs controlling most production and promotion at any given time.

To begin the recording process, bandleaders must secure sufficient funding to cover the expenses of recording, rehearsing, and promotion. This requires an executive producer who is willing to make a risky investment in the new band. Executive producers are most often record executives who fund the recording, promotion, and early formation of new bands as investments for their own companies. Their preceding commercial successes with other bands allow them to afford the possible monetary loss if the new band's record does not sell. Sometimes bandleaders who have been unable to secure a record deal with an established record company turn toward affluent friends or local drug dealers, or they form a cooperative among several musicians who provide the initial financial support in hopes of capturing the attention of a record company with the self-produced recording.

A producer also must be hired to begin the recording process. The producer's first job is to coordinate all the individuals involved in making the recording, and then to give the recording its identifiable sound. The producer chooses the recording studio; hires the engineer, arrangers, composers, music copyists, and studio musicians; and coordinates the scheduling of the recording sessions.[4] Additionally, the producer may assist in choosing the repertoire and then compose and arrange some of the selections. In the studio, producers dictate musical and sonic decisions and direct the mixing and mastering sessions. Producers frequently perform on the recording and often will continue to play with the group during the rehearsal period and through the first few performances. Their presence ensures the proper interpretation and execution of the arrangements.

Freelance songwriters who sell their compositions to bandleaders and producers provide most of the repertoire on new salsa recordings. Composer Mimi Ibarra explains, "I customize my songs to any given artist depending on their style, and the kind of work they have done in the past . . . I first write to please myself, then I shape the work to reflect the style and persona of the artist."[5] A few bandleaders, such as Danny Rojo and Ramon Rodríguez, compose their own songs, but they are the exception. Remakes of songs from other musical styles are also popular. Examples include Nieves's version of "I'll Always Love You," originally sung by American pop singer Taylor Dayne, or Marc Anthony's version of the Mexican ballad "Hasta Que Te Conocí" ("Until I Knew You"). Remakes of older Cuban *sones* are popular choices as well.

Composers seldom arrange their own compositions; instead, arrangers are employed to adapt the songs to salsa orchestration, formal structures, and performance practices, as well as to the specific needs of the bandleader (key choices, personal style, and specific instrumentation). As such, arrangers exercise considerable influence on the various stylistic directions of salsa. As bandleader Sepulveda states, "I always meet with my producer several times to discuss what tunes to record. He suggests some, I find some, and then I leave it up to the producer to pick the arrangers and leave the rest up to them. I come to the studio when they are ready for me to record" (R. Sepulveda, pers. comm.). George, who produced some of Sepulveda's recordings, prefers to have complete control over repertoire choices: "I have to get a song that I like. The song must make me say 'Wow, I like that song, I like where it is going, I like the melody—I think I can take it over here, over there, anywhere.' The passion begins with the song. That's why for all the artists I produce, I pick all the songs. The only exception has been Marc Anthony. I just laid back and let him get his own identity. He gathered the material and later consulted with me" (S. George, pers. comm.).

Composers typically provide arrangers with a demo recording containing the text, melody, a simplified harmonic structure, and preliminary ideas concerning the arrangement (number of *soneos* [lead vocal improvisations] and *coros* [chorus] between sections, and melodic suggestions for the instrumental accompaniment). Arrangers then proceed by reharmonizing the overall structure, composing the instrumental sections (introduction, interludes, mambo, *moña* [instrumental interlude], and coda), and orchestrating the accompaniment parts during the vocal sections. According to arranger Ricky

Gonzalez, these decisions are not only based on musical considerations, but commercial ones as well. One aim of the arranger is to provide a product that will achieve commercial success. It must be in line with consumer expectations, but also stand out in some way. Often, a memorable hook or melody serves this purpose well. Gonzalez comments, "I try to write simple but interesting melodies that will be, in some way, memorable . . . I start with the melody and text to determine the overall feel of the composition, either laid-back or with a lot of energy. Then I decide where energy level changes are going to take place. Energy change is important. A tune that is always laid-back and never moves anywhere is boring. Similarly, if it is always at a high energy level, it is boring. You change the energy level by the use of different instrumentation and orchestrational techniques" (R. Gonzalez, pers. comm.).

As a seasoned arranger, Gonzalez knows how to manipulate the orchestrational and instrumental choices for the desired effect. His constant orchestrational shifting of instruments creates a dynamic presentation that provides direction and motion in the music. Often musicians will comment on the "aliveness" or "deadness" of an arrangement. These terms refer to the expanding and contracting movement that accompanies energy shifts. This movement serves to engage listeners and dancers by maintaining motion and keeping the music "alive."

Arrangers rarely do the time-consuming task of copying individual instrumental parts of their arrangements. Instead, they supply a notated score to music copyists who are hired to provide legible parts for the studio musicians to read during the recording. These same parts will be used later for live performances. With the advent of computer software, more arrangers have become computer literate and skilled in using notional software such as Finale and Sibelius. Computer-generated charts have become the standard, whether created by a copyist or the arranger.

The salsa recording community in New York is small, with only a handful of producers, arrangers, and studio musicians working regularly (less than 100). The community remains limited because of the financial advantages gained from hiring experienced musicians who expeditiously can execute their respective parts with few corrections. Costly studio time requires a well-prepared production and prompt completion of the recording process. Performance errors necessitate multiple takes, with each take causing direct economic consequences; hiring higher-priced producers, arrangers, and studio musicians ensures a higher level of performance, less correcting and rerecording time, and, in the end, a less expensive production. Negatively, the limited recording community has reduced stylistic variety in the New York scene and restricts opportunities for less experienced players, resulting in numerous recordings that sound alike.

Budgetary constraints play a role in affecting the characteristic sound of the final product because they dictate the quality of the studio, equipment, and engineers that are used, as well as determine the amount of session time a producer can spend in the studio. Sessions with limited budgets often must leave less-than-acceptable performances in the final product because of the lack of time to fix parts. The expenses of recording can be high, with rates ranging from $75 per hour for small studios to $450 per hour at large commercial studios. A salsa record typically requires six to ten eight-hour recording sessions, three to four eight-hour mixing sessions, and two to three eight-hour mastering sessions. Producers are paid per production. Their rates range from a few thousand to more than twenty thousand dollars, depending on their prestige and the success of past productions. At times producers negotiate points on the recording, meaning they receive a percentage of the profits from record sales. Arrangers are paid per arrangement, usually between $250 and $750. Their rates also depend on experience and prestige. Music copyists are typically paid between $50 and $250 per arrangement. Studio musicians are paid for each overdubbed track they record. Rates begin at $50 and can be as high as $200 per track.

Most productions are paid for in cash, with no subsequent residuals or royalties paid to arrangers and musicians. Even though U.S. copyright laws require record companies to pay royalties to composers and publishers, throughout the 1980s and 1990s the Latin music record industry lagged in legalizing its business practices; only in the late 1990s was royalty compensation sporadically paid. One of salsa's most prolific composers, Ramon Rodríguez, commented, "I have over 150 salsa songs recorded on Fania and for RMM, and I never received any royalty money for them until last month [September, 1993]. ASCAP sent me a $3,000 check, saying it was for 'artistic appreciation.' This is the first time that I have been recognized and benefited from the American system. They don't view what we do as important enough" (R. Rodríguez, pers. comm.). Puerto Rican composer Tite Curet Alonso complained that after he joined the Asociación de Compositores y Editores de Música Latinoamericana (ACEMLA), which, like BMI and ASCAP, collects money from radio and television stations to pay royalties to its composer members, Puerto Rico's main salsa stations agreed to exclude his songs from their programming to avoid any extra expense. As a result, the record industry has been reluctant to record his songs, fearing that they will not receive airplay in Puerto Rico (González 1999: 23). This reluctance to conduct business in a legal manner and avoid royalty payments eventually led to the demise of RMM Records. In November 2001, Mercado was forced to seek Chapter 11 bankruptcy protection and close his company as a result of the successful copyright infringement lawsuit composer Glenn Monroig brought against

RMM Records. Monroig's case was an exception though; most musicians, composers, and producers never expect to receive anything past their initial one-time cash payments. In fact, musicians view the one-time cash payments as both positive and negative; they receive a predetermined amount regardless of whether the record sells or not, but no benefits are gained from highly successful recordings.[6]

In the Recording Studio

The ethnographic work of Louise Meintjes on recording studios as significant sites of cultural production is helpful in thinking about how musicians deal with the specific challenges presented in the studio, all of which have significant repercussions in how the music will be used, signified, and interpreted later. She writes that "recording and mixing is a dramatized struggle over signs embodying values, identities, and aspirations. In their struggle, studio musicmakers rework or reaffirm their sociological and professional positioning," creatively using the studio's technological resources (Meintjes 2003: 9). Seasoned studio musicians and savvy producers must create artistically satisfying records while attending to the social and economic climes of their constituency (the market). In the studio, this struggle is played out on the micro level. Since salsa recordings are built part-by-part and section-by-section, with each step scrutinized by producers and musicians alike, the effect of the final product is constantly in negotiation. How perfectly a note should be played, its rhythmic placement, its timbre, and its feeling are subjective decisions that can fuel contentious debates. The participants' artistic sensibilities, reputations, and sociopolitical positionings are at stake, all of which cannot be divorced from their concerns for their livelihoods and future economic prospects. Further, these negotiations are particularly charged because it is on the micro level that the shaping of musical style is forged; that is, style as a performed and multilayered sign that expresses, constructs, and embodies values, identities, and affiliations (Feld 1982, 1988; Keil 1985; Meintjes 2003; Urban 1991). As musicians finish their respective parts, though, they leave the studio. Only the producers remain throughout the entire process and, ultimately, have the final say over such decisions. Throughout the recording process, producers must imagine the final product in play, on the radio, and on the dance floor, conceptualizing the incitations of movement and the cultural identifications that are part and parcel of live salsa performance events.[7]

Seemingly antithetical to the incitations of pueble (collectivity) that will play a part in the future soundings (both live and mediated) of the salsa recording, multitracking, a practice borrowed from pop music studio techniques in which each instrumental and vocal part is recorded separately, has become a standard practice in salsa productions. This overdubbing process sonically isolates each part on a different track, which in turn maximizes the subsequent editing and balancing possibilities during the mixing sessions. The most typical order for recording is to first record a click track (a metronomic beat on every quarter note). All musicians hear the click as they record their perspective parts, ensuring that all play with a uniform sense of pulse. The use of the click facilitates future computer editing as well, since all sections of the arrangement maintain the same tempo. The supportive rhythm section parts follow the recording of the click track. Since most rhythm section instruments play throughout a salsa arrangement, recording their parts first facilitates the brass and vocal parts, both of which do not constantly play throughout a selection. The piano and bass are typically first, either recorded separately or together. The percussion follows, usually with the congas first, then timbales, followed by the bongos and bells. The maracas and guiro are sometimes recorded immediately after the other percussion, or later after the brass parts are completed. The brass section is then recorded. Its order depends on the producer's choice of instrumentation. If the band includes trumpets, they will be added first, followed by the trombones and saxophones. Brass parts are usually recorded individually, with each instrumentalist sitting alone in the studio, though some producers prefer to have the entire section recording simultaneously to simulate the sound and balance of a live performance. Extra keyboard or synthesizer effects (for instance, sound effects or samples) come next. After all instrumental parts are completed, background vocals are added. The lead vocals are the last addition before the mixing begins.

Most arranging decisions are made in preproduction, before the recording process begins. However, producers often make adjustments during recording sessions. Issues of execution and performance practice are the main focus in the studio (how melodic lines are to be phrased, which timbre choices to employ, and where notes are to be placed in relation to the beat—"laid-back," "in the pocket," or "pushed ahead"). Though multitracking allows the producer more postproduction sonic control, this style of recording confronts musicians with several unique performance issues. First, because recording standards have changed to favor the clean and perfected productions established in Puerto Rico throughout the 1980s, musicians rarely record a complete track in one take; instead, they usually work on one section or phrase at a time. Difficult passages may be pieced together note by note, thus disrupting the flow of the performance. Both musicians and producers must compensate by trying to simulate the type of flow found in a complete run-through by taking care to match dynamic levels, timbre, feel, and energy flow from take to take. Second, musical interplay between players found in live performance is minimized because musicians can react only unidirectionally; that is, only to the musicians who have preceded them. Studio musicians must attempt to create a sense of spontaneous interaction in this unidirectional environment by being attentive and responding to the reactional changes incorporated by the preceding players. Third, recordings are geared toward radio airplay, making the length of each track (arrangement) limited to less than five minutes. This short format reduces instrumental and vocal improvisatory sections. When musicians perform solos, they are forced to adjust their playing styles by infusing the type of excitement that can be created within a thirty-six-measure solo in a live performance setting into just four to eight measures.

The Rehearsal Process

Once the recording has been commercially released, bands begin to rehearse new material. However, for new groups, several components must be in place before rehearsals begin. First, a band manager or booking agent will be hired to begin arranging performance opportunities. Bandleaders contend that it is very difficult, if not impossible, to perform regularly without management from one of the several booking agents in the New York area. Associating with booking agents allows bandleaders respite from hustling work and from seeking new performance venues. Furthermore, bands can take advantage of the close relations agents often foster with club owners. At times, agents negotiate exclusive agreements that reserve priority for booking their clients. Agents collect a commission of 10 to 25 percent, which is deducted from the band's fee, for each gig booked.

While bandleaders front the band and are the personalities that attract audiences, musical directors are hired to conduct the band on stage, ensuring that performances run smoothly. Their other duties typically include hiring, firing, and paying the musicians; scheduling and directing rehearsals; giving musical cues during performances; and serving as the liaisons between the leaders and the musicians. Often, the producer will serve as the musical director throughout the rehearsal period and through the first few performances. The bandleader and musical director work together to assemble musicians who are willing to commit to playing steadily with the group and who will fit stylistically with the new band.

Finally, a "band boy" (a roadie or stage manager) will be hired. His (I have not seen a female hold this position) duties include carrying the rhythm section's instruments to and from their cars, setting up the instruments on stage, and passing out and retrieving the music. This last duty is the most important;

since copies are seldom made of the parts, recopying or reprinting can be costly, or even impossible. When Ray Barretto's entire book was stolen from the trunk of his car in the mid-1990s, he had no backup scores. Literally decades of salsa history were lost. Band boys are paid around $35 per gig and often are tipped by the musicians for whom they carry and set up instruments.

Most rehearsals take place in centrally located Manhattan studios; the Boys and Girls Harbor School and Montana Studios in Midtown are preferred spots. Studio rates run from $20 to $50 per hour. Rehearsals are normally held after 7:00 P.M. to accommodate musicians with day jobs. The majority of established bands rehearse only when they are adding new material to their repertoire or adding new members. If only one new member is added, he or she is expected to learn the music on the bandstand or at home from the recording before his or her first performance. Ray Sepulveda, for instance, will rehearse two or three times when adding new material to his group's repertoire. He usually incorporates two to three new songs from each recording, depending on radio airplay. Most rehearsals last between two to three hours. Salsa rehearsal techniques tend to rely on multiple run-throughs of arrangements as preparation for performance.

Newly formed bands tend to rehearse once a week for one to two months before their debut performances. However, many never make it past this rehearsal stage. The first problem is the difficulty in striking a reasonable management deal for an unknown band. The morale of a band that has rehearsed but does not have many gigs fades quickly. The second problem is that musicians are rarely paid for rehearsals. Financially, musicians cannot afford to maintain a rigorous weekly rehearsal schedule without the benefit of paying gigs. On those rare occasions when musicians receive rehearsal payment, $25 to $50 is the norm. The third obstacle is that, during the first few rehearsals, inexperienced bandleaders often complain that the music does not sound enough like their recordings. Most often this is caused by the bandleader's or music director's poor selection of musicians, which is often based more on camaraderie than musicianship. This type of complaint can cause friction between musicians and bandleaders, and can lead to a disbanding. Fourth, the demand for commitment that bandleaders place on musicians is nearly impossible for working musicians to satisfy. One missed rehearsal can justify replacement, especially if the musician is recording or playing with another band (jealousy runs deep between leaders). Most salsa musicians cannot afford an exclusive relationship with a band that is not working full time. This leads to frequent personnel changes, which disrupt the coherence of the developing group. Once bands have established their personnel and have adequately prepared their music for live performance, they seek professionally paid gigs.

On the Gig

Salsa performance is entwined in the fabric of daily life for the people in the salsa community. Performative events range from nonformalized ones, which occur frequently and at times spontaneously, to highly formalized professional music-making. Examples of nonformalized events include aspiring *soneros* (lead singers) walking down the street singing salsa lyrics aloud; a maraca player jamming with a boom box at Orchard Beach in the Bronx on a Sunday afternoon; car stereos, with heavy emphasis on the anticipated bass, blasting through the streets of upper Manhattan with the driver and passengers singing along; percussionists who gather in the summer afternoons on street corners in El Barrio, or in Central Park, jamming a cappella or with a radio playing old Hector Lavoe hits; and weekly rehearsal bands comprised of amateur musicians who gather to jam on their favorite salsa covers in makeshift rehearsal studios in tenement basements. This book is concerned primarily with the highly formalized salsa performance events; that is, performances of professional salsa bands in their most stylized form—a large band, typically twelve to fifteen musicians, playing sophisticated arrangements of songs in a salsa format (instrumentation, style, rhythm), receiving compensation, and performing in a style that clearly delineates between performers and audience and is distinguishable from other daily routines and rituals of the participants. However, it is important to note that the distinction between informal and formal performance events is an artificial one that I have created to limit the scope of this project. Each type of event is ripe for and worthy of deep ethnographic interpretive analysis. For many, informal events serve as an introduction and first educative step into salsa. Furthermore, the activity of musicians who work in the formalized scene often bleeds into the less formalized type (they may be driving those cars blasting a record they just recorded). That said, I now turn to addressing the following questions concerning the performances of professional salsa bands: Where do salsa bands perform? What does a salsa performance event consist of? And, in addressing issues of performance practice, how do they perform?

Performance Venues

Most professional salsa performance occurs in nightclubs. Other performance opportunities include private parties, such as wedding receptions and holiday parties held at community centers, churches, and catering halls; indoor arena and concert hall performances; outdoor salsa festivals; and live television and radio appearances. As an example, of the ninety gigs that Sepulveda's band played in 1994, sixty-three (70 percent) were in salsa dance clubs in the greater New York metropolitan area; five (6 percent) were in out-of-town salsa dance clubs (Rochester, Philadelphia, Washington D.C., and Boston); twelve (13 percent) were at private functions; nine (10 percent) were at outdoor salsa festivals at Orchard Beach and street festivals in Brooklyn, Manhattan, and the Bronx; and one (less than 1 percent) was at Madison Square Garden. Since nightclubs provide the majority of performance opportunities, I mainly focus upon the particulars of club performance in the following analysis. First, however, I briefly introduce the other performance venues mentioned above before embarking on that discussion.

Since the 1980s, the largest concert events were produced by Mercado and held at Madison Square Garden. These concerts often drew more than twenty thousand audience members at each event and were programmed several times a year. The advantage for concertgoers was that, for the price of one ticket ($35 to $75), they could see numerous salsa acts performing the most popular music. These concerts were integral to the success and sustained dominance of RMM Records because they provided large audience exposure and were used to introduce RMM's newest salsa acts. Both Marc Anthony and La India made their salsa debuts in one of these concerts. Mercado also produced smaller-scaled concert events that typically featured three to five bands performing at Carnegie Hall, Lincoln Center, and Town Hall.

Outdoor street festivals, held during the warmer months, are often sponsored by New York's largest Latin music radio station, La Mega (WADO 97.9 FM), in conjunction with either cigarette or beer companies and New York City borough governmental offices. These festivals, along with the Puerto Rican Day parades of Manhattan and the Bronx, provide the widest exposure of live salsa performance to New York City audiences. The summer outdoor festivals are usually free and tend to attract large numbers, including many who are unable to afford the expensive admission prices of indoor concerts and salsa clubs. For instance, one of the largest ongoing festivals is held at Orchard Beach Park in the Bronx. It runs every weekend throughout the summer months, attracting over two thousand people daily and featuring two to four different bands each week.

Other performance opportunities are provided by the New York–area Spanish-language television stations Channel 41 (WXTV) and 47 (WNJU), which include live salsa performances in their programming. Radio station WBAI (99.5 FM) often features in-studio live performances on its Sunday afternoon Latin music program, and La Mega frequently airs live broadcasts from its sponsored street festivals and club events. I now turn to the New York dance club scene in order to examine who performs salsa in New York and what performance events typically consist of.

Salsa Club Soundscapes

During the 1990s, there were fifty nightclubs that regularly (at least once a week) programmed live salsa performances in the greater New York metropolitan area (a list of those venues can be found in Appendix 2 of this volume).[8] These venues were the mainstay for salsa performance in New York throughout the decade, generating the lion's share of income for *salseros* and providing avenues for bands to develop and build their audiences. The following section focuses on the overall soundscape of salsa clubs—that is, the club environment and experience, and how salsa performance operates within that milieu. In particular, I examine salsa clubs not by focusing on one particular performance event or venue, but by exploring the commonalties shared by the premier New York salsa clubs of that decade—the Copacabana, Les Poulets, Club Broadway (later renamed the Latin Quarter), Broadway Too, Wild Palm, and Sidestreet.

The performative frame of salsa club performance is set apart from the daily lives of the participants, creating a heightened event atmosphere. Simultaneously, though, salsa club performance is fully steeped in the cultural environment from which the music style emerged, and its cultural "rootedness" (and "everydayness") is often the focus of performance. First, I turn to the former and investigate the distinctive cues that frame salsa performance as an event set apart. As Norma McLeod and Marcia Herndon write, "The framing of performance involves communication about communication through the means of culturally conventionalized meta-communication . . . this means that each musical group, performer, or society will employ a structured set of distinctive cues from among its communicative resources in culturally specific and culturally conventionalized ways. These cues will then announce to the audience and to the performers, 'This is a performance'" (McLeod and Herndon 1980: 190).

Clubs are located throughout the New York metropolitan area; however, the premier salsa clubs tend to be centrally located, not necessarily in neighborhoods where the majority of their patrons reside. Attending a salsa club requires some type of travel, either by taxi, car, or public transportation. It does not involve leisurely walking to the corner restaurant and dropping in to hear a local band perform cover songs. Further, club decor tends to be formal, and most clubs adopt dress codes that are enforced at their entrances by security personnel who ensure that patrons dress up for the occasion. The presence of large and intimidating bouncers conducting body and purse searches and metal detectors at club entrances attest to the imminent danger of the club scene. Conversely, it also provides a sense (perhaps not necessarily true) that clubgoers are entering a protected and potentially less dangerous space than the one they just left.

After passing the dress requirements and weapons inspection, clubgoers must pay an entrance fee. The pricey admission fees ($15 to $35 for men, slightly lower for women), along with high drink minimums (two to four drinks) when sitting at a table, limit audiences to those of certain economic means. A night of salsa dancing can easily exceed $100 for a couple. The incentive of lower admission prices for women is to ensure enough dance partners for men and to entice more men to come. Age requirements also reflect this desire to ensure the attendance of equal numbers between the sexes. For instance, at the Wild Palm in the Bronx, only men twenty-five years of age and older and women twenty-three years of age and older were admitted. This practice is not uncommon. Clientele come to salsa clubs primarily to dance and to see their favorite performers; secondary reasons include meeting new people, finding new sex partners, escaping from the routines of daily life, and fraternizing with friends. Salsa is a highly stylized couple's dance requiring available partners of the opposite sex. Rarely do audience members dance alone or with members of the same sex. On occasion some women do dance together; however, men are rarely seen dancing together. At times, highly competent male dancers will take on two female partners simultaneously. Furthermore, "sex sells"; a club with the reputation of having many single and potentially available women and men is a strong marketing tool for attracting large crowds. Bandleaders often play up this attraction by announcing between songs: "[Name of club] is the most elegant in New York, with the most beautiful women." The requirements to travel and dress up, the elegant and sexually charged atmosphere, and the expense of attending a salsa club posit it as a special occasion for many, making clubgoing an appropriate choice for escaping daily routines. Bandleaders typically receive four to ten requests to give public birthday wishes or announcements of anniversaries each night; this attests to the "special" event status that is often coupled with clubgoing.

The overall sensory effect clientele receive upon entering a salsa club also contributes to the heightened, specialized event status. Upon entering, clubgoers' senses are immediately overloaded, cueing participants that they are crossing a threshold to an alternative soundscape. Visually, this effect is created foremost by the lighting design. Lighting is kept dim, which softens edges and blurs lines, making it difficult for clubgoers to see clearly their surroundings. It also serves to focus attention on the lighting effects of the dance floor and stage. Clubs frequently employ lighting engineers to operate their systems in an interactive way, in which the vibe, tempo, and mood of the music are accentuated by lighting changes. Most typically, traditional discotheque lighting is used, multicolored lights that are electronically manipulated to rapidly change the color, amplitude, and shape of their projected fields. Strobes, laser lights, fog machines to enhance light displays, and mirrored reflecting balls are frequently employed as well. Mirrors often are placed throughout the club to distort attendees' fields of vision by amplifying the size of the space and number of patrons, and to accentuate the light show. Video screens located throughout the club project images of bands performing live, commercial Latin music videos, clips of scantily clad women and men, or sports events. These also distort space and add to the perpetually transforming color sphere. Further, the sartorial style of the club's employees contributes to a formalized and sexualized atmosphere. Male waitstaff and security personnel often don formal clothing, such as tuxedos or tailored suits. The female waitstaff tends to be young and to dress suggestively, often in miniskirts, low-cut tops, and exposed midriffs.

To further enhance their clubgoing experience, many patrons consume alcoholic beverages upon entering; others indulge in recreational drugs (most drug activity is centered in the club's bathrooms). These substances contribute to an alternative state and serve to set the user's club experience apart. Moreover, club performances tend to start after 11:00 P.M. and last until 4:00 A.M. This nocturnal time frame, when bodies and minds can become fatigued, enhances feelings of being in an alternative state of mind, further differentiating the participants' club experience from their diurnal lives.

The loud volumes of both the recorded music and the live bands make conversing difficult. Not only are patrons' ears filled, but the sound also is felt physically pulsating inside their bodies. The loud volume dictates much of the physical movement in the club. Besides the movements on the dance floor, people move in their seats, stand alone at the edge of the dance floor or at the bar swaying to the music, and play along with the band by slapping tabletops as makeshift conga drums or by clapping the clave beat. The constant music is rarely broken by silence as deejays bleed endings into beginnings of their selected playlists, creating a seamless club soundtrack that segues between salsa, merengue, and house-music styles.

The architectural layout of clubs also contributes to the formalized atmosphere. Dancing is the most prominent activity during club events. Its significance is reflected in the space that is designated for that activity, the dance floor. Dance floors are centrally located, with specialized hardwood floorboards that allow for unimpeded foot movement, and are set apart from the rest of the club, with most of the lighting system directed toward them. Deejays work from booths that are typically set to the back or to one side of the club. Their workspace most often is elevated to provide an unobstructed view of the dance floor. Their job is to provide a continual party atmosphere and keep the patrons dancing and enjoying themselves. Deejays constantly monitor the numbers on the dance floor, attempting to read what style of music is preferred. They typically play three to five selections in each style, depending on crowd response. The music they play is representative of the participants, reflecting their nationality, experience, and skill level (for example, salsa for Puerto Rican couples and skilled dancers, merengue for Dominican couples and others who cannot dance salsa, and house music that caters to younger audience members and those who prefer to dance without a partner). Deejays frequently vocally interject over the sound system, often provoking interactive responses from audience members. This is done by using rap-mixing techniques, such as superimposing snippets of other songs into their mix, and by enticing audiences to sing along with records. For instance, during coros, the deejay momentarily mutes the system, leaving a sudden silent break lasting only as long as the length of the coro. Audience members quickly pick up the cue and begin singing in those empty spaces, momentarily transforming the dance floor into an impromptu participatory performance through call and response. Deejays begin as the clubs open, alternate sets with bands, and then continue after bands have finished and until the clubs close. The deejay sets serve to frame salsa band performance, and they often musically ease the transition from recorded to live performance mediums by playing salsa tracks before bands begin to play. They also often call the musicians to the stage two songs before they end their sets to ensure that the band begins within moments after they end and to alert audience members that the band's performance is imminent.

Salsa bands perform on a stage, a place that is often elevated or set aside for the performers only. Sound amplification equipment, instruments, and stage lighting delimit this space. Often, security personnel will be employed to ensure that only performers enter that space before, during, and after performances. The stage abuts the dance floor to facilitate communication loops between the dancers and musicians. The stage lighting remains dim until just before a band begins to play, and it returns to a darkened level immediately after the band's performance is over. The dance floor light show is kept to a minimum during a band's performance, focusing attention on the stage area. When the band is set up and nearly ready to play, the deejay ends his or her set, creating the first lengthy silence (lasting one to three minutes) of the evening. Because of the preceding constancy of sound, this silence provides a striking contrast and serves as an overt cue that a performance is about to begin. Occasionally an emcee, usually a local radio personality, is hired as the evening's host. The emcee makes a brief appearance before each set to introduce the band, tell jokes, and inform audience members of upcoming events.

Once the band begins, it is confronted by one the biggest obstacles of the event: inconsistent sound quality. Since deejays begin early in the evening and the busy schedules of New York musicians prevent them from arriving early, sound checks rarely are conducted. Microphone, monitor, and house-system volumes must be adjusted during the first few minutes of performance. Salsa on the professional level is always performed at loud volumes and requires amplification, usually in the form of a sound system that includes amplifiers, a mixing board, house speakers, monitors, microphones (for vocals, horn section, and percussionists), and direct boxes for the piano and bass.[9] Sound systems are provided at most venues, along with sound engineers. However, most engineers have never heard the individual bands perform and are not sensitive to each band's specific needs. Due to the high expense of quality sound systems, most equipment found in clubs is inadequate. The lack of sound checks and competent sound engineers (again, a significant expense) often results in poor sound quality during live performances. Groups that are financially well off, such as those fronted by Marc Anthony and Ruben Blades, compensate for sound system and engineer problems by bringing their own sound people to all performances. Mikey Jimenez, sound engineer for Marc Anthony, comments, "What happens is when you're on stage and there are five thousand people in the club or wherever you're at and you feel the vibe of the people, it's hard to tell the band to keep it down, because the band wants to get into it . . . If they can play louder, they will play louder. Most of the clubs in New York, they don't have what salsa needs. For them [the musicians] to hear themselves, they got to play a lot louder just so they can feel each other."[10] It is imperative for salsa bands to learn to adapt quickly to the acoustics and sound-system deficiencies of each venue and learn how to perform with adverse sonic conditions. Regardless of the musicians' abilities, poor sound quality negatively affects performances and the overall clubgoing experience for audiences and is a frequent source of complaints.

The reluctance of club owners to purchase costly sound equipment and hire experienced engineers highlights their fundamental interest in profit-making. As long as the paying customers are not complaining too much, the owners will avoid the added expenditure. Club owners hold salsa events for profit. The admission charges and drink prices are calculated to maximize profitability. Bands are hired to draw patrons to the club. During the events, the role of salsa bands is to generate dancing and to entertain. The nights are organized around the live performances; the first set begins around midnight, when audience numbers peak, and the last set ends just before the club closes to entice patrons to remain. If a band can encourage dancing, the patrons buy more drinks, thus increasing the club's profitability.

The interplay between art and commerce plays a fundamental role in how bands perform. From the perspective of some musicians, this is a conflict rooted in the perceived disjuncture between salsa as the "essence" of the New

York barrio and Latino culture and salsa as an international popular music style tied to various commercial agendas. Often the disparities between the goals of business people (executive producers, promoters, and club owners) and those of performers (who are portrayed as artists rather than business people), as well as conflicts arising from a music style rooted in an urban working-class experience and the structure of big business, are marked as irreconcilable points of contention. This dynamic between business and artistic expression permeates performance and is a source of complaints and frequent comments from bandleaders and musicians. Percussionist Milton Cardona provides one example among many: "Frankly, salsa . . . is here to make money, and this attitude, above all, prevails. The promoters and record company heads, for the most part, do not give a damn about Afro-Caribbean music in its true form" (Torres 1976: 143).

Regardless of this pervasive discourse, a large part of being a member of a professional salsa band involves profitability. The business structure described above is constructed for that purpose, and bands do not perform if they are not compensated. As such, salsa performance, especially in the formalized structure of clubs, involves an intricate balance between economics, artistic expression, class struggles, and national and ethnic identifications. The role of salsa bands is to choreograph performances in such a way that these seemingly contradictory agendas are attended to, and they enact and embody a number of affiliations and social positions simultaneously through their performance practice. These, of course, are imbued with the variety of social forces in play during "a night out dancing." José Limón's work on Mexican American music and dance is informative in this regard:

> As a professional group, the band to some degree embodies the profitable political economy of the dance, with its marked tendency to treat the dancers as commodities and consumers . . . But there is another kind, a paradoxical choreographer at the dance, one sited directly on the human body itself. The inseparable triad of hard, working-class labor, substance use, and sexual desire may initially motivate the dancing—a desire to relax tired muscles; a sexual desire consummated in a cheap hotel or a car seat; and alcohol as a desire that drives the other two. (Limón 1994: 164)

Salsa bands accomplish such goals by privileging pueble over other concerns; obscuring the formalized boundaries established by the structures of salsa club performance events; performatively crossing or breaking boundaries set in place by club management; downplaying the business structures that enable the public performance in the first place (managers, booking agents, record executives, and so forth); and constructing their public identities as oppositional to, or in some way not associated with, the economic underbelly of the music industry ("soy otro humano cualquiera" ["I am just a regular guy"]).

As liaisons between the public and the bands, industry, and clubs, salsa bandleaders accomplish these tasks by informalizing the performance environment, encouraging group participation, and allowing audience members to cross boundaries. For instance, bandleaders use the breaks between songs to converse with audience members, addressing individuals directly to announce celebrations, to relate personal anecdotes associated with the songs they are about to sing, and to incite cultural pride. In New York they often use a combination of Spanish and English in order to include as many audience members as possible. Audiences are encouraged to dance, and, at times, are invited onto the stage to dance with the leader. Further, singers often sing directly to individual audience members by making eye contact, thus personalizing the song text to that individual. Establishing a rapport with audience members sets a communication loop in motion between performers and listeners in which the actions of each affect the other.[11] In salsa, the fourth wall of the stage remains pliable in disregard of the club's security personnel who often are posted at the foot of the stage. Audience members typically cross that line by passing notes scribbled on napkins or scraps of paper, requesting birthday greetings or even making sexual propositions. Bandleaders frequently shake hands, hug, or kiss people who approach the stage. At times, bandleaders engage in dialogues with audience members who shout from the dance floor song requests, qualitative statements concerning the bands' performances, or expressions of personal desire ("We love you, Tito!"). Singers respond over the microphone. This discourse often occurs while leaders are singing, and, at times, they are forced to omit a few lines of a song in order to shake hands or give hugs. These interchanges preempt the delivery of the song texts and take precedence over the rendition of the song: people before art.

This type of behavior informalizes the performance, reducing the distance between performers and audience inherent in its staging. Aaron Fox's ideas concerning this phenomenon, which he labels the "poetics of de- and re-naturalization," are pertinent to salsa performance. Fox writes that denaturalizing and renaturalizing effects are basic to the poetics of live performance in country music. "After denaturalizing themselves through a marked form of fancy dress, highly stylized stage movements, and other familiar trappings of the distanced, aesthetic experience of staged musical performance, country musicians partially re-naturalize the marked distinction between the stage and the dance floor by breaking the performative 'frame' which separates them from their fans" (Fox 1992: 55–56). Similarly, salsa bandleaders engage in such "partial re-naturalizations" by "staging" themselves as approachable, accessible, and equal with audience members. For instance, during gigs in Brooklyn, Sepulveda never fails to mention that he was born and raised in the neighborhood. Between sets he frequently mingles with the crowd, as opposed to remaining secluded in a backstage area. And during the set, he encourages audiences to sing along, a strategy many leaders use. One frequent way they employ this strategy is by pointing their microphones toward the dancers, temporarily inverting the performative frame where audience becomes performer and performer becomes spectator. This most often occurs during the coros, when the lead singer can then engage in a call and response with his or her fans. Arranger George discusses the significance of this type of group participation and the role it plays in his arranging choices:

> For the coros? I have a formula. I imagine myself in front of a stage watching a band. What is the band going to do to keep me hooked and interested? The coro! Remember that I have the ear of the people. I choose not to have the ear of a musician who wants to impress another musician. I am just like the average individual in the crowd singing along . . . I ask myself, "Is this coro a sing-along coro? . . . If I think people can sing to this coro, that's it." I don't mind giving away my little "secrets," but you've got to have coros that are dynamic, swingin', and, most importantly, coros that people understand and follow.[12]

George was the most successful arranger and producer in salsa in the 1990s, and he single-handedly shaped the stylistic trends of the genre for ten years—hardly the actions of "an average individual in the crowd." Regardless, as a producer working in studios, isolated from audiences, George felt compelled to adopt a "pueble stance" to inform his composition, arranging, and producing choices. As he suggests, the key to his commercial success was the prioritization of the average listener over musical concerns: people before music.

In salsa clubs, familiar contextual markers that permeate the soundscape assist bandleaders in their constructions of pueble. Though club performances are cued and set apart in a formalized fashion from the participants' daily lives, they are not separate entities divorced from quotidian experiences, but rather accentuated microcosms of the world where the participants live and work. The club's sensual overload is an extension of the soundscape, albeit an intensified and heightened one, found in the urbanized barrio environment from which salsa emerged, where the constant din of close city living, car alarms, sirens, occasional gun shots, traffic noise, and the constantly changing color sphere of the city at night are ordinary experiences. Several clubs actually incorporate the type of rotating flashing lights found atop emergency vehicles as part of their light shows. On the streets of El Barrio, salsa is not a private aesthetic, but a communal experience. Listened to loudly, it crosses over private spaces into public ones. Owners of *bodegas* (small family-owned grocery stores) frequently place on their storefronts speakers that project salsa onto the street, transforming the sidewalks into gathering places where older men play dominoes, kids hang out, and passersby stop to socialize. On the weekends, it is not uncommon to have stereo speakers placed facing outward on windowsills of private apartments. The sound is projected onto the streets even though the apartment may be filled with revelers. Cars cruise the inner-city streets with their tinted windows and hatchbacks opened to enhance sound dissemination, blasting salsa into the street. The music is shared, not sequestered. Like these impromptu salsascapes of the street, salsa clubs mimic such shared spaces, albeit through more controlled and intimate versions. Even the drug dealers, usually found selling their goods from street corners, relocate inside clubs to conduct business in the bathrooms throughout the evening.

During club performances, bandleaders gauge the effectiveness of their performative choices by the feedback they receive from audiences. As McLeod and Herndon write, "Performance involves the assumption of responsibility to an audience—as culturally defined—for the display of competence. This competence in display rests on both knowledge, and the ability of the performer to manifest a musical product within a socially acceptable range . . . and the ideal of style held by listeners seems to function as a negative and positive sanction on musical behavior" (McLeod and Herndon 1980: 190, 180). Salsa audiences communicate their positive and negative responses to musicians through both verbal and body language. Applauding, whistling, hollering, singing, and dancing serve as modes of interaction. Even the spaces where audiences choose to be during performances communicate degrees of approval or disapproval. When bands are particularly popular, audiences tend to crowd the stages, infringing upon the bands' space. They appear to desire to climb onto the stage, becoming part of the performance. The crowds in front can become so dense that dancing becomes impossible. Couples who want to dance must do so well away from the stage area. Conversely, if a band's performance is poor, few dancers will remain on the dance floor. The few who remain typically will dance in spaces farthest from the stage area. Large enthusiastic audiences can greatly enhance performance. The energy audience members exude serves to heighten the energy exuded on stage, and vice versa. Musicians often allude to and comment upon crowds that either respond greatly or remain despondent. For instance, after performing for an overly exuberant crowd in Colombia, trombonist Jimmy Bosch commented, "I like playing for Colombian crowds. They are always so responsive. You can feel all that energy" (J. Bosch, pers. comm.). And trombonist Dave Chamberlain remarked, "To me, one of my favorite things about playing Latin music is when the band is swinging, and we come in with a moña, and you can feel the entire band change gears and lift off the ground. You can see the dancers respond on the dance floor, and then the whole thing takes off" (D. Chamberlain, pers. comm.).

In order to foster this communication loop, bands construct their sets primarily to cater to dancers' needs. Sara Cohen writes, "Dance can thus not only integrate members of the audience but can effect and act as a mode of communication between audience and performers, establishing a relationship between them which heightens the sense of community and group identity and intensifies the social interaction occasioned by the musical performance" (Cohen 1991: 87). How bands perform their material reflects the importance of generating dance. Since recorded selections tend to be radio friendly and under five minutes, songs performed live need to be elongated (between eight to fifteen minutes) to accommodate dance club etiquette. Dancers briefly listen to a song before venturing to locate a prospective partner. Once obtained, they make their way to the dance floor. By the time they reach the dance floor, the band will have been playing for two to three minutes. If the band plays the number exactly as it appears on its recording, the couple would have only one to three minutes to dance. By adding solos, extra soneos, instrumental mambos, and moñas, the musicians provide sufficient dance time. During live performance the bandleader or musical director will make decisions concerning the length and repetition of each section. These decisions are made by surveying the reactions of audience members and are then communicated to the other group members by a set of cues. The loud volume of performances makes vocal cueing difficult, though, at times, singers will incorporate directions to the band in their soneos, such as "Vamonos al mambo" ("Let's go to the mambo"). More typically, though, salsa performances are directed by a series of standardized hand cues given by the bandleader or musical director, each of which indicates when the next section will begin. For instance, a raised index finger signals the mambo section; a raised index finger circling in the air indicates the repeat of the last cued section; a fist twisting in front of the forehead or a hand simulating grabbing the front of one's hair signals the moña; and a raised fist in the air signifies that the coda is to follow. Each of these cues is then followed by a four-, three-, or two-measure count off, depending on the arrangement, which is indicated by fingers raised in the air. In this way, bands tightly control the pacing of performance events, prescribing the vibe of the music and how long audiences dance, all with the aim of inciting collective participation. If a bandleader sees that no one is dancing, the selection may be cut short; conversely, popular songs are extended to accommodate greater participation: participation over music.

As bandleaders frequently seek to foster communication loops with audience members, they begin to recognize which formulas work and often return to those devices. Their nightly efforts to cater to audience expectations often cause them to remain tied to performative norms. These normative practices in and of themselves not only standardize, but also formalize, performance practices. Salsa performance, especially in clubs, tends to be uniform. It is quite easy to speak of typical practices because behavioral variation is kept to a minimum. Clubgoers can expect much of what has been described above (for example, salsa bands on a stage will present music sets lasting forty-five minutes in length, their performances will include such visual enhancements as choreographed dance steps and wardrobe coordination, etc.). In this way the interaction with audience members creates a dialectic between denaturalized formalities of highly stylized professional salsa performance practices and renaturalized images that bandleaders incorporate into the performances. In other words, even the renaturalized gestures can become formalized by their repetition. Audiences who come to see Sepulveda perform, for instance, can expect each performance to include Sepulveda's own opening introductory statement for his band. He begins by exclaiming, "Esto es Ray Sepulveda y su orquesta, la suya no la mia" (literally, "This is Ray Sepulveda and his orchestra, yours not mine"). This statement serves the utilitarian purposes of introduction, both for himself and his band, but at the same time conveys his perspective on the interpersonal relationships he shares with his audience that are central to his performance practice. Sepulveda comments, "I always begin by telling everyone that my band is their band. It lets them know that we are playing for them" (R. Sepulveda, pers. comm.). His introduction serves to renaturalize both his position and his band's relationship to the audience. Regardless of the fact that the official name of the band includes the possessive pronoun *su* (his), Sepulveda's staged discursive move of "relinquishing" ownership (*suya* [yours]) publicly veils his actual position as leader, a role that is embedded in the business structures involved in running a band, booking gigs, making records, and paying the musicians. On stage his message purports that not only is his band performing for all present, but the audience members are an integral part of the performance and are the actual possessors of the band. The music belongs to them: people above all. Pueble is central in this renaturalization process. This message's repetition and the audience's expectation of its inclusion are a formalized part of the band's performance.

Who are the gente (folks) who supposedly possess Sepulveda's band, and who are those involved in other assertions of pueble? To address this question, I briefly examine a recurrent strategy integral to the performance of salsa bands in which pueble is brought to the fore through the public performance of identity politics that simultaneously attend to specific national affiliations and purport broader cultural alliances. During a music set at Club Broadway, Les Poulets, the Copacabana, Sidestreet, or any other Latin dance club in the greater New York metropolitan area, bandleaders invariably shout out over the sound system, "Are there any Puerto Ricans in the house?" Elated cheers, hoots, and whistles accompanied by raised hands, and an occasional raised fist, are most certain to follow. The shout is not a real question, but rather an incitation for all Puerto Ricans present to proclaim their cultural pride and do so in an overtly public manner. Needless to say, if the crowd consists of mixed nationalities, the question "Are there any Dominicans in the house?" may follow, along with any number of additional cries of "Are there any [fill in your Latino nationality of choice] in the house?" And invariably there is a punctuating "Are there any Latinos in the house?" that follows, which creates excessive cheers and heightened levels of elation exuded by the audience. Most participants get to cheer not once, but twice, demonstrating multiple modes of identification. However, as an overhyphenated Anglo American—that is, one who is half Ukrainian American, a quarter Russian Jewish American, a quarter Scottish American, and often the only non-Latino present during such invocations—I have often wondered, "When do I get to cheer?" (I have never heard "Are there any Anglo Americans in the house?" or anything that closely represents an ethnicity that I personally identity with.) How is it that I, and others like me, can be participants in this scene and never get the chance to cheer? Further, why do salsa music performances often include these incitations? How can both exclusive nationalistic pride and a more inclusive pan-Latino ethnic pride be incited simultaneously?

It is my contention that the specifically hybrid nature of salsa musical culture explains why it is used with such pliability for a variety of cultural identifications. This hybridity reaches beyond mere stylistic influence to an overt, performatively practiced expression—a "staged hybridity." Salsa bands not only embody this hybridity in their membership, production, and business structures, but also serve as vessels for the public enactments of such expression. As Frances Aparicio points out, "Within the post-colonial conditions of the diaspora, U.S. Latino/a communities engage this music as a space for cultural reaffirmation . . . The plurality of ideological sites and discursive locations . . . illustrate the value of this music as metaphor for national identity, difference, hybridity, and oppositionality" (Aparicio 1998: xvii and 68). On stage these cultural affirmations are accomplished through repetitive incitations like the ones described above, and through other performative strategies that delve into the interplay of cultural and national diversity as well as establish "sameness" amidst difference.

What is at issue here is the role of salsa performance in the construction of fluid social identities. Informed by the works of Stuart Hall, Simon Frith, and Christopher Waterman, I adopt a conception of identity that accounts for these malleable attributes, whereby identity is an imaginative and emergent process rather than a thing in and of itself, and where music and its performance both reflect social conditions as well as serve as a constitutive force in the construction of those conditions. In this way, salsa band performance serves as a useful lens into broader social forces at play, but remains a central and significant component in identificatory processes. Hall writes, "Though they seem to invoke an origin in a historical past with which they continue to correspond, actually identities are about questions of using the resources of history, language and culture in the process of becoming rather than being: not 'who we are' or 'where we came from,' so much as what we might become, how we have been represented and how that bears on how we might represent ourselves . . . They relate to the invention of tradition as much as to tradition itself" (Hall 1996: 4). Frith shares a similar position, reminding us that identity is a process that is fluid and mobile, "a becoming not a being." For Frith, music participation "constructs our sense of identity through the direct experience it offers the body, time and sociability, experiences which enable us to place ourselves in imaginative cultural narratives" (Frith 1996: 275). Waterman also points to a similar notion of identity when he writes that "the role of musical style in the enactment of identity makes it not merely a reflexive but also a potentially constitutive factor in the patterning of cultural values and social integration" (Waterman 1991: 66). The identity politics involved in salsa performance, and for pueble in particular, serve as examples par excellence of such reflexive and process-oriented notions of collectivity, especially concerning invocations of a "pan-Latino identity." Because of the diversity of cultures, nations, classes, and races associated with and integrated in the production of salsa, the gente involved in pueble during performance must be imaginatively constructed as homogeneous collectives, or, at the very least, a heterogeneous group sharing commonalities. And the deep divisions between these groups involved in salsa performance (e.g., Puerto Ricans versus Dominicans) must be downplayed or temporarily ignored.[13]

No matter how fleeting, real, or imagined, these public constructions are rooted in specific social and political movements of the recent past. Stemming from the 1960s and rooted in the civil rights movement, proponents for Latino self-empowerment in the United States called for a stronger political voice within the mainstream Anglo American establishment, and it became increasingly important to present a unified political front. This extended beyond national boundaries, and calls began for a unified Latino community and for the assertion of a pan-Latino ethnic identity. Daniel Bell (1975) terms this type of contemporary ethnic allegiance as a "political ethnicity," meaning a strategic choice based on political interest rather than on common cultural considerations. Maria Eva Valle writes, "Accordingly, ethnic and racial identity undergoes a dynamic transformation from a source of discrimination and structural disadvantage into a strategic political tool that can be utilized to assert power" (Valle 1991: 74). This inclusive move also has been labeled *Latinismo* by Felix Padilla (1985), referring to the ferment for unity and ethnic revitalization that began in the 1960s and coincided with the rise of salsa. Padilla sees this as part of a larger phenomenon of panethnic movements worldwide that have been fueled largely by political and economic pressures. A common unity empowers a minority group with mass mobilization toward a common goal. Latinismo exists in constant tension with country-specific national identification and requires both a common interest and identity for success often solidified by a common overarching symbol system, or what Laurie Kay Sommers refers to as a "cultural umbrella" (Sommers 1991: 35).[14] Salsa's emergence was intrinsically tied to this political current, and its performers capitalized on these fervent ambitions, something that has continued to the present.

Since the 1960s, notions of a pan-Latino ethnic identity have been adopted and further inculcated by such mainstream institutions as the growing Latino media, which tend to address the Latino population in the United States as a homogeneous entity. Miguel Tinker-Salas observes, "Latino immigrants in the United States receive a daily barrage of Venezuelan, Mexican, Puerto Rican, and Brazilian soap operas. They view musical and talk shows hosted by Chileans, Cubans, and Mexicans. The dominant trend in this arena is decidedly pan-ethnic and has a definite impact on the formation of identity among recent waves of immigrants" (Tinker-Salas 1991: 68). However, the results of this push toward a pan-Latino ethnic identity have been more heterogeneous in nature; exclusive national identities are maintained along with new broader inclusive identities. To account for this heterogeneity, Valle (1991) prefers to make the distinction between "private" and "public" forms of ethnicity that coexist to serve a new type of emerging cultural community and set of political opportunities.

Salsa music performance serves to promulgate both "private" cultural identities drawn along nationalistic lines as well as to promote a "public" pan-Latino ethnic identity. The interactions between performers and audience members are particularly illustrative of this point. In his discussion of black identity, Paul Gilroy writes that significations during musical performance "produce the imaginary effect of an internal racial core or essence by acting on the body though the specific mechanisms of identification and recognition that are produced in the intimate interaction of performer and crowd. This reciprocal relationship serves as a strategy and an ideal communicative situation" (Gilroy 1990: 127). One illustrative example occurred during a 1994 concert in California. Marc Anthony, still a novice salsero at the time who was used to performing primarily for Puerto Rican and Nuyorican audiences in New York, borrowed a typical crowd-warming strategy he had heard veteran salseros use: He proclaimed, "I am Puerto Rican." However, he was completely surprised by the lack of response from the predominantly Mexican and Colombian West Coast audience, misjudging their ethnic makeup. One could see his consternation and determination to somehow correct his mistake once he realized it. So, after a short pause, he dramatically dropped to his knees and continued, "but, more importantly . . . I am Latino." This statement was followed by an explosive response from the audience. Pueble was operative, and Anthony achieved the identificatory connection he was seeking. As he turned to the band to quickly count off the next tune, he rolled his eyes and mouthed a relieved "whew!" to us.

Inclusive incitations such as this, and the others described above, occur frequently during salsa performances. They not only serve to acknowledge the different individual national identities of the participants in the salsa scene, but they call for solidarity based on Latino-ness as well. In these ways, the commonalities of experience—such as their shared immigrant or migrant status and the Spanish language—are accentuated, and divisions within the Latino community are deemphasized. This unified image is constructed, fostered, and displayed by the participants in an overtly public manner. This is nowhere clearer than when salsa bands are invited to perform during the annual meetings of various Latino or Hispanic organizations, such as the Latino Police Officers Association of New York or the Hispanic Union Workers of New York. These organizations establish social networks that are designed to assist Latinos in advancing their positions in society while maintaining their culture. The members of these organizations comprise many nationalities, so the speeches, food, and entertainment in some way must support an inclusively panethnic environment. The speakers include prominent Latino politicians and business people. The food served is most often *arroz con pollo* (rice with chicken), beans, and other dishes that are found in most Latin American and Caribbean countries. The music entertainment is most often a salsa band. In these situations, salsa bands are served up as translatable cultural set pieces, like rice and beans, and are chosen because the music supposedly holds some type of significance for all present.

Savvy bandleaders assess both their audience and performance context in order to attend to cultural differences, using pueble as their most effective avenue. One strategy Ray Sepulveda uses is to geographically label and locate each musician while making band introductions. For instance, he will say, "from San Juan, Puerto Rico—[name of musician here]," or "from Caracas, Venezuela," and so forth. Including the musician's hometown along with his or her name not only serves to incite nationalistic pride from audience members who share the same local ethnicity as the musician, but it also demonstrates the "pan-Latino-ness" behind the music-making. He rarely offers any other information during these introductions, preferring to privilege place over other personal details. And typically he concludes his introductions with one of his favorite incitations: "La raza latina, together forever!" or "¡Que viva la raza latina!" ("Long live the Latino race!"), both of which always receive many cheers. Gerald Creed and Barbara Ching (1997) point to the importance of incorporating locational politics into explorations of identity, and this incorporation is something that is prominently engaged in salsa performance, albeit in a fluid and changeable way. For instance, over time I noticed how Sepulveda would deemphasize and even exclude certain localities over others, depending on his perceptions of the performance context and of the ethnicity of audience members. For him, contextual factors heavily determine his presentation of ethnicity and identification. For concerts in Brooklyn, Sepulveda says, "I'm Puerto Rican, but I grew up in Brooklyn." For concerts in New Jersey, he makes sure to include that he now resides in Fort Lee, New Jersey. For a performance at a Peruvian wedding, Puerto Rico was not mentioned once, but the national Peruvian call "Chimpún Callao!"[15] was heard repeatedly. For Sepulveda, along with other bandleaders, establishing a sense of commonality with audiences—pueble—remains a central goal, and they rely on this fluid identificatory performance practice to accomplish such sentiment.

Interestingly, as the only non-Latino in Sepulveda's band, I was never introduced "from Bath, Ohio"; instead, he began introducing me, in jest, as being from Ponce, Puerto Rico (something that he continued to do for over three years). This always elicited many laughs from my fellow musicians and perplexed looks from audience members. Even though I do have a modicum of cultural pride concerning my rural Ohio roots, I took the jesting in stride and interpreted it as a complimentary gesture signifying my acceptance into the salsa scene. However, I was the only band member whose birthplace was treated in this jocular manner. For Sepulveda, it was necessary and acceptable to deemphasize and even exclude my North American-ness and Anglo-ness because it did not play into, or contribute to, a cohesive and unified pan-Latino ethnicity. This is why I was never given a chance to cheer during "in the house" incitations; such an incitation would only diffuse the types of feelings associated with the cultural pride that Sepulveda and other bandleaders try to elicit: people, but not all people, before music.

This accentuates a fundamental component of pueble—that is, exclusion. Hall addresses the exclusionary nature of constructing inclusionary identities. Drawing on the writings of Jacques Derrida (1981), Ernesto Laclau (1990), and Judith Butler (1993), Hall writes that "identities emerge within the play of specific modalities of power, and thus are more the product of the marking of difference and exclusion, than they are the sign of an identical, naturally constituted unity . . . Throughout their careers, identities can function as points of identification and attachment only because of the capacity to exclude, to leave out, to render 'outside,' abjected" (Hall 1996: 4–5). Though it was in the United States that salsa developed, it is against the exclusionary backdrop of a "mainstream America" that the various Latino and pan-Latino ethnicities are constructed during salsa performances that take place within the United States. "Cultural outsiders" are able to participate as long as their presence does not interfere too greatly in those constructions. Even during gigs where I have been the musical director, dictating the pacing of the performance event and arranging most of the music, the exclusion of my own culture and ethnicity and my subsequent silence during those incitations was never commented on by other participants. Their silence points to the inherent exclusion that is couched in every construction of cultural identity.

Practices of pueble are so essential to salsa performance that sometimes incitations, such those described above, are composed into song lyrics, ensuring their inclusion in all subsequent performances, and, in a way, canonizing this type of performance practice. "Llegó La India" serves as one of many illustrative examples.[16] Eddie Palmieri composed this song as the title track for the debut salsa recording of La India in 1992 (*Llegó La India Via Eddie Palmieri,* RMM Records, RMD-80864). Linda Bell Caballero, known professionally as *La India* (the Indian), is representative of the second generation of salseras and salseros. She is a second-generation Nuyorican, born and raised in New York City. Her musical roots lie primarily in house and soul music, and she draws from these musical styles, mixing them with *salsa romántica*, to produce a more contemporary pop-oriented sound (see Chapter Five for an analysis and discussion of her performance practice).

This recording marked a dramatic stylistic shift in her musical career; in her performance of "Llegó La India," India is positioned as a nascent but authoritative voice invested with a newly discovered cultural pride. The narrative of the lyric unfolds in a series of declarations sung in a mixture of Spanish and English (reflecting the Nuyorican barrio experience of both her and her intended audience), incorporating both locational markers and overt declarations as to the reasons behind her reinvention as a salsera, as well as specific clues as to whom she is singing. The coro begins by dramatically announcing, "Llegó La India cantando son a todos los barrios de Nueva York" ("India has arrived singing son to all of the New York barrios"). Alternating with her solo statements, this repetitive statement reinforces its message throughout. Her audience is a specific demographic connected with the barrio experience. She responds with "A todos los barrios le canto ahora el ritmo suave del rico son . . . Y dedicado a mi raza latina, que con orgullo le canto yo . . . Porque el son es más divino, que usted puede imaginar" ("To all the barrios I now sing the smooth rhythm of the rich *son* . . . I dedicate it to the Latino race, to whom I sing it with pride . . . because the *son* is more divine than you can imagine"). These statements aim to invoke feelings of Latino solidarity and a shared cultural pride. Praising the beauty of the music, and thus by extension the cultural milieu for which it emerges, is a frequent strategy in salsa lyrics. In this case, the beauty of "her/our" music is "divine." Her public proclamation of her proud feelings, along with her call for group participation, serves as an invitation for others to feel that pride, as well as for them to join her in a cohesive communal experience and participate by dancing. This call comes first in English and later in Spanish. No one in her targeted demographic is left out. "You're going to dance the montuno with me now, so grab me hard, love, and hold me tight."

An extended vocal interlude is then sung in English, serving as a musical journey of sorts. "So now into Queens and to Brooklyn, and to the Bronx and Manhattan, too . . . New York, how I love you New York, I want to shout out to everyone. To the Bronx—is where I'm from, and to Brooklyn, and Staten Island, too. We can't forget about Queens, and all the Latins in Manhattan." The listing of the names of the five boroughs creates a feeling of inclusion for all New York listeners, and the use of English when addressing those people not only reflects the bilingual environment of the city, but also India's own generation of Latinos who were born and raised there (India did not have a command of the Spanish language prior to her salsa career). The use of jargon from the hip-hop and underground dance music scenes (such as "shout out") further locates this song within the New York musical milieu. While singing the word "Bronx," India sings the flatted third d-flat over the b-flat dominant seventh chord, a note associated with the blues scale. This is also coupled with a glissando and a growling raspy sound quality in her voice that serves to accentuate the word "Bronx" in a specifically bluesy manner. This gesture for her home borough acknowledges the rich African American traditions associated with the city that played a large role in her own musical development—New York as a crosscultural contact zone. Further, the words "I love you New York" seem reminiscent of the numerous New York praise songs written in the American popular music tradition. She is a New Yorker, and this song serves as a public proclamation of her love and pride for her hometown and her fellow New Yorkers.[17]

The realm of "Llegó La India" continually expands, reaching beyond the limits of New York City. "Le canto a las Américas para que escuchen mi son" ("I sing to the Americas so they can listen to my son"). Then, this broadened inclusive tract continues to expand further on the last line of text that includes an all encompassing "everyone": "Vengan todos pa'que bailen conmigo, mi rico son" ("Everyone come and dance with me, my rich [beautiful] son"). However, the inclusionary nature of the lyrics has limits. Similar to the examples provided above (e.g., Sepulveda's treatment of my cultural origins), India's "everyone" serves exclusionary purposes as well. The exclusionary elements become overtly stated when India shouts out to "all the Latins in Manhattan." The "everyone" then, is a qualified one. It also appears in her declaration, "I dedicate myself to the Latin race." This is particularly significant because this recording was the result of her decision to make a career change, moving from the underground dance music scene to salsa, a more culturally specified style in terms of its identification with Puerto Rican culture and its use as an identity marker of Puerto Rican, Nuyorican, and Latino culture. For India, performing salsa was her way of rediscovering her cultural roots and calling for pan-Latino pride and participation.

The pliability and flexibility of cultural identification that pervades the salsa scene is evident in the changes "Llegó La India" undergoes as performance contexts vary. Similar to Sepulveda, India deemphasizes certain localities over others depending on her perceptions of the performance context and of the ethnicity of audience members. For instance, at the Copacabana, New York's premier salsa club, "Llegó" was one of the highlights of the performance in terms of audience response and interaction with India. This became especially pronounced during the listing of the New York boroughs. Audience members would cheer as their home borough was mentioned, with each group trying to outcheer the other. However, in a concert in Los Angeles, even though she included the five boroughs, the lyric "I love you New York" was replaced by "I love you L.A." In Miami, "I want to shout" became "I want to shout out to los Cubanos" (the Cubans). In Puerto Rico, the English sections were replaced by praises of Puerto Rico that were sung in Spanish. And for concerts in Colombia, Venezuela, and Argentina, the song was not included. When deciding the repertoire for concerts in South America, Sergio George remarked, "We can't play that song. It doesn't make sense. They would not get all the New York references. And the English doesn't work down here either. We got to play what these people can relate to" (S. George, pers. comm.).

As John Blacking writes, humans make music; however, "there is also a sense in which music makes man, releasing creative energy, expanding consciousness and influencing decision making and cultural invention" (Blacking 1979: 3). Through the performance of such songs as "Llegó La India" and incitations during salsa performances, salseros and salseras arouse feelings of cultural pride; a sense of belonging and identification with a group or groups, whether they be Latino, Puerto Rican, or Nuyorican, is fostered.

Salsa particularly is well suited for such purposes. As a hybrid or polysemic symbol of identity, its aesthetic and performance parameters make possible several simultaneous and even contradictory "identifications." The political climate that coincided with the emergence of salsa as a music style, along with the hybrid nature of salsa's music structure, explains why it can be used with such pliability for cultural identification, and why performances can promote both exclusive nationalism and inclusive pan-Latino ethnicity. Its performers, producers, dancers, and listeners are primarily Puerto Ricans, but also include many others with various cultural affiliations. This diversity creates a multiethnic environment that enables salsa to function as a tool for evoking nationalistic and cultural pride and creating a sense of inclusion for its participants in a variety of different cultural contexts.

The dynamic play that salsa bands engage, which pits denaturalization against renaturalization and the formal against the informal, serves the salsa community well and is reflective of its values. Through blurring or crossing boundaries, salsa performers are able to maintain a connectedness to the urban barrio culture from which salsa emerged. Even within a highly structured professional performance environment, the music remains a "people's music." The salsa community continually reifies the notion that music is an integral part of its daily life by the number of actively performing bands it supports on the New York scene, how the music permeates the barrio streets, and the numerous events where salsa performance is included. As salsa becomes increasingly more commercialized, informalizing and renaturalizing gestures during performance play an ever-larger role in keeping the people—as opposed to record companies, radio stations, and promoters—as the possessors of the music: people first.

2

"The music is so good, but the scene is pure dues!"

Salsa Musicians

"What do you expect? This is salsa! The promoters couldn't care less about the musician's welfare. They just think about the money. If they only realized that we would play a lot better if they treated us well. It would be better for their show. But it never changes."

—Pianist Arturo Ortiz

Salseros (salsa musicians), those who make the sounds that incite dance—the sounds and movements that signify *familia* (togetherness), otherness (exoticism), nationhood, *la raza latina* (ethnicity), multiple historical discontinuities (Caribbean), disjointed immigrant marginalization (colonialization), and so much more—operate in an alternative space, set apart from daily life, bearing the burden of a highly contested cultural terrain. Their "everynight" lives and unique experiences weave a tightly knit collectivity by which adversity and infectious musical expression serve as sinews, both of which are the fundamental building blocks for the salsa "scene"—people celebratively grooving in spite of . . . Yet this scene, inhabited by a community of salseros, remains unbounded and fluid, in transit, existing between cultures, yet informed by the cultural trappings of the dominant groups among the salseros in New York: Puerto Ricans and Nuyoricans.[1] Stuart Hall points out that Caribbean migrants to New York City have a different relationship to the classical model of diaspora in the sense that they are "twice diasporized" (Hall 2003b: 190). Everybody who lives in the Caribbean today, with the exception of a minority of indigenous peoples, came from somewhere else and are products of the creolization process. By definition they are transnational communities, differing from homogenized national identities, possessing multiple foci of identification, maintaining pluralistic ties to homelands, and belonging to what Hall labels a "new zone of cultural emergence" (Hall

2003b: 190). Salseros operate within such a zone. Juan Flores explains, "Puerto Rican culture today is a culture of commuting, of a constant back and forth transfer between two intertwining zones . . . the Nuyorican experience is showing how it is possible to struggle through the quandary of biculturalism and affirm the straddling position. Not with the claim to be both . . . but 'not neither'" (Flores 1992: 201). James Clifford describes this transitory mindset of part-time residents of both Puerto Rico and New York: "Everyone is more or less permanently in transit . . . Not so much 'Where are you from?' as 'Where are you between?'" (Clifford 1997: 37, 39). Salsa as cultural expression—underpinned by transit, between-ness, deterritorialized cultural pluralism, and multiple sites of identification—remains emergent, and by its very nature, it straddles various positions simultaneously, thereby remaining unlocatable and at the same time signifying the "rooted" essence of Puerto Rican-ness. Indeed, Jorge Duany writes, "Popular music is one of the main symbolic resources through which Caribbean people define, assert, and promote their cultural identity" (Duany 1996: 177). But Mary Lee Mulholland counters, "Salsa travels so well because it is 'contaminated' and its 'messy' nature resists being located or claimed because its origins are ambiguous" (Mulholland 1998: 78). Both are right.

Complicating matters, though, is money. As Jacques Attali observes, wherever there is music, there is money, and this is especially the case with a popular commercial musical expression like salsa. Salsa is big business. Real economic capital is at stake with every contested signification. Further, as Attali reminds us, "no organized society can exist without structuring differences at its core. No market economy can develop without erasing those differences in mass production" (Attali 1985: 5). Salsa musicians work on the front line of these dividings and erasings, between-ness and rootedness, and must navigate delicately through this sometimes-adversarial domain. Becoming an insider to this salsascape does not require one to be Puerto Rican or Nuyorican, just open to straddling, of being "not neither." Salseros grapple with these ambiguities in a multitude of ways. In the process, they have developed a set of behavioral norms, despite an overt social informality, that are structured in a highly formal and stylized manner that frames and counters this inherent fluidity. Strategically, they have come to rely on these norms in the machinations of their professional lives, but, as we shall see, these structured conventions can be as permutable as the definitions and significations of salsa itself.

In this chapter, I am concerned with the everyday and -night lives of salsa musicians, focusing mainly on the group of performers known as "sidemen."[2] A "sideman" or "sideperson" is any member of a band other than the leader. They are employed by bandleaders to play supporting roles within the group structure (they make the music). I discuss their attitudes, working environment, education, business practices, and reasons for playing salsa. Their perceptions of and ideas regarding the salsa scene are directly incorporated herein in an effort to paint a clear picture of the life of a salsa musician in New York City in the 1990s. By ethnographically documenting the structures within which they work, play, and live, I trace the fluid negotiative dances of social relations in which each salsero must engage, which are at times complicit with the process of specific contestations, and, at other times, contrary, but all informing how the music is sounded and performed.

Salsa Musicians

Who are salsa musicians? The cultural climate of New York City provides diverse opportunities for musicians, probably more so than any other place. Many, including musicians who play salsa, take advantage of New York's cultural diversity by performing simultaneously in a variety of styles and scenes. Indeed, the high cost of living in the city often necessitates learning to be musically literate in a number of cultural arenas, as well as taking every gig that comes along, just to make ends meet. This results in the constant shifting of musicians from one style of music or scene to another, and a jockeying for higher paying and more prestigious positions within those scenes. These comings and goings lead to significant fluctuations among musicians participating in the salsascape of New York at any given time, making it difficult to describe a "typical" salsa musician, though a general picture based on ethnicity, age, gender, and competence level can be drawn. What follows is that general picture. In the following discussion, I rely heavily upon my experience as a regularly performing member of the Ray Sepulveda band from 1993 to 1998. During that time, I developed intimate friendships with many of the musicians in his band, and their ideas and viewpoints invaluably inform my discussion. Throughout the 1990s, Sepulveda's band was one of the busiest and most in-demand groups on the scene, and the ethnic makeup and competence level were similar to many of the top salsa bands performing in New York City.[3] They are as "typical" as a diverse and fluid community gets.[4]

Most of the musicians performing salsa in New York City (roughly 80 percent) label themselves as either "Puerto Rican" or "Nuyorican." This distinction, as used in this book, signifies whether they (a) were born and raised in Puerto Rico ("Puerto Rican"), or (b) are first-, second-, or third-generation Puerto Rican American, having been born and raised in New York City ("Nuyorican"). The remaining 20 percent, listed from the largest to the smallest in number, consists of musicians from the United States, the Dominican Republic, Cuba, South American countries (mostly Colombia and Venezuela), and

Figure 2.1 The Ray Sepulveda Band performing at Orchard Beach in 1995. (From Left to Right: Ricky Gonzalez, Abiud Troche, Ray Sepulveda, William Cepeda, Junior Perez, Claudette Sierra, Chris Washburne, Pablo "Chino" Nuñez, John "Pee Wee" Fernandez, Hector Colón, and Ralph Figueroa). *(From the Christopher Washburne collection: photographgrapher unknown.)*

a small number from Central American nations.[5] For instance, in 1996, Sepulveda's band had four Puerto Ricans, four Nuyoricans, one Dominican American, one member who was born and raised in New York City with one Puerto Rican parent and one Cuban parent, a Venezuelan, and one "Anglo" (a white North American)—that is, me.[6]

Salsa musicians range in age from their early twenties to mid-forties (Sepulveda's band ranged from thirty to forty-five years). Musicians over fifty years old are rare. The rigorous performance schedules with incessant sleep deprivation caused by late performance hours (most club performances end at 4:00 A.M.) is taxing and forces older musicians, some with families and those with weaker constitutions, to seek employment elsewhere. Also, newer salsa bands that adopt hip-hop styles and practices, and who cater specifically to younger audiences, often prefer younger musicians. This hiring practice further limits opportunities for older musicians.

With few exceptions, women musicians are absent from the performance scene. The women who do perform most often are vocalists, though there are a few horn players (Sepulveda employed a female *coro* singer for three years). I have never witnessed a woman playing a rhythm section instrument in any of the top New York bands. Notwithstanding, female musicians often participate in the salsa workshops and lessons held at the Boys and Girls Harbor School; a few perform with lower-level bands; and there is a small number of all-women salsa bands, though none have attained the status or reputation of the top level in New York. Reasons for the absence of female players are complex and intrinsically tied to the gender dynamics found among the various cultures represented by both performers and listeners.[7] I discuss some of these issues at greater length in Chapter Five of this volume; however, at this point, I would like to mention two generalized factors that limit the participation of women performers. First, historically salsa has been (and remains) a male-dominated industry offering few performance opportunities for women. Duany writes, "most salsa songs . . . are conceived and written by a man, sung and executed largely by men" (Duany 1984: 204). Until the debut recording of La India in 1992, Celia Cruz was the only female bandleader working regularly on the New York salsa scene.

Exclusionary attitudes toward women performers persist. On several occasions when I sent female trombone substitutes to cover for my absence, bandleaders requested that they not be called again. One leader responded, "Don't get me wrong. She plays good. She knows Latin music. But it looks strange to have a woman with all the guys in the band. It makes people uncomfortable" (Anon., pers. comm.). Second, the late hours and dangerous neighborhoods of some performance venues present many dangers for a woman traveling alone. One woman who performs occasionally in salsa bands remarked, "Sometimes it is a drag when I play in a salsa club. As soon as we finish a set, it seems I am always harassed by some drunk guy asking me to dance or for my phone number. It gets tiring after a while . . . sometimes they follow me out of the club. I always have to arrange rides with one of the guys to get home. I hate to have to rely on men just to make my living" (Anon., pers. comm.). As of the writing of this manuscript, there was an increase in female vocalist bandleaders due to the success of La India, but female musicians performing in salsa bands are still rare.

There are three general distinctions based on competence that salsa musicians make among themselves: "studio musicians," "steady band members," and "newcomers," amateur players who are establishing their music careers. A further distinction is that of "freelancer," which is not necessarily tied to competency and refers to a musician who is not performing regularly with any band, or who is floating between several bands simultaneously. Judging musical competence is a rather subjective enterprise that not only involves talent, ability, and taste, but also an understanding of how these qualities are contextually employed. Knowing how, when, where, and in what fashion to use acquired abilities can be just as important as possessing those abilities in the first place (McLeod and Herndon 1980: 185). Regardless of the subjective nature of the judgments involved, though, among salsa musicians these categories are well defined and clearly delineated at any given time. There is a sharp dividing line between who gets called for what type of work, and these divisions are maintained through exclusionary peer networks that attempt to maintain the status quo (I explain this in more detail shortly). Even though these are not static categories—a musician's status can change over time, depending on performing abilities and changing stylistic demands—it can be difficult for musicians to break into higher levels of work.

The most accomplished musicians are those who do the majority of the studio recording and are thus known as "studio musicians." Extensive recording experience endows a player with high prestige among bandleaders, fellow musicians, and audience members alike, and it places a high demand on their participation. When a new band or salsa singer debuts, the musicians who worked on the original recording are the first to be called to perform. Their familiarity with the music reduces costly rehearsal time, their high competence makes the band sound good, and their presence serves to elevate the prestige of the new artist. These studio musicians usually remain with new bands for the first several months, reaping the financial benefits of work generated by the radio airplay of newly released material and by the novelty of a new salsa personality arriving on the scene. As the initial wave of work diminishes, the studio musicians usually move on to another group or return to freelancing. Often the busiest players hold positions in one of the most prestigious bands, such as those of Ruben Blades, Marc Anthony, and Eddie Palmieri, while maintaining a freelancing career on the side.

The second competence level includes musicians who prefer to "play steady" with one band. They are usually seasoned salsa musicians who either do not possess the sight-reading skills and stylistic flexibility for freelancing, or the nerves to stomach the inconsistencies of a freelancer's work schedule. Playing steady with a group requires a commitment that involves turning down offers of possibly more lucrative work that conflicts with the band's schedule, attending rehearsals, and accommodating any last-minute scheduling changes that the band may make. In return for their sacrifices, sidepersons are given a modicum of job security, are included in all of the work generated by the band, and are accorded the elevated status of being a member of a popular band.

The third competency level consists of musicians who are striving to acquire a steady position in one of the top bands and those who are establishing freelancing careers. They are often newcomers to the salsa scene who gain experience by playing with cover bands[8] and groups that are based in New York's outer suburbs, Connecticut, or New Jersey. They are the pool of musicians that freelancers draw from to supply substitute players ('subs') on especially busy nights, such as Saturdays and holidays.

Those who freelance are either vying for a steady gig or are musicians who prefer the variety that comes with performing with many groups at one time. Trumpeter John Walsh comments, "I enjoy freelance work the best. Because of the challenge of being in different situations every night, I rarely get bored. I get as much artistic satisfaction out of sight-reading a book all night, especially when things are going well, as I do when I get a lot of solo space" (J. Walsh, pers. comm.). Throughout the 1990s in the New York salsa scene, there was only a small number of musicians (fewer than 100) who made their living as freelancers.[9] These numbers remain small due to the limited freelancing positions that the salsa scene accommodates (i.e., a certain number of bands and performance venues at any given time) and to the arduous demands this type of work places on individual musicians. The first requirement for freelance work is the ability to sight-read extremely well, since most bands do not rehearse regularly. That means playing the arrangements close to perfection at first sight and quickly adapting to the stylistic idiosyncrasies of each band, skills that can take years to acquire. Further, the erratic lifestyle that accompanies freelancing, with no guarantee of employment, discourages many. For instance, while freelancing in November 1995, I had six gigs in the first week, none in the second, three the third week, and eight in the fourth week. This was not considered an unusual freelancing schedule. Because dry spells are hard to predict, freelancers are compelled to accept all offers of work. This erratic schedule can easily cause tensions at home with regard to scheduling family events, such as vacations, and can cause stress with respect to economic planning. Furthermore, freelancers can receive calls up to one hour before a gig or recording session. If they turn down the invitation, the bandleader or musical director may not call again for several weeks or even months. According to trumpeter Ray Vega, "You need to say 'yes' to everything. It is like being a slave to your phone, beeper, and cell phone. But that is the way to work in this business. You need to love to play. If you say 'no,' people assume that you are busy and don't need the work. So they don't call back for a while" (R. Vega, pers. comm.).

A successful freelancer must develop exceptional skills for maintaining good relations with colleagues. Freelancers acquire work and maintain a busy schedule through an intricate referral system. When a musician recommends another for a job, or hires another as a "sub," there is an unspoken agreement that the favor should and will be returned and that the gig will not be stolen by the sub. Often small groups of musicians—usually ones who frequently socialize together—will form a consortium of sorts, whereby each limits his referrals to the other members of the group. This relationship is indicated when one musician says of another, "That's my boy!" These circles can be tightly guarded and difficult to break into, ensuring employment for members and limiting employment possibilities for nonmembers. Another, more formal way musicians establish reciprocating relationships is by asking a fellow musician to be the godfather of one of their children, thus becoming "*compadres*." The tradition of "*compadrazgo*" in Puerto Rican culture is a significant social institution that promotes solidarity and reciprocal obligations between men.[10] These practices help to maintain the status quo and limit the number of working freelancers, and these male-dominated social territories perpetuate the exclusion of women. For women who do participate, these male cultural spaces necessitate the adoption of roles that conform in some way to these exclusionary constructions. For vocalist Claudette Sierra, who worked with Sepulveda, it was necessary to negotiate a quasi-gender-bending relationship with the men in the band in order to grapple with these social dynamics: "I do not want to be treated differently. I don't want the guys to feel they have to act differently when I am around. So I don't let all the crude talk and comments about other women bother me. I know that just shows that the guys are comfortable with me being in the band. I just try to be one of the boys in the band" (C. Sierra, pers. comm.).

Juggling gigs on busy nights is another skill that is required for optimum profit or artistic fulfillment for freelancers. Saturdays can produce double and triple bookings. When called for a higher paying job or for a more creatively fulfilling opportunity, a freelance musician must search for a suitable sub (one that the bandleader and musical director will approve of) and diplomatically excuse him- or herself from the first job. This can be a delicate task that requires political acumen to avoid elimination from the call list of the dismissed band. Aware of this policy among freelancers, and in an attempt to secure the best musicians for a gig, bandleaders will at times turn to deceptive practices, promising fabricated upcoming gigs, travel, and recordings. The following provides a typical situational example. In May 1996, Bandleader A called me on a Monday for a gig on Saturday night. I was free, so I accepted. On Wednesday I received a call from Bandleader B, asking me to play on Friday, Saturday, and Sunday nights. He wanted someone to commit to all of the nights and would not accept my offer to play on Friday and Sunday only. So I accepted B's offer for three nights of employment. I then proceeded to call a sub to cover my Saturday night gig and carefully negotiated for my release with Bandleader A. On Thursday, I was called by a Bandleader C to play on Sunday. I turned him down because of my prior commitment to B. After Friday's gig, Bandleader B announced that the gigs on Saturday and Sunday were canceled, providing no excuses. At that point it was too late to cancel my sub for Saturday's gig. I had lost two nights of work. On Saturday afternoon I telephoned the club where one of the canceled gigs was supposed to take place. The club owner stated that B was never scheduled to play. My impression was that both the Saturday and Sunday gigs never existed. Bandleader B had deceived me to insure that I would be at the Friday gig, knowing that I would not jeopardize three nights of employment by sending a sub. As a freelancer I had no recourse but to accept the financial loss and the possible repercussions of turning down two other bandleaders, and to vow not to perform for Bandleader B again. This scenario is not unusual in the salsa scene, and seasoned freelancers develop a "sixth sense" to evaluate the validity of the employer's promises made in lieu of written contracts. Trombonist Cookie Lebron offered this advice: "Take all the work that they call you for and don't sub it out until the last minute, even if you are double booked, because the way things are, you will probably have one of those gigs canceled, or the time will change and you will be able to do both. And always play with the band that offers the most money. Look out for yourself because they [the bandleaders] aren't going to look out for you" (C. Lebron, pers. comm.). Lebron's comments capture sentiments shared by many. With the lack of written agreements or formal institutions, such as a union, musicians have little recourse against exploitive practices (like the one by Bandleader B, described above). The relatively disempowered position of musicians within the salsa industry at large, often at the mercy of unethical and selfish bandleaders and promoters, fosters an adversarial environment between cliques of musicians and frequently perpetuates an "every man for himself" stance. This "divide and conquer" strategy is one way those who possess power maintain their hold; however, these common adversarial experiences also serve as a communal glue, forging deeper feelings of solidarity and strengthening personal relations among musicians, and are one of the reasons behind the formation of "That's my boy" networks.

Salsa Education and Getting Gigs

How are musicians educated in salsa? For most, salsa education comes primarily through practical training in which competence is developed through performance experience. Through various educative processes such as observation, imitation, and trial and error, accompanied by the guidance of established salseros and colleagues, musicians work to establish their professional salsa careers. In addition, individual practicing, private studying, jazz and classical training, listening to recordings, transcribing, reading supplemental literature on salsa performance practice and Latin music history (reading *Latin Beat Magazine*), acquiring and developing accepted behavioral skills, and fostering positive relations with colleagues are all necessary for attaining the highest levels of competence and preparedness for acquiring and retaining performance work that is both creatively and economically fulfilling.

The reliance on Western music notation in salsa performance is standard; all rhythm and horn section parts are written out and most salsa musicians read those notated parts during performances. With the exception of vocalists, who mostly rely on aural learning, performance opportunities are limited for illiterate musicians. This requires musicians to seek some type of musical training. In New York there are two schools that cater to amateur and beginner salsa students, offering salsa instruction with renowned Latin musicians: the Johnny Colón Music School, founded in 1971 by the boogaloo artist; and bassist Ramon Rodríguez's music program at the Boys and Girls Harbor School, founded in 1973.[11] Both schools are located in El Barrio on East 104th Street, and offer affordable private lessons, clinics, and coached ensembles.

Latin music instruction in New York City that is geared toward young aspiring professional salsa musicians is limited to the few Latin music ensemble offerings at the New School Jazz and Contemporary Music Program and the Manhattan School of Music, the private percussion instruction available at the Drummer's Collective, and a few advanced ensembles at Boys Harbor. This dearth of formal education in salsa forces many young musicians to enroll in established jazz and classical programs at universities and conservatories around the country; the Manhattan School of Music in New York City and the Berklee School of Music in Boston are popular choices.[12] These programs serve to sharpen sight-reading skills; provide instruction in Western music theory, history, composition, and arranging techniques; and provide private instrumental instruction, all necessary components to becoming a professional musician. However, they offer little assistance in developing competence in salsa performance and knowledge of the music's history and theoretical underpinnings. In the past few years, a small number of schools around the United States have begun offering salsa and Latin music ensembles as electives, but these ensembles are viewed as supplemental and remain on the periphery of conservatory and music school curriculums. These nascent offerings, though, have spawned a publishing industry catering to this new market that specializes in Latin music (e.g., www.3-2music.com). As of the early 2000s, arrangements of the most popular salsa and Latin jazz songs were commercially available for the first time.

Regardless, most musicians rely upon less formalized settings to obtain the essential knowledge and practice needed to establish a professional salsa career. A number of self-instructional books and videos on salsa performance practice were published in the late 1990s to assist in this process (e.g., Mauleón 1996; Sher 1997; and Sanabria 1996). More importantly, though, learning about music by listening to recordings, playing along with records in an attempt to emulate performances of studio musicians, and "hanging out" (socializing and "talking shop" with colleagues) plays the largest role in the educational process of salsa musicians. Percussionist George Delgado comments, "I never studied music at a university or a music school. I learned from a very different type of place. It's called the 'University of the Street.' I just learned by playing and listening to a lot of bands. And older guys like Manny Oquendo showed me a lot of stuff, too. That's the way most guys I know learned to play" (G. Delgado, pers. comm.). During set breaks at clubs, percussionists often can be observed collectively playing along with the recordings played by the deejay. These "play-along sessions" demonstrate the prowess of each percussionist's ability to learn aurally the rhythmic breaks from the most popular bands. They also serve as ways of sharing musical knowledge. "Show me that break again," "Slow that one down," or "How do you play that?" are commonly heard expressions during these sessions.

In general, older salsa musicians generously share their knowledge and experience with younger or less experienced players. Some offer private study or mentorship, and others prefer a less structured sharing of knowledge where guidance is given during performances. The professional bandstand can become a classroom of sorts when younger players have the opportunity to perform with and observe seasoned veterans. For instance, trombonist Barry Rogers often suggested alternatives to the way I phrased a particular passage or recommended different approaches to soloing during performances. The set breaks were often filled with salient anecdotal information that played an important role in my own salsa education and initial perceptions of the Latin music scene.

Working with amateur and semiprofessional bands before progressing to more proficient ones is an essential part to becoming a professional salsa musician. Valuable experience is gained by playing with cover bands and other locally based groups that primarily work the private party and small club circuit in New Jersey, Connecticut, Long Island, Westchester County, and the *cuchifrito* circuit made up of small restaurants and neighborhood bars located throughout the New York metropolitan area. Performance practices as well as the repertoires of the most popular bands are learned in a low-pressured atmosphere. This type of performing is referred to by professional salseros as "paying dues," a borrowing from the jazz lexicon, which posits these performance settings as investments for preparing oneself for more high profile work. Bandleaders often will inquire with whom a particular musician has performed (how many dues have been paid) before accepting him or her for subbing work. If a musician working in the cuchifrito circuit is given a "break," invited to play with a well-known band, and judged to be insufficiently prepared for the higher gigging level, he or she is excluded from further work with the band and generally will return to lower-level gigs to further hone his or her Latin music skills.

In addition to learning correct phrasing, proper rhythmic placement, and other essential musical elements, salsa education also includes the acquisition of accepted behavioral skills (learning how to conduct oneself on the salsa scene). Proper behavior expectations rarely are stated overtly unless a musician blatantly ignores an unspoken rule. Instead, newcomers must decipher social cues by observing the behavior of experienced musicians, while establishing their places within the salsa scene. Well-developed social skills can play a large role in establishing and maintaining a career in salsa. Salseros are expected to display a certain degree of professionalism on and off the bandstand. This is accomplished by conducting oneself in a dependable fashion; arriving at gigs and rehearsals in a timely manner; and respecting and observing established performance etiquette, such as not stealing a gig that one is subbing on or by respecting older or more experienced players. For instance, horn players can show respect by allowing older musicians to choose which parts they prefer to play, leads or supporting ones. This maintains positive relationships with colleagues who may be in positions to recommend fellow musicians for future work.

Musicians who repeatedly display antisocial behavior or unreliability automatically limit their professional opportunities. However, other benefits can arise from their conduct. Bandleaders often refuse to hire subs who have acquired notorious reputations. While discussing with me possible musicians for subbing, Sepulveda remarked, "How can you even think of sending that guy to play with me? You can never be sure if he's going to show up, and if he does come, who knows what shape he will be in? You've heard the stories." Sepulveda was referring to a trombonist who gained notoriety within the salsa scene from an incident that occurred during a wedding reception. In a drunken stupor, he jumped off the bandstand during the first dance and "cut in," taking the bride away from the groom, dancing with her for the remainder of the song as the astonished groom looked on. Though his blatant impertinence caused a great disruption, elicited threats from the bride's and groom's families, and subsequently diminished his future employment possibilities, over time his antics, as is often the case with other episodes of antisocial behavior by salsa musicians, have served as fodder for the "stories" Sepulveda referred to. When gathered in groups, such as in the back room of a club on set breaks, musicians frequently tell and retell stories relating to the salsa scene. I have heard the wedding story recounted on numerous occasions with embellishments added on each retelling. Not only do these narratives serve as entertainment, passing the time between performances, but they also transmit an oral history among insiders. Though the focus of the anecdote is the trombonist's actions, information offered on the periphery, such as which band was performing, which musicians were present, and so forth, provide vital historical data. Further discussion often will ensue concerning the band's repertoire, recordings, or other salient information. In this way, shared information and experiential data are passed on to colleagues, younger musicians, and new arrivals to the scene during the "hang" between sets, bus rides to gigs, rehearsal breaks, or while having breakfast after a gig; this process plays an integral role in the education of salsa as well as creating a stronger sense of group cohesion among salsa musicians. This "salsa lore" is a "canon" that salsa insiders exclusively share with one another, reinforcing their relationships.

Social behavior and rituals prevalent among New York Latinos, mostly New York Puerto Ricans, also dictate acceptable behavior within the salsa scene. For instance, one is quick to recognize the prominence of greeting rituals in clubs and rehearsal studios. Regardless of the number of people in a room, upon entering, a newcomer is expected to greet everyone with a handshake and introduce him- or herself to those with whom he or she is unacquainted. Obviously, this is not done when entering a large club, such as the Copacabana, that may be filled with one thousand strangers; however, it does apply if someone enters the band's dressing room. This may seem like an insignificant formality to the newcomer, yet musicians who do not conform to this practice are often labeled as antisocial, strange, unfriendly, or rude, which in turn can negatively affect their future gigging opportunities. One bandleader comments about a musician, "I don't like to use W in my band because he's so negative. He never takes the time to say hello to anyone. Man, he's a strange cat!" (Anon., pers. comm.). Walsh remarks, "I always find it odd when I play a jazz gig. No one says hello or greets anyone like in a salsa band. I have been playing Latin music so long that I have become more comfortable with shaking everyone's hand. So I do it on my jazz gigs as well. If it makes them feel strange, that's their problem" (J. Walsh, pers. comm.).

Knowing how to dress for gigs is also an important skill for maintaining work. The dress codes most salsa clubs implement reflect Latino attitudes concerning appearance and being properly attired for an occasion. New York Latino patrons tend to dress up for a night of dancing and, in turn, salsa clubs refuse entry to those not in compliance. This concern for proper attire applies to band members as well, and bandleaders take care in choosing the appropriate clothing for each particular performance setting. For salseros, the way a band looks on stage is a significant part of the performance. When a band chooses not to wear a uniform, bandleaders will request that sidepersons wear specific types of clothing. For instance, Sepulveda chooses from the following apparel options, listed from dress used on the most formal occasions and progressing to the most casual: tuxedos for weddings and special occasions, such as New Year's Eve; a black suit with a white shirt and a matching tie for clubs with strict dress codes; a suit (musician's choice of color) and tie for less formal private parties and clubs with less strict dress codes; casual "but in good taste" (meaning not jeans and tennis shoes) for clubs with relaxed dress codes; all black stylish clothing for clubs with relaxed dress codes; and T-shirt with jeans and tennis shoes for summer beach parties or outdoor festivals. Musicians jokingly comment on Sepulveda's habit of accompanying his greeting of band members with a "once-over look," inspecting their clothing before every performance. Musicians are admonished by both bandleaders and fellow musicians, and often can receive friendly ridicule throughout the performance if they arrive at a gig donning anything other than the requested clothing. Being overdressed for an occasion is as much of a concern as being underdressed. When Sepulveda's band arrived wearing suits and ties for a party that was billed as a beach party, to which patrons were encouraged to wear beach clothing, the club owner protested and insisted that all band members change clothing before the performance. He provided shorts and T-shirts worn by the club's softball team to musicians who did not have other clothes with them. The club owner and Sepulveda both agreed that appropriate dress was essential for the party, regardless of the fact that the combination of softball uniforms and black socks with formal black dress shoes proved to be quite a sight!

Many musicians express a preference for choosing their own clothes as opposed to having uniforms dictated by bandleaders. Having his or her own choice allows each musician to assert his or her own individual identity. Furthermore, when musicians are required to wear the same clothing, their uniform appearance easily identifies them as band members and aligns them with other uniformed service providers working in the club, such as the waitstaff and security personnel. This is significant to musicians since many are routinely treated in disrespectful ways by club management. For instance, Marty Aret, the owner of Club Broadway (later renamed the Latin Quarter), barred musicians from entering through the front door, insisting that they use a rat-infested service entrance. And on a steaming hot August night in 1995, when the club's air-conditioning failed, he refused to let a bartender serve band members water. When I objected, he replied, "I don't care who you play with. Just because you are a musician doesn't entitle you to any special treatment. You have to buy a glass of spring water at the bar for $4 just like everyone else." This animosity was confounding. Wasn't his club filled with patrons because of the band that was performing? In response to this type of treatment, some bands, such as Marc Anthony's and La India's, chose to wear jeans and T-shirts to all performance venues, including those with strict dress codes. Even though this clothing choice further distinguished musicians from both employees and patrons in the club, musicians viewed this choice as an important stance against uniforms and a way for them to receive preferential treatment (i.e., being allowed to enter without conforming to the club's rules). In both Anthony's and India's cases, the uniform change also reflected their desires to appeal to younger audiences. India's musical director Bobby Allende commented, "If you want to capture younger Latino audiences, you got to dress hip. They don't want to see a bunch of guys dressed in stuffy suits and ties" (B. Allende, pers. comm.).

Gigging

Salsa music-making on a professional level is defined economically and tied intrinsically to commercial enterprise. Professional salsa musicians play salsa only when they are paid. Money determines where and when salsa is performed and who attends. A professional salsa performance is referred to as a "*guiso*" or "gig." Both terms are used interchangeably. The former is a Spanish slang term meaning "a happening" or "an event" (literally, "stew"). The latter term is borrowed from jazz argot, meaning a paid professional engagement. Salsa musicians are paid per performance, and their pay scale ranges from $50 to $1,000 per gig, depending on the type of venue and the performance context. For instance, a performance with a cover band on a weekday night at a small restaurant in Queens will pay $50 per musician. A Saturday night performance at Madison Square Garden with Ruben Blades or Marc Anthony is likely to pay up to $1,000. In general, each job consists of one to three sets of music, each of which is thirty minutes to one hour in length. The most famous bands usually play no more than two sets, each consisting of four to six songs. In 1996, the median pay for the top salsa bands was $125 per musician for club performances in the New York metropolitan area, and $250 for out-of-town venues. Pianists and bassists tend to receive $10 to $20 more per gig to offset the additional expenses incurred from the cartage of their instruments (e.g., taxi fare and parking garage fees). Lead singers who are not bandleaders receive $30 to $50 more than the average. The musical director and bandleader typically receive "double scale" (twice the average pay). However, depending on their commercial success (number of records sold and number of hits currently receiving radio airplay) bandleaders can receive considerably large sums for each performance. Anthony was charging close to $10,000 for each performance in 1996. Most bands charge between $750 and $2,500 to perform in a club or disco, and more for other occasions, such as weddings and other private affairs.

Variables affecting particular musicians' pay scales include their acquired level of prestige and competence, the popularity of the bands they perform with, the types of events at which the bands perform, the night of the week of the performance, the amount due to booking agents (if there are any), and the greed of the leaders. The prestige of a musician is determined by his or her playing abilities, the amount of recording, and the number of famous bands on his or her resume. Television and music video appearances also can heighten prestige levels. A higher level of prestige allows for greater leverage when negotiating pay scale with bandleaders.

Hiring and firing practices can vary greatly from one bandleader to another. The hiring process rarely includes a formal audition. Often, subbing on a band serves that function. When a position becomes available, musicians who frequently have subbed on the band are most often the first choices. Their familiarity with the band's repertoire and performance routines helps to minimize rehearsal time. Furthermore, subbing musicians can establish their musical and personal compatibility with the steady members of the group. Since each new member brings about a certain degree of change within the group dynamic, disruptive or incompatible personalities can be weeded out before someone is hired. Being hired typically comes by way of a formal invitation from the bandleader or musical director. Once the terms are agreed upon by both parties, the agreement remains a verbal one. Written contracts are rare for sidepersons. An exception is the agreement made by a lead vocalist who plans on recording with a nonvocalist bandleader. Binding written agreements are viewed as essential to ensure that the singer does not use the recording to launch his or her own band, abandoning the bandleader who provided the recording opportunity. Beginning in the late 1980s and continuing throughout the 1990s, salsa bands became increasingly more lead-vocalist oriented, due in part to the growing number of singer-led bands. As a result, the personal singing style and performance image put forth by the lead singer are viewed as essential to the group's identity. As Sepulveda remarked, "When I left Johnny Zumont [Zumont and Sepulveda's band was known as 'Johnny and Ray'], he wanted to sue me, because he knew that the reason why people were coming to see his band was because of my voice. It is my voice that brought the people, not his conga playing" (R. Sepulveda, pers. comm.).

When hiring sidepersons, bandleaders require that their own bands be given priority over other freelance opportunities. Freelancing by sidepersons is permitted only when the band is not working. Regardless of the amount of work a bandleader has to offer, this level of commitment is always requested. Bands offering more than three gigs per week easily can maintain musician loyalty and retain a consistent membership. Conversely, bands that work less often have a high turnover rate in their personnel. As performance opportunities declined throughout the 1990s, only a small number of bands were able to offer enough work to maintain consistent memberships. Both bandleaders and musicians agree that constantly changing personnel has a negative effect on the music. Without a consistent group of musicians performing together over a period of time, the rapport so essential in the development of a cohesive and personalized group sound never evolves. The preponderance of freelancers also contributed to a nebulous and somewhat indistinguishable sound that many bands shared in the 1990s. Bassist Guillermo Edgehil observed, "In the sixties and seventies, and even before that, you could always identify whose band was playing from the recordings. Now all these new bands sound the same" (G. Edgehil, pers. comm.). Trumpeter Walsh added, "When I am not playing steady with any one band, I never get a chance to develop musical intimacy with other musicians. It never allows the music to be taken to another level" (J. Walsh, pers. comm.). Trumpeter Vega concured and added, "The trouble with bands today is they have not creatively pushed Latin music forward because they can't. There is too much freelancing because most bands are unable to offer enough work to provide the incentive for the same musicians to work steady with them. What ends up happening is that the best musicians freelance, and less-skilled players who can't freelance stay steady with the bands. The level of musicianship has fallen since when I began playing Latin music in the early 1980s" (R. Vega, pers. comm.).

Amicable partings, such as when a musician is hired by a more prestigious group, are usually accompanied by two weeks' notice. Confrontational firings are usually carried out with more immediacy. Firing procedures often are erratic and vary greatly. For instance, in January 1997, Sepulveda wanted to make some personnel changes. He called a band meeting and had Ricky Gonzalez, his musical director, announce that he was breaking up the band as of February 1 (four weeks' notice), then rehiring some musicians and firing others; everyone would be personally called and informed of his or her status. Gonzalez consolingly exclaimed that it was out of respect for the band members that they were providing the extra notification time; in this way, they were allowing more time for the musicians to seek work with other bands. In contrast, in December 1996, Sepulveda just stopped calling one of the coro singers without any notification. No formal firing took place until the singer called to inquire why the band had not worked for several weeks. Sepulveda responded that he had decided to make some changes, and that was the end of the conversation.

Another case of desultory hiring and firing occurred in 1992, when Junior Gonzalez invited me to play with his band. During the hiring, he effusively stated how much he desired to have me play with the band and offered, "If you are ever hired by another band for more money, I will match their price to make sure that you play with me." I was surprised by this generous and uncommon offer. My first scheduled performance with Gonzalez was the following Saturday. On Friday, Tito Nieves called and asked if I was available to play on Saturday for a price that was $10 more than Gonzalez was paying.

I called Gonzalez to take him up on his price-matching offer. He responded by exclaiming incredulously, "How dare you ask me for more money? We have an agreement. You're fired!" and then he hung up. The lack of written agreements reflects the capricious nature of job security in the salsa business. However, counter to the examples provided above, there are some bandleaders, mostly older salseros who have led bands since the 1970s, who faithfully reward band loyalty. Tito Puente, Manny Oquendo, Eddie Palmieri, and Ruben Blades have been using many of the same sidepersons for years, and in return the musicians make every effort not to miss any of their gigs.

On the Gig: Salsa Is Hard Work

On and off the bandstand, salsa musicians face a variety of occupational hazards and difficulties that include the presence of violence, the abundance of drugs, the sheer physicality of performing music that demands such a sustained high level of intensity, harmful loud volumes, persistent sleep deprivation, dwindling performance opportunities, and the preponderance of exploitative and erratic business practices.

Inside salsa performance spaces (clubs, concerts, and street festivals), there is widespread alcohol consumption and drug use. The use of these mind-altering substances, along with the late-night hours and the sexually charged atmosphere of these performance settings, can foster a volatility that exposes musicians to dangerous individuals and acts of violence. Clubs directly connected with the illicit drug trade tend to be more prone to outbreaks of violence; however, disturbances also occur at legitimately run clubs (I explore the roles of both violence and drugs in detail in Chapters Three and Four, respectively). Salsa performance spaces often are located in neighborhoods associated with high crime rates and rampant drug dealing, so concerns for personal safety continue outside of the venues as well. Commuting to and from gigs, especially when carrying expensive instruments from cars or on public transportation, can be hazardous. Several musicians routinely carry weapons, such as guns, knives, and mace, for self-defense. The safety of their vehicles while at the gig, usually parked on unattended and deserted streets, is also a problem. Vehicle break-ins are not uncommon (my own car was broken into twice while gigging).

The physical toll of salsa performance is another area of concern. When a musician does become injured while performing, no workman's compensation is paid. There are no sick days granted. If a musician does not play, he or she does not get paid. Often brass players with split lips, percussionists with blistered hands, singers with injured vocal cords, and musicians who are so ill they should be in bed are forced to perform. Musicians adapt and learn how to play through physical pain, but performing while injured or sick takes a toll over time. Muscular damage, tendonitis, and damaged vocal cords are persistent problems, some career-ending. Additionally, the stentoraphonic volume levels employed during performances satisfy the expectations of clubgoers who have grown accustomed to the potentially deafening volumes produced by club deejays mixing dance music. Unfortunately, this has resulted in a large number of musicians suffering from tinnitus or other forms of hearing damage and loss. Poor sound systems and incompetent sound engineers in some clubs further exacerbate the problem. Many musicians complain about constant ringing in their ears, and some have been forced to retire from live performance when the problem grows unbearable. As musicians slowly become educated about the risks of exposure to constant loud volumes, more are performing with earplugs. However, for many, the education has come too late in their shortened careers.

The late and extended working hours, especially on weekends and during tours, can result in excessive sleep deprivation. One typical example of a performance schedule appears below. It was the schedule of Raulín Rosendo's band on a Saturday and Sunday in October 1993. This was a typical weekend for the group throughout 1993 and 1994.[13]

- Saturday night, 11:00 P.M.: We depart for the gig.
- 11:30 P.M.: We arrive at the club, Las Terrazas in the Bronx.
- 12:15 A.M. to 1:00 A.M.: We play one set and leave for the next club.
- 1:30 A.M.: We arrive at the second club, Studio 84 in Harlem.
- 1:45 A.M. to 2:30 A.M.: We play one set and depart for the next club.
- 2:55 A.M.: We arrive at the next club, Las Vegas in Washington Heights. The owner cancels the gig, claiming there are not enough patrons in the club to cover the expense of the band.
- 3:00 A.M. to 3:45 A.M.: We meet at a restaurant for dinner.
- 4:00 A.M.: We arrive at the next club, Elegante in the Bronx, an illegal after-hours bar.[14]
- 4:30 A.M.: The owner tells us to wait until more people arrive before playing.
- 4:30 A.M. to 5:50 A.M.: We wait as patrons begin to arrive.
- 5:50 A.M. to 6:45 A.M.: We play one set.
- 6:45 A.M. to 7:15 A.M.: We wait to get paid.
- 7:15 A.M.: We receive payment and leave for home.
- 8:00 A.M. to noon: We sleep.
- 1:00 P.M.: We depart for a 2:00 P.M. performance at a street festival in Brooklyn.
- 1:45 P.M.: We arrive at performance venue.

- 1:45 P.M. to 3:30 P.M.: The gig is delayed as we wait for the arrival of the bandleader (he overslept!).
- 3:30 P.M. to 6:00 P.M.: We play two sets with a break in between.
- 6:00 P.M. to 6:30 P.M.: We wait to get paid.
- 6:30 P.M.: We leave for home.
- 7:25 P.M. to 10:00 P.M.: We eat and sleep.
- 10:30 P.M.: We leave for an 11:00 P.M. gig at the Las Vegas club.
- 3:15 A.M.: We leave for home.
- 3:45 A.M.: We arrive home.

This type of rigorous schedule requires musicians to perform in sleep-deprived and fatigued states. During the gigs listed above, the effects of musician fatigue on the performances were markedly noticeable as the night progressed. The singers and horn section players danced on stage less, and the tempos played by the rhythm section tended to lag throughout the later sets. The sore and tired hands of the rhythm section players, the swollen lips of the horn players, and the tired and hoarse vocalists resulted in a comparatively subdued performance at the Sunday afternoon gig. Trumpeter Joe King shared his view concerning these performance conditions: "Many guys complain about the late hours, but you have to accept it. That's our business. If you want to work, you have to be able to play whether you have slept or not, whether your face hurts or not, whether you are sick or healthy. Because no one is going to pay you if you don't play" (J. King, pers. comm.).

Out-of-town performances that require air or bus travel can cause the hours to become even more rigorous. In an attempt to minimize expenses, promoters tend to purchase the cheapest tickets available, which often are early morning flights. Musicians performing until 3:00 or 4:00 A.M. frequently are required to catch flights that depart at 6:00 or 7:00 A.M. Percussionist Junior Perez said, "During [Sepulveda]'s West Coast tour we didn't sleep for almost a week. We played every night. We would get back to the hotel at 3 or 4 in the morning and would have to be in the lobby at 5 or 6 to get to the airport. If we were lucky, we would get to take a nap in the afternoon. Night after night it was the same thing. By the end of the week we were so tired that everyone wanted to kill everybody else" (J. Perez, pers. comm.). Pianist and musical director Ricky Gonzalez added, "I was so sick for days after Ray's last tour, we didn't get to rest for an entire week" (R. Gonzalez, pers. comm.).

Throughout the late 1980s and early 1990s, performance venues and opportunities for salsa bands dwindled. This was due to the growing preference for hip-hop, house music, and rap among Latino youth in New York City; the popularity of Dominican merengue; the government crackdown on the drug trade (see Chapter Four); and the cuts made to the National Endowment for the Arts and other governmental funding programs that supported performances in poorer neighborhoods and at street festivals. This added economic strain to musicians who played salsa exclusively and forced many to engage in other types of nonmusical employment. In 1992, the Nieves band was one of the busiest bands in New York, averaging sixteen gigs a month. At that time the average pay per gig was $90. A steady member who did not participate in any additional freelance work earned $1,440 as a monthly salary. Considering the cost of living in New York City and the additional costs of supporting other family members, the musicians were hard-pressed to make ends meet. Six of the twelve members held regular nine-to-five jobs. Each job needed a level of flexibility to accommodate occasional touring and the late hours (e.g., a boss who was a Nieves admirer and enjoyed complimentary concert tickets). Those jobs included car salesperson, schoolteacher, hospital maintenance worker, bank teller, and packager at a fashion warehouse. One band member worked as a studio musician, recording for a variety of other bands. Only five drew all their income from the live performances of the band and occasional freelance work.

Balancing diurnal work with a busy nightly gig schedule involves a degree of sacrifice in both the personal and professional lives of musicians. Many hours are spent away from family life, and suffering from continual sleep deprivation can affect productivity both on the bandstand and in the daytime work place. During 1992, two of Nieves's musicians holding day jobs were fired from their daytime work because of excessive absenteeism caused by touring and the late hours. Complaints concerning the physical strain of ending a gig between 3:00 and 5:00 A.M. on a weekday morning and having to work an eight-hour shift that begins only a few hours later are frequent. Trombonist Orlando Peña comments, "You can't imagine how hard it is for me to wake up some times, let alone make it throughout the day until five. When I get home it takes all my effort to practice and try to keep my chops up. That's the thing I miss the most about not having a day gig—the time to practice. But I've got a family to support and I get health benefits for them, so it's worth it. You got to do what you got to do" (O. Peña, pers. comm.).

The ways in which salsa business is conducted—which encompass both legitimate and legal means (reported to the IRS), illegitimate and illegal means (unreported cash), and a disregard for practices long established by the U.S. mainstream music industry—present an array of difficulties and often result in the persistent exploitation of musicians (many of the illegal practices are rooted in the illicit drug trade, a topic I discuss in depth in Chapter Four). Throughout the 1990s, roughly 30 percent of working salsa bands conducted business in a legitimate fashion. During negotiations, musicians must distinguish the modi operandi of the employers with whom they are dealing, which are not overtly stated. Paperwork and record-keeping can prove to be difficult tasks. Often it is unclear if a 1099 tax form will be submitted for a gig, even if all transactions were in cash. At year's end, many are faced with paying tax on work they thought would remain unreported. Additionally, no salsa bands offer insurance benefits, make Social Security and Medicare contributions, have pension plans, provide unemployment benefits, pay royalties, or provide payment guarantees for canceled gigs.

To understand these business practices, it is helpful to briefly examine their historical precedents. Jerry Masucci of Fania Records established these now-standard practices in the 1960s, and, according to Larry Harlow, he adopted his business approach from Morris Levy, who ran Roulette Records and had reputed ties to the Mob. Allegedly, in order to avoid paying extra money for pension and health benefits, royalties, and so forth, and to avoid operating his business in a legitimate fashion, Masucci struck a covert deal with the American Federation of Musicians Union Local 802 (A. F. of M.) in New York City not to organize or represent musicians working in the salsa scene. This set the precedent for future generations.

In the early 1980s, to compensate for these inequitable practices, singer Blades attempted to organize Latin musicians through the A. F. of M. Blades comments about that period, "it was very complex because . . . musicians here in New York were not treated very fairly, not only by the record companies but by the booking agencies" (Polin 1996: 7). Though there was some interest by musicians, his plans never came to fruition. The record companies, bandleaders, producers, managers, and club owners viewed his plans as threats to their continued prosperity and quickly worked to divide musicians over the issue. The A. F. of M. was not overly receptive to the idea, either. Trumpeter Joe Schuffle, who assisted Blades in this effort, remarked, "Without the overwhelming support of every musician, we could not get anything organized. Everyone was worried about losing their gigs. The bandleaders knew that if they had any trouble from their sidemen they could easily replace them and they told them so . . . so many other musicians wanted to steal their gigs anyway. The union wasn't very helpful in the whole process that eventually failed" (J. Schuffle, pers. comm.).

Taking their cue from Masucci, producers have continued covert negotiations with Local 802 officials to ensure the status quo is maintained. As a result, union officials have not interfered with the Latin music recording and concert industry. Salsa musicians have never received residual payments for audio recordings, videotaped performances, and television appearances (unless the performances were covered by the Screen Actors Guild [SAG] or the American Federation of Television and Radio Artists [AFTRA]); and they do not enjoy union leverage or assistance during arbitration. In 1994, a serendipitous conversation with a Local 802 union official revealed that the laissez-faire relationship advanced in the 1960s between the union and Latin music producers was still in place. I was scheduled to perform at the Cathedral of St. John the Divine in New York City a composition written for seventy-seven trombones by Wendy Chambers, a new music composer. She planned to record the concert and release the performance on CD. She personally funded the project. The night before the performance, an official at Local 802 contacted me, stating that Chambers did not have a recording agreement with the union. Consequently, they were going to set up a picket line and, as a union member, I was not permitted to cross. A partial transcript of the conversation is included below:

CHRIS WASHBURNE: Why are you even bothering to go after such a small-scale project? She is employing seventy-seven trombonists and paying them only slightly under union scale for a project that barely has a chance to recoup its investment. How many people do you think are actually going to buy a record with seventy-seven trombones on an independent label (CRI) with a small distribution deal?

UNION REP: That is not the point. She does not have a recording agreement with us and therefore will not be paying into your pension fund or health benefits. Plus we can't let people get away with recording without contracts because then we cannot protect the musicians if she reuses the music for television or radio.

CW: I agree. Then, if that is the case, why weren't you picketing at my recording session yesterday? Wendy's record will sell maybe five thousand copies at best. The one I did yesterday will have worldwide distribution and could potentially sell over five hundred thousand copies.

UNION REP: Who was it with and where was it?

CW: It was at Variety Studios on West 42nd Street and was for Oscar D'Leon.

UNION REP: What kind of music was it?

CW: Latin music, salsa.

UNION REP: Who was the producer and what label was it for?

CW: Ralph Mercado, RMM and Sony Records. Isn't Sony a union signatory company?

UNION REP: Oh, well then. Sony does have a recording contract with us, but . . . ah . . . Ralph Mercado is insulated.

CW: Insulated? What is that supposed to mean?

UNION REP: He's insulated. I am not personally aware of the details of our relationship with him.

CW: How does one become insulated?

UNION REP: Um . . . I am not sure of the details of that either. But if you want to officially complain, you can submit a formal complaint in writing.

CW: Thanks for your help!

These separate standards for Latin music, related to but set apart from mainstream U.S-music-industry practices, permeate the salsa scene and are indicative of the marginalized position Latinos often are forced to inhabit. When I shared this exchange with musicians, the majority was shocked by the candidness of the union representative, but not by Mercado's "insulation." Salsa musicians are aware of alleged corruption and in general have become complacent, growing accustomed to the continual abuses. For instance, in 1996 at Broadway Too, a salsa club in Queens, a videotaping crew set up and began recording for a Bronx cable television station during a performance of the Sepulveda band. Permission was not sought from band members, and no musicians were informed of how the tape was to be used. Only the club owner had authorized the taping session. This would not have been possible with a union contract. Upon interviewing several band members during the set break, all agreed that it was wrong of the crew not to seek permission for the taping and not to have informed the group about its purpose. Nevertheless, no member chose to protest. When questioned about their reticence, one musician remarked, "What good would it do anyway? [Sepulveda] isn't going to do anything about it. Besides we were already playing. If we refused to continue to play the club would just send us home and not pay us for the night" (Anon., pers. comm.). Responding verbally in that situation also risked stigmatization as a "troublemaker," possibly jeopardizing future employment. No one was willing to take that risk.

This type of videotaping has resulted in a substantial loss of revenue for musicians. Throughout the early 1990s, performances at the Palladium dance club in Manhattan were videotaped and the filmed images were projected onto screens throughout the large club. What was not revealed to the performers was that these tapes were compiled, edited, and commercially released throughout Latin America. Members of the Nieves group related an account of their first trip to Peru in 1991. When a crowd of admirers met the band at the airport, the musicians were amazed by the fact that the fans were familiar with all of their names. This was especially perplexing since most band members had not recorded with Nieves (thus they would have had their names listed on the album credits), nor had they traveled to Peru with other bands prior to this occasion. It was revealed later that their performances at the Palladium, which included their credits, were frequently shown on Peruvian television and routinely projected onto screens at salsa clubs throughout Lima. These video recordings also were available commercially in video and record stores throughout the country. No musicians ever signed release forms for the use of their images, nor were they offered any compensation. Without union representation there was no viable recourse, so nothing was done.

These exploitive practices as well as the continued marginalization of salsa business within the U.S. mainstream music industry partially stems from the lack of competition within salsa business. Throughout its history, the business of salsa has remained monopolized by two moguls: first, Masucci and Fania Records; later, Ralph Mercado and RMM Records. Without competition within the business sector, relations between "business people" and "artists" became more antagonistic and adversarial with fewer negotiable possibilities. If you didn't accept RMM's conditions in the 1990s, for instance, no alternative record companies or booking agencies were available. Mutual disrespect and distrust ran rampant. Musicians often remarked that RMM really stood for "Rob My Money" and "Ruin My Music." In fairness to Mercado, he took the international infrastructure set up by Fania and pushed for further growth and explored new markets. He used his powerful position to influence airplay, push records, and present concerts throughout the world. Some artists he represented financially benefited. However, many members of the salsa community still feel that he did little to improve upon the exploitative practices of the salsa scene. Bandleader Eddie Palmieri, who was not signed with RMM, comments, "But now we have a political booking situation that I cannot fight, because when you fight for your rights, it's, 'This guy's a problem; this guy's unmanageable,' only because you have decided not to refrain from thinking. You have a mind, and my main concern is respect, to me and the musicians I bring to the bandstand" (Birnbaum 1994: 17).

Another example of exploitative treatment of musicians occurs when club owners and promoters, occurring when crowds are not deemed sufficient to cover the band's wage. As a result club owners routinely cancel such performances, even after the band has arrived and set up on stage. For instance, in September 1998, Sepulveda was hired to play at Jimmy's, a club in the Bronx. The band arrived at 12:30 A.M. and began setting up for a 1:00 A.M. start. The promoter informed us that he wanted us to wait until more people showed up (the club was half filled). At 3:15 A.M. he called Sepulveda into the office and informed him that the gig was canceled because he did not have enough money to pay us. Sepulveda stated, "I asked him why he waited to cancel us and he said he thought more people would come. He blamed us for not bringing more people. What could I say? When I asked him to at least pay me for the guys or even give us gas money, he said, 'no!' There's nothing I could do. I had no contract, so there was no deposit. If I complain too much, he won't hire us again. The only thing I can do is ask for the money up front next time. He probably won't accept though. So I guess this is the last time we play here" (R. Sepulveda, pers. comm.). Without even partial compensation, the musicians were incensed and disgusted. Trumpeter Pete Nader complained, "I'm so sick and tired of this shit, with promoters always treating us with such disrespect" (P. Nader, pers. comm.). One musician was seen damaging microphones by dropping them on the floor. The sound company accused the band members of stealing a microphone. When the soundman told us that the promoter would have to pay for the missing equipment, one musician remarked, "Maybe we should take the whole sound system and then see if he would like to pay for that instead of paying us" (Anon., pers. comm.). Another musician said, "Man, this gets me so depressed. We have no place to sit. There's no back room for us. We can't get free or discounted drinks at the bar, and then they cancel us without pay. This is just how I wanted to spend my Saturday night!" (Anon., pers. comm.).

The constant disrespect that musicians receive is discouraging, and many stop playing after a while because of these poor working conditions. In her study of food-service workers, Robin Leidner discusses that a sense of self is formed in childhood, but throughout life it remains vulnerable to messages from others. If car salespeople are treated with suspicion (Lawson 1991), phone solicitors with rudeness, restaurant servers with condescension or familiarity, or domestic servants as nonpeople (Rollins 1985), how will they react? Certainly they need not accept the implied judgment of the service recipients. But they need to construct some means of defending themselves as demeaned (Leidner 1993: 13). Musicians protect themselves by often expecting insolent behavior before they actually receive it. One percussionist remarked, "We play on the 'come mierda' circuit. If you play on this scene, you know sometimes they are going to make you 'eat shit'" (Anon., pers. comm.). On occasions when things go well and musicians are treated with some respect, it can be surprising. When musicians are pushed past their limits, they often lash out, such as with the damaging of microphones described above. Another example occurred during a Frankie Ruíz performance at Madison Square Garden. Ruíz made a blatant mistake during one of his songs. At the end of the tune, he admonished the band, blaming us for the mistake, and announced to the audience of twenty thousand, "These musicians need to go back to school because they don't know how to play." The band reacted by playing poorly, which sabotaged the rest of his performance. The horn players played in the wrong key and played the mambo and *moña* sections in the wrong place, and the percussionists sped up and slowed down throughout his second number. As he stammered off the stage, disgruntled, the horn players destroyed his sheet music.

The greed of certain bandleaders and musical directors is another issue with which musicians must contend. Such leaders, some with notorious reputations, usually allow no negotiation regardless of a musician's prestige and frequently pay less than the average, or even attempt not to pay at all. One example is L.G., the longtime musical director for Nieves, who was eventually fired when it was revealed that he had been skimming thousands of dollars from the musician's pay. Many musicians were aware of his actions for years, but they were reticent to complain to Nieves, fearing the loss of their jobs. It wasn't until the entire band decided to confront L.G. collectively in front of Nieves and in the middle of a club (something very unusual), that Nieves asked L.G. to leave the band (I coincidentally happened to be subbing on the band during that fateful evening). No money was collected from him and no further action was taken; however, the band's pay suddenly increased, revealing just how much L.G. had been stealing each night ($10 to $100 from each musician on every gig). More accomplished musicians try to avoid performing under such conditions; however, the large numbers of novice musicians attempting to break into the salsa scene become easy prey, allowing such unethical practices to continue. Another example occurred in 1995, when bandleader D.L. put together a Hector Lavoe tribute band after the passing of the famed *sonero*. He organized a concert series to raise money for a Hector Lavoe AIDS fund that was to help infected children living in El Barrio. He hired musicians who had performed with Lavoe to play for a considerably underscaled fee, justifying the low wage because it was for a "good cause." After the second concert, none of the musicians had received any payment. As protests arose from the players, further inquiry revealed that the only fund the donated contributions (including the musicians' pay) were endowing was D.L.'s personal bank account. Protests were met with extreme aggression, including threats of bodily harm. One musician who attempted to collect his money by visiting D.L.'s apartment was escorted off the premises, in his own words, "by two large thugs." Regardless, D.L. remained on the scene and, by employing young and inexperienced musicians, continued his unethical practices. In 1998, pianist Oscar Hernandez remarked, "There are so many people with dirty hands. I'm so happy I'm doing what I'm doing; not working in the salsa scene so much anymore so I don't have to deal with them" (O. Hernandez, pers. comm.).

But in 2000, Hernandez did return to salsa in a profound way, founding the hugely successful Spanish Harlem Orchestra, a band dedicated to revitalizing the hard driving salsa *dura* sound. In 2006, after winning a Grammy Award the previous year, Hernandez's band was the best salsa gig in town. Why did he choose to return to a scene that just two years prior he dismissed with disdain?

Why Salsa Musicians Play Salsa

Studies by Carlo Lastrucci (1941), Howard Becker (1963), and Bruce MacLeod (1993) document the social segregation that the music business necessitates and the disruptions this can cause in the personal lives of musicians. This is not something unique to salsa. Further, compared with other nonmusic professions, the income musicians receive is not commensurate with their abilities and the amount of time they spend practicing, rehearsing, commuting, and performing. Considering these stark economic and social realities of making a living as a musician, along with the hardships, hazards, and exploitations that are specific to the salsa scene (documented above), it makes one wonder: Why do musicians continue to play salsa?

Posing this question to a number of musicians reveals that the act of salsa music-making and the sounds themselves remain central motivating factors in their continued participation. Some consider the social and cultural aspects associated with the music scene as significant in their determination to perform. For most, though, the desire to attain the highest degree of competence as well as the musical, personal, and soulful fulfillment of achieving a "hard-swinging groove" keeps them performing. Increasing competence not only provides opportunities to perform and record with the most famous bands, but, in the view of many, offers more fulfilling performance experiences as well. Trumpeter Hector Colón comments, "The salsa business sucks. That is a given. If you are going to play in this scene you have to accept that fact. What keeps me playing is the music. When the band is really swinging, there is nothing like it. It just washes away all of the other stuff" (H. Colón, pers. comm.). Colón suggests that through collective effort in live performance, musicians can transcend their daily and nightly hardships and achieve a sense of euphoria. As Sara Cohen writes, in this way the music fulfills a significant "need for loss of self, to emotions, sensations, and thought invoked by and through the performance that take one over, obscuring all sense of normal self with the place, time, obligations, and responsibilities" (Cohen 1991: 98). Indeed, musicians hold the intensity of the salsa musical experience so special that hardship and difficulties are eclipsed and become accepted as part and parcel of the scene. Trombonist Barry Olsen adds, "The music business in general can be very negative. But I am [a] person who was born and raised in a non-Latino culture and I have found that Latin music has become a part of my being, so deeply that I am unhappy if I am not playing the music. I think it is my favorite music to play. I would rather be playing a Latin gig than a 'club-date' any day, even if the Latin gig pays less"[15] (B. Olsen, pers. comm.). And trumpeter Barry Danielian sums it up by simply stating, "the music is so good, but the scene is pure dues" (B. Danielian, pers. comm.). These intense feelings for the music and strong desire to play, in some ways, facilitate the widespread exploitation musicians experience. Producers, promoters, and bandleaders at times take advantage of this passion to play in spite of inequity.

For some Latino musicians, cultural issues associated with salsa play an important role in their performance. Specifically, Puerto Ricans and Nuyoricans often use salsa as a cultural identity marker, viewing the music as specifically representative of and signifying their culture. Salsa performance can evoke feelings of cultural pride.[16] For Puerto Ricans who claim ownership of the music (and many do), performing salsa is performing something of one's own, and it asserts their cultural affiliations and affirms their cultural roots in a public manner. Emblematic of this relationship is Nieves's decision to place an embroidered microphone wrapped in a Puerto Rican flag on the back of his band jackets. Roberta Singer writes, "As musicians, as New Yorkers, as Puerto Ricans and Latinos and for many, as socially and politically conscious individuals, they have at their disposal a range of musical tools with which to express a sense of self, a philosophy and ideology. At the very least, performances of Latin popular music communicate and reinforce pride in New York Puerto Rican and Latino selfhood. According to one musician [pianist Oscar Hernandez], 'There's a nationalistic sense of pride when people hear salsa. They say "that's our music'" (Singer 1982: 7). Marisol Berrios-Miranda concurs, stating that salsa provides "Puerto Ricans in New York with a sense of historical and cultural continuity" (Berrios-Miranda 2000: 17).

Latino musicians from countries other than Puerto Rico, as members of a wider delineated pan-Latino culture, also view salsa as their own. For instance, Dominican trumpeter Ité Jeréz comments, "When I play salsa and see non-Latino people enjoying it and dancing to it, I feel good that I am able to share my culture with them" (I. Jeréz, pers. comm.). This pan-Latino association of salsa stems from what Felix Padilla labels a "Latinizing" process that occurred in the 1960s and was consciously marketed by Fania Records: "To Fania, the Latinizing of salsa came to mean homogenizing the product, presenting an all-embracing 'Pan-American' or Latino sound with which people from all of Latin America and Spanish-speaking communities in the United States could identify and purchase" (Padilla 1992: 349). Motivated primarily by economic factors, Fania's push for countries throughout Latin America to embrace salsa did result in an expanded market. But in addition, throughout the 1970s, salsa groups from Colombia, the Dominican Republic, and Venezuela, among other Latin American nations, emerged, composing and performing music that related to their own specific cultural experiences and affiliations, which posited salsa as a cultural identity marker for those nations as well. For instance, Colombian festivals in Queens will feature a number of performances by Colombian salsa bands; likewise, Dominican festivals in Washington Heights include salsa performances by Dominican bands.

Other musicians are drawn to the social aspects of gigging, such as inclusiveness, group participation, audience interaction, and other uniting qualities of salsa performance. Many of these qualities are the social benefits that come with being a regular member of a band. The intensity of these bonds often is spoken of in familial terms. Trombonist Dan Reagan speaks of his longtime membership in Conjunto Libre: "I always go out of my way to make Libre gigs. When I was living on the West Coast, I would fly in to New York just to play one night with them. I would always lose money but it did not matter, because playing with Manny Oquendo is like playing with family. He creates such a positive energy within the group, that it always feels good" (D. Reagan, pers. comm.). Bandleaders also share similar sentiments toward their sidepersons. Sepulveda says, "It's important to me that the band feels like a family because when we do, we sound better. And it's more fun to play" (R. Sepulveda, pers. comm.). Performing regularly with a band offers musicians chances to develop intimate relationships with others, fulfills needs for belonging, and elicits feelings of loyalty and solidarity.

These relationships are forged and developed in live performance and remind us that, for musicians, gigs are the central focus of their working lives. It is on the gig that they are able to develop and achieve their creative potential, affirm cultural affiliations, and use music as a means of communication with fellow musicians and also with audience members. Audiences play critical roles in live salsa performance. Cohen's work is insightful here: "Live performance thus unites participants in common activity. They collectively concentrate on, contribute to, and experience the production of a spectacle, and the relationship and dialogue between audience and performers can be such that even if they do not know each other a rapport is established, highlighting the social role of the gig. This bonding and uniting of participants can be achieved through dance, music, or through the gig's symbolic forms" (Cohen 1991: 39). And salseros often acknowledge the importance of audience interaction in their gigging experiences. Trombonist Dave Chamberlain says, "It's great when you are playing well, the band's swinging, and the audience is digging it. If they're into it, it can take the band to another level. It just lifts the whole thing up" (D. Chamberlain, pers. comm.).

In spite of salsa affiliations with specific Latino communities, salsa performance spaces also can create inclusionary vistas of intercultural exchange where diverse peoples gather and participate in a shared and unifying experience. This diversity often cuts across ethnicity, nation, culture, class, and generation. Similar to the Chicano dance events that Manuel Peña studies, dance

Figure 2.2 Dance floor of the Latin Quarter in New York, 2005. *(Photograph by Christopher Washburne.)*

events create communitas (Turner 1969) whereby participants confirm, establish, and maintain community through the ritual of the dance (Peña 1985). Trumpeter Walsh remarks, "One reason I continue to play salsa is because the scene is multigenerational, which is really unique. You can go into a club and see seventy-year-olds dancing right next to people in their twenties. Dancing to the same beat and enjoying it to the same degree. And it is even multicultural where people from all over Latin America and North America are dancing together. I love that. I love to be a part of that" (J. Walsh, pers. comm.).

The financial benefits of performing salsa, however modest, also provide incentive for continued performance in the scene. The large number of bands working in the 1990s, using up to six horn players, several singers, and three percussionists, created a high demand for competent musicians, especially on Saturday nights. Musicians who were building careers in jazz, Broadway, or studio playing, or were planning on leading their own bands, often took advantage of the money earned from salsa performances to support their other musical interests. Trombonist Pete McGuinness says, "When I first came to town I played a lot of Latin gigs. I really enjoyed it. It is a good scene, especially for cats who are new in town. You meet a lot of players and earn some money. Now that my Broadway and club-date work is picking up, I don't play

Latin gigs anymore. But I really miss it" (P. McGuinness, pers. comm.). Singer Aires Martínez offers another perspective: "I enjoy that I can make money doing what I love to do . . . sing. My goal is to have my own salsa band. And I'm working on getting the arrangements done and I plan to record a demo. But everyone has to pay the rent. So I'm singing coro with a bunch of different bands in the meantime" (A. Martínez, pers. comm.).

As demonstrated by these perspectives, the reasons for playing salsa are as diverse as the people who inhabit the New York salsascape, reflecting the deterritorialized cultures in motion within which they operate. Straddling, "not neither," adversity, familia, gigging, and intense collective music-making are fundamental in the nightly lives of New York salsa musicians. It all keeps them playing.

3

"Play like there's a gun to your head!"

The Aesthetics and Performance Practice of Sounding Violence in Salsa

October 1995, 11:00 P.M. Singer Pete "El Conde" Rodríguez has a gig at Fuego Fuego, a New York Latin dance club aptly named "Fire Fire." As the band members arrive, we are confronted by a group of insolent security staff the club employs. We are refused entry in a verbally abusive way. "The main entrance is for paying customers only," they bark. We, along with all employees, are forced to use the service entrance around back, located in a dark, deserted alley. As we approach the back door, nearby two drug dealers are engaged in a heated argument. The service entrance is locked and unattended. The argument is escalating. The quarreling dealers block our only way of returning to the front of the club. As we pound loudly on the door, one of the dealers walks past us. Just on the other side of our group, he pulls out a gun and points it in our direction, aiming at the other dealer. His adversary does the same. We are pinned between both gun-wielding parties as they exchange insults. As we hunch together, making ourselves as flat as possible against the building, the door is finally unlocked from inside. We all rush into the club without injury and leave the two dealers to their own devices.

Though the band members were visibly shaken, no one suggested going home or not playing. One musician exclaimed, "Well we're here. None of us got shot, so we might as well play." Others chuckled nervously in response. We all stayed, and played. In some ways the gig proceeded as though nothing had occurred, though there seemed to be a heightened emotional edge on stage. One musician remarked, "Man, the music has such a dark vibe tonight."

Figure 3.1 Pete "El Conde" Rodríguez performing at Orchard Beach in 1992 (From Left to Right: Vincent Velez, Ralph Figueroa, Cita Rodríguez, Chris Washburne, Pete "El Conde" Rodríguez, Hector Colón, and Skip Howlett). *(From the Christopher Washburne collection: photographer unknown.)*

New York salsa has long been associated with urban street life, a life that is commonly permeated by violence. It is a widely held belief among scholars and musicians alike that "the street" as topos is an essential quality of salsa and one of its defining characteristics. Mayra Santos-Febres writes that "[salsa] espouses the values of the street, of that space that creates an alternative criminalized market economy and . . . lies outside the margins of power of the bourgeois nation-state" (Santos-Febres 1997: 180). Other urban music styles, such as rap, hip-hop, and dance hall, also share this fundamental relationship with "street culture," but what makes salsa unique is the social particularities of the "street" that it espouses. This street is not just any urban thoroughfare, but specifically references a subaltern experiential imaginary rooted in El Barrio of New York City, encapsulating the unique blend of intercultural exchange and friction (Tsing 2005), capitalism, and rigorous competition so prevalent in that locale. Since the 1930s, Latin music in New York has been associated with El Barrio to various degrees; however, it was El Barrio of the 1960s and 1970s that served as, what Peter Manuel (1995) labels, a "cauldron" for artistic creativity that was spawned by newfound political fervor and activism amidst dire social conditions. Jorge Duany describes El Barrio as embodying a unique blend of urbanity—with all of its resplendent decay—and a provincial rusticity transplanted directly from rural settings in the Caribbean. He writes, "[El Barrio is] framed by economic deprivation and ecological isolation. It preserves much of the face-to-face quality of a rural community through reciprocity networks . . . but is marked by violence, crime . . . and physical deterioration" (Duany 1984: 196). The violence associated with this socially and physically marginalized urban or rural space, then, stems from various historical and societal factors, including poverty, racism, unemployment, family instability, inadequate education, the illegal drug trade, gang activity, lack of opportunity, and others. The belief that salsa emerged from, and continues to be informed by, this particular cultural milieu perpetuates an imagined sense of cultural "rootedness," an indispensable authenticity that remains at the core of salsa performance practice.

Because of this deep-rooted connection with El Barrio, as well as the fact that many salsa performances take place in locations conducive to dubious behavior (after-hours nightclubs in crime-ridden neighborhoods), and that the infrastructure of salsa business often is linked inextricably to the illicit drug trade (sustaining that "alternative criminalized market economy"), *salseros* frequently encounter acts of violence. While a number of studies have addressed the role of violence in salsa song texts, especially in connection with salsa *dura* of the 1970s (e.g., Rodríguez 1988; Manuel 1995; Waxer 2002), none have focused on sound structure and performance practice, let alone the role of violence in the professional lives of salsa musicians. This chapter explores how violence manifests itself in aesthetics, how tropes of violence are adopted by musicians and inform salsa performance, and how violence has served as an integral and shaping force, one of many I might add, throughout the music's history.

Addressing issues of violence in music is inherently problematic, in part due to the absence of methodological models to draw upon, but also (and, perhaps, more importantly) owing to the elusive process by which social phenomena get rechanneled or transposed into aesthetic constructs. With few exceptions, ethnographers and musicologists have shied away from such taboo topics.[1] The reasons for this avoidance are numerous and are partly due to the complexities of the cluster of phenomena associated with violent behavior and its thicket of social and cultural connotations.

Philippe Bourgois points to a threefold problem that he believes is rooted in anthropology's functionalist paradigm, "which imposes order and community on its research subjects" and thus cannot always attend to the disorder and breakdown of community that violence often entails. Further, and probably more to the point, is that "the methodological logistics of participation-observation," where researchers are required to be physically present and personally involved, can create insurmountable challenges when dealing with sensitive topics that profoundly affect the people to whom the researcher is empathetically engaged. Obtaining consent and gaining access can be prohibitive. Finally, extreme field settings involving human tragedy can be both psychologically overwhelming and physically dangerous (Bourgois 1996: 14). On a very basic level, I would add that violent encounters rarely are accessible directly or indirectly to the researcher. Being present when violence occurs or gaining access to the experiences of others is difficult and often dependent on happenstance.

Moreover, when the ethnographer is present or does gain access, by definition, he or she remains always on the margins of the violent encounter and thus must struggle to develop indirect discursive strategies or narrative formats that can encapsulate something fundamentally unrepresentable. Contact with the violent experience is always distanced by a degree and demands a very specific set of communicative strategies when dealing with informants and participants in violent settings, especially if one of those participants is the ethnographer him- or herself.

Beyond fieldwork and methodological difficulties lie numerous interpretive quandaries due, in part, to the opaque and inaccessible nature of violent experience and the "discursive eclipse" that surrounds it. Elaine Scarry, who is a pioneer in this realm, warns, "A great deal is at stake in the attempt to invent linguistic structures that will reach and accommodate this area of experience normally so inaccessible to language; the human attempt to reverse the de-objectifying work of pain by forcing pain itself into avenues of objectification is a project laden with practical and ethical consequence" (Scarry 1985: 6). Bat-Ami Bar On dovetails this critique, adding that violence cannot be controlled theoretically and, when done so, is only "a momentary achievement since violence cannot be neatly organized under the categories that it is assigned . . . Theoretical abstraction is a kind of forgetfulness . . . with its appearance of surface normality" (Bar On 2002: 28, 25). In light of this, however, she offers an intriguing partial solution that I adopt in the following pages. She advocates for a holistic approach to the subject through which multiple modes of engagement (theory, autobiography, and biography, and my addition to this mix—ethnography) are combined and negotiated to serve as "interior modes of thinking about violence" (Bar On 2002: xiii). Thus, I adopt a multivocal approach in order to circumvent the inherent blockages vis-à-vis the discourse on violence by means of certain metaphorical and narrative strategies that can begin to approach the unspeakable. The advantage to this approach is that it is rooted in and reflects the everyday strategies that salsa musicians employ in order to deal with their violent encounters. Through embracing, avoiding, humoring, distancing, denying, ignoring, and other creatively imaginative acts, painful experience often is translated into performance in highly complex and creative ways, making New York salsa sound, look, and feel the way it does.

To begin, a working definition of violence is in order, along with the delimitation of what constitutes a violent encounter per se on the New York salsa scene.[2] On the most basic level, acts of violence involve at least two agents and are multileveled affairs.[3] As Robert McAfee Brown writes, in the most general sense, violence encompasses "a violation of personhood, in the sense of infringement, denial, abuse, or disregard of another physically or otherwise" (Brown 1987: 7). I take "otherwise" to mean acts that depersonalize, reaching beyond bodily harm into the sphere of long-term, psychological, and transpersonal affairs. Barbara Witmer adds that perpetrators of violence can include both singular persons or institutions and, in addition to overtly physical destructive behavior, "there is covert personal violence which does psychological damage to another, and institutional covert violence where social structures violate the personhood of groups" (Witmer 1997: 22), which can come in the form of action or discourse. This expands the domain of violence to include the effects of corruption, indignities, exploitation, and the mere threat of physical violence. John McDowell embraces this position and posits violent acts as fundamentally forms of communication "in which destruction of property and the infliction of physical harm is the essential mode of signification" (McDowell 2000: 17–19). Thus, I am defining violence as injurious or destructive discourse or action.[4]

However, there is a larger historical context in which the types of microlevel everyday encounters defined above must be viewed, especially with regard to the New York salsa scene. Indeed, they are informed and undergirded by overarching macrolevel modes of violence stemming from the long colonial history of both the Caribbean and Latin America and their subsequent postcolonial positions, especially in relation to the United States. Antonio Benítez-Rojo observes that forms of Caribbean artistic expression perpetually resonate in "the swirling black hole of social violence produced by the *encomienda* and the plantation, that is, their otherness, their peripheral asymmetry with regard to the West" (Benítez-Rojo: 27). Stuart Hall echoes this sentiment, reminding us that Caribbean culture cannot be disassociated with notions of trauma, rupture, and catastrophe: ". . . [T]he violence of being torn from one's historic resting place, the brutal, abruptly truncated violence in which the different cultures were forced to coexist in the plantation system, the requirement to bend and incline to the unequal hegemony of the Other, the dehumanization, the loss of freedom . . . are always . . . recurring tropes of transplantation and forced labor, of mastery and subordination" (Hall 2003a: 35).[5]

These recurring tropes find expression in salsa in the forms of metaphors, imagery, and narratives that express exile, exclusion, and struggle for survival and recognition. Thus, a difference in agency is what distinguishes macrolevel from microlevel violence. Obviously all types of violence involve individual agents, but violence as it operates on the microlevel possesses a fairly distinguishable pattern of agency, whereas violence as it operates on a macrolevel is more subtle and diffused insofar as it is institutional and systemic in nature, embedded in complex transpersonal and ultimately discursive dynamics. Large-scale violent crimes, such as genocide or long-term colonial repression, never have one simple individual agent, but must be traced through a system of tropes and institutional structures.

Framing violence in this discursive manner, both on macro- and microlevels, adds a significant interpretive component to a given corpus of field materials when determining what actually constitutes violence and who can claim to be a victim, especially when dealing with the historically inflected nonphysical and psychological forms. Adding to this emergent murk is the experiential multileveledness of violence that is marked by its socially centrifugal nature. This is due to how its effects typically reach beyond that of perpetrator and victim, extending to what McDowell labels an "optional" but equally significant role, that of the witness. Witnesses "can be found at varying distances from the epicenter of action, ranging from an eyewitness present at the scene to those who 'witness' the action vicariously" through the accounts of others (McDowell 2000: 17–19). In this way, one relatively isolated incident potentially can reverberate throughout a community within a relatively short time, ultimately affecting large groups of people and, thus, highlighting the simultaneously personal and communal nature of violence. This is the case I make for the salsa community in New York City. Typically it is not those who were pinned against the back door at gunpoint, but rather those who received the hearsay at one or more steps removed who avidly disseminate the effect of that experience through retellings and subsequent reinventions. In many ways, it is this emergent postviolence discourse that ultimately has the greatest impact. As Paul Ricoeur observes, it is only through the use of language and discourse that the dialectic of violence and meaning is born. Violence confronts meaning only in discourse (Ricoeur 1975 [1967]: 88–101).[6]

That night at Fuego Fuego, the musicians were barred from entering the club's front door, a slighting policy considering that live music is the main audience draw for such businesses. Once inside, no concern was shown by the club owners, managers, or other employees for our well-being, even after we recounted our experience. When asking for a glass of water at the bar, I was told that no complimentary drinks were granted to musicians and that the only option was to pay $5 for bottled water, regardless of the presence of a functioning faucet and an abundance of cleaned and empty glasses. Though the club had informed the bandleader that we were to start at midnight, it was not until 2:45 A.M. that we began our first set. In the meantime, we were forced to wait in a back hallway segregated from the paying customers. No reason was given for the delay or why we were discouraged from mingling with the club's patrons. As we waited for the second set to begin, the club started to empty. And so at 4:00 A.M. the manager informed us that the second set was canceled and we would only receive half our pay. We were then sent home without any recourse. This was not an atypical night inside Fuego Fuego, though, admittedly, the gunfight outside was a bit unusual. The band performed on many other occasions at this club after that evening, often experiencing similarly exploitive, disrespectful, and abusive treatment, and even witnessing several fights inside.

What I have described above aptly captures the range of violent encounters, both personal and institutional, physical as well as psychological, that salsa musicians working in New York City routinely experience. That evening no musicians were harmed physically, nor did they witness any such act. However, the threat of both, as well as the nonphysical exploitative violence they encountered, was seriously real. I do not mean to reduce salsa performance to a mere list of violent encounters. Indeed, performing salsa encompasses so much more. However, the constant presence of these types of experiences in the lives of salsa musicians does affect the music they make, and it is this underexplored component of salsa music-making I focus upon presently.

Compared to other locales, the violence on the New York salsa scene is localized and relatively contained. New York City, after all, is a place that offers many occupational alternatives. Most musicians inhabit social strata that grant some type of mobility, providing avenues of escape from the violent environment of their work places for safer professions. And, indeed, many do eventually opt to leave the profession. Salsa, after all, is not an imposed war zone; it is a chosen path. As percussionist Marc Quiñones remarks, "Hey, shit happens. You just have to accept that you can't change things. If you play in these clubs night after night, you are going to see things going down. It's just part of the scene" (M. Quiñones, pers. comm.). The club environment, with its alcohol consumption and drug use, can foster particularly volatile situations.[7] Clubs that are associated with the drug trade tend to be more prone to outbreaks of violence; however, disturbances also occur at well-established, legitimately run venues. Even though club owners take precautions by employing well-armed and ominous-looking security personnel and by installing metal detectors to limit the weapons being brought inside, serious fights are not uncommon. On occasion, fights commencing inside escalate once the individuals involved are thrown out of the club. For instance, in 1990 while I was performing at the Palladium with Johnny Rivera, a fight erupted. The security staff expeditiously ejected the perpetrators, but not before the bouncers inflicted some bodily harm. Later in the evening one of the men involved in the altercation returned. As he drove by the front of the club, he shot the two bouncers who had thrown him out, killing one and injuring the other. The band played throughout the fight and during the shooting.

Consciously aware of their occupational hazards and adverse conditions, musicians sometimes refer to their working environment as "the trenches," or "the salsa trenches." Echoing the observations of Benítez-Rojo and Hall, musicians accuse those in positions of localized power (club owners, producers, bandleaders, and promoters) of adopting a "plantation mentality," referencing their exploitive practices. This discursive choice suggests that musicians perceive their own status as an enslaved servitude, albeit freely exposing themselves to continual abuse by those in power. But precisely because this is a free choice of profession, this discursive move illuminates a strategic self-conception that consciously locates their experiences within a broader colonial and postcolonial historical context. Worn as a badge of courage, this discourse serves as a self-empowering and self-defining tactical maneuver, a trope of struggle, survival, and mastery achieved despite the adversity.

Thus, no matter how localized or contained, specific conflicts must be viewed within the wider discursive and institutional continuities in which they are embedded. As Vivienne Jabri writes, "the linguistic constructs used to provide versions of a conflict . . . derive from pre-existing discursive modes which are implicated in the construction of the conflict. Furthermore, the linguistic modes surrounding a particular conflict have potent consequences more widely in the temporal and spatial domain in the reconstruction and reproduction of the discourses and institutions which render violent human conflict a social continuity in patterned social systems" (Jabri 1996: 128). It must not be overlooked then, that many New York salsa musicians live or were raised in economically depressed, inner-city neighborhoods, and that the experience of disempowerment, alienation, and violence are familiar. One musician comments, "I grew up on the corner of Broadway and 157th Street, just across from Fuego Fuego. I remember that every weekend there would be gunshots on the street below. My whole family would be watching television in the evening and when the shooting would start my parents would make us all lay flat on the floor and stay away from the windows. We would all lie there and just continue watching television. It was just another normal Saturday night" (Anon., pers. comm.). Another adds, "My father played with all those bands in the 1970s and lived in El Barrio. He and my mother moved us to Long Island when we were kids because they wanted to get away from all the violence on the street. I mean, my uncle was shot over some small argument. When I started playing on the scene, I began to realize all of the difficulties my parents faced living in that place" (Anon., pers. comm.).

El Barrio, once again, emerges as a definitorial trope. To some extent, these musicians' acceptance of their adverse working conditions and their willingness to persevere despite inequities are the results of the conditions they face in their daily lives, and it reflects their investment into the potency of El Barrio experience.[8] Through continual exposure to both physical and nonphysical violence, a normalization of this type of social behavior takes place. What follows is a shift or decentering of norms that fosters an adversarial terrain where violent acts and actions are routinized, and, ultimately, are embraced as significant forces affecting how musicians discursively relate to and physically perform the music ("trenches" being a prime example). Percussionist Ralph Figueroa says, "When I moved to Florida after playing in New York all those years, I tried to tell the local musicians there about all the things we experienced playing in New York. When I tell them the stories, they just say 'Yeah right!' They don't believe me! They want to play like New York musicians, but they can't since they have not experienced what we did" (R. Figueroa, pers. comm.).

Attesting to the potential paradigm-shifting power imbued in acts of violence, other musicians not familiar with this type of social and economic milieu adopt similar attitudes over the course of time through continued exposure. For instance, my own perspective was so greatly affected by these constant encounters that I would sometimes lose sight of my own behavioral norms. The ease with which I adopted an attitude of "We might as well play, get paid, and go home" was unsettling as I struggled to maintain an objective distance for my ethnographic project.

Rarely do musicians become directly involved in altercations of physical violence; however, such events sometimes do occur. Saxophonist Mitch Frohman offers the following anecdote: "Once I remember being awakened by a call at noon on a Sunday. A bandleader was calling to hire me for a gig that afternoon beginning at 4 o'clock. I said, 'Boy the club is starting early today.' And he responded, 'No they're not. We are playing the last set of Saturday night and I need you to play because our sax player was shot last night outside of another club'" (M. Frohman, pers. comm.). Alternatively, musicians desensitized by their working environment may opt to engage in violent physical action as a legitimate and acceptable form of recourse under certain circumstances. Though violent altercations between musicians are rare, they are not unprecedented (recall Eddie Montalvo's decision to damage Ramon's car, as described in the Introduction).

Seeking out the reverberations of these violent encounters in the music, one finds both short- and long-term effects on the aesthetic modes of expression. The short-term effects are more difficult to pin down, and, certainly, the struggle musicians have in specifically articulating this phenomenon reflect the "unspeakability" of violence. Hannah Arendt contends that one can speak about violence only at a distance and in forms that divorce us from lived experience because of the coercively silencing character of trauma (Arendt 1969). Accordingly, musicians often turn to metaphor, a distancing move, and speak indirectly of the "vibe" of specific performances, venues, and the scene in general. For example, after witnessing a fight at the Palm Tree, a club in Queens, saxophonist Bob Franceschini commented, "Did you notice how the whole 'vibe' changed after the fight? Everything got real intense. It was so dark" (B. Franceschini, pers. comm.). But what is this vibe that they are referring to? How is darkness expressed in music? Certainly it involves interpretive and perceptional aspects as well as very real sonic phenomena.

Originating from African American parlance, "vibe" is derived from "vibrations" and refers to a feeling, sensation, emanation, aura, or an atmosphere experienced or communicated. Geneva Smitherman adds a further sense by defining it as "an elusive, indefinable quality of something that cannot be described, you have to feel it" (Smitherman 1994: 291). Turning to this ambiguous and subjective terminology aptly captures how we personally experience music, the effects of violence, and the intersection of both. The perceptional and emotional shifts that take place in the aftermath of violent encounters are indeed elusive, personal, highly variant, and unique to each experience and subject. Violent experience shifts how we hear and make music, as well as how we speak about it. However, it also highlights the fundamental disjuncture between speech and experience. What is not being said—that which remains unspoken, that which can only be revealed through musical expression—is significant when examining the relationship between music and violence.

Bar On writes that "[v]iolence itself exerts a strong silencing force," and there is "a sense that violence leaves behind an unspeakable remainder and thus seems to produce the distinction and then exist between speakability and unspeakability" (Bar On 2002: 15). To my mind, music and performance provide a medium for the expression of this "unspeakable remainder" that manifests in subtle and not-so-subtle elemental shifts. Musicians may be silenced verbally, but the nature of musical expression provides a distanced and ambiguous space for cathartic release, a place for the unspeakable, a sonification of the silence. Scarry writes, "Physical pain does not simply resist language but actively destroys it, bringing about an immediate reversion to a state anterior to language, to the sounds and cries a human makes before language is learned" (Scarry 1985: 4). The nonverbal nature of instrumental music can facilitate

Figure 3.2 LP Cover of Willie Colón's *Lo Mato*. *(Album cover courtesy of Fania. Used by Permission. All rights owned by Emusica Acquisitions Corporation, 575 Blue Lagoon Drive, Suite 230, Miami, FL 33126.)*

precisely those primal cries of physical or psychological pain within the framework of a very public and socially acceptable arena. For instance, at Fuego Fuego, even though Rodríguez sang primarily about romantic love and cultural pride, interspersing only occasional improvised *soneos* that referenced the violent encounter, the band seemed to play slightly louder than usual; the percussion section pushed many of the tempos; the horn players responded with more intense solos, emphasizing their higher registers; the piano solos included more fast and dissonant runs than usual; and virtuosic rhythmic flurries permeated the percussion fills. The overall timbre choices the musicians made were brash and raw, at times pushing their volumes to distortion and even mimicking cries, yells, hollers, growls, howls, and screams within solo passages. None of these factors are foreign to the "hot" aesthetic of salsa performance. Notwithstanding, these combined elements, along with the aftermath of witnessing and experiencing violence, added to the "edginess" of the performance, "the vibe." These elemental changes are significant because, over time, they have the potential to evolve into standard performance practice, and many eventually do. Thus, the sonification of violent experience is direct and indirect, immediate and postponed. The long-term effect reinforced by continual violent encounters is musical change, where the residue of past violent encounters lingers and perpetuates in both aesthetics and performance practice. As trumpeter Tony Barrero told me, in order to have the right feel in your soloing for New York salsa, you have to "[p]lay like there's a gun to your head!" In other words, play as though your life depends on it. At Fuego Fuego, on some level it seemed to.

The use of tropes of violence is historically rooted in the salsa *dura* of the late 1960s and early 1970s, which openly embraced and co-opted violence as an aesthetic, and violent images as marketing tools. This seminal stylistic period, which was strongly tied to El Barrio, continues to hold considerable sway over salsa performance practice. A number of early salsa dura song texts dealt with the volatility of El Barrio life; at times, musicians adopted public images that portrayed and romanticized violence, most notably Willie Colón. Colón's "Calle Luna, Calle Sol" (from *Lo Mato*; Fania 444, 1073) provides an illustrative example where the following warning is sung: "Listen lady, hold on tight to your purse, you don't know this *barrio*, here they attack anyone . . . In the barrio of *guapos*, no one lives at peace, careful what you say or you won't be worth a kilo, walk straight ahead and don't look to the side." Of such salsa dura texts, Manuel writes that these lyrics portray "the alienation, violence, and lurking malevolence of barrio life" where "there is an ambiguous mixture of attitudinal stances. On one level, these songs are simply 'telling it like it is,' baring barrio reality . . . But the lyrics also convey a tension ridden adrenaline high and suggest at least a hint of fascination with the ghetto's lawlessness and with the figure of the guapo, the macho hoodlum who has achieved power in the marginalized and oppressed world of the barrio" (Manuel 1995: 76–77). This ambiguous mixture points to the tropes of struggle, survival, and mastery, discussed above, where successful survival is not only glorified, but, simultaneously, the satirical and metaphorical nature of such content serves as an apt platform for launching a very public social critique.

In their study of gangsta rap in Los Angeles, Steve Loza, Milo Alvarez, Josefina Santiago, and Charles Moore (1994) explore the adoption of violent images and discourse as an aesthetic in musical performance (an aesthetic of violent acts). They argue that, similar to cars and fashion, acts of violence can be stylized and discussed in terms of their artistic qualities, goals, and levels of fulfillment. Through such artistic expression as film and music, this aesthetic constantly is simulated, whereby that expression becomes a reflection of the

Figure 3.3 LP Cover of Willie Colón's *The Big Break–La Gran Fuga*. *(Album cover courtesy of Fania. Used by Permission. All rights owned by Emusica Acquisitions Corporation, 575 Blue Lagoon Drive, Suite 230, Miami, FL 33126.)*

cultural milieu from which it emerges. They write, "the experiential aesthetic of violence becomes the basis for artistic cognition and aesthetic energy engaged in the composition and performance." Thus, the experiential corresponds to the imaging of metaphor that conveys "intellectual insight," serving as a creative mode of representation (Loza et al. 1994: 159). In salsa, the most obvious adoption of an aesthetic of violence are the images found on Colón's record jackets, in which he is portrayed in a variety of situational poses that align his public persona with criminal activity and violent acts.

Wilson Valentín-Escobar reminds us, "Album covers become more than textual self-representations but also self-reflexive meta-performances of diasporic identities and musical style" (Valentín-Escobar 2002: 167); indeed, such an interpretation is called for. In some ways, these depictions superficially

Figure 3.4 LP Cover of Willie Colón's *Cosa Nuestra.* *(Album cover courtesy of Fania. Used by Permission. All rights owned by Emusica Acquisitions Corporation, 575 Blue Lagoon Drive, Suite 230, Miami, FL 33126.)*

play into racist stereotypes of violent Latino street culture. However their parodic exaggerations (the trombone as weapon, trombone as phallus, etc.) imbue the images with irony and humor, which calls for an alternative read: music as weapon against social injustice, music as empowerment. Which music? *Cosa Nuestra* (Our Thing)—not yours, not theirs, but an exclusionary "ours," which serves as a strategic countermand to the exclusionary and marginalizing practices of the hegemonic powers. The marginalized barrio is centered and, through tropes of exclusion, survival, and mastery, is posited in these depictions as a tool for empowerment.

Throughout the 1980s and early 1990s, the number of song texts dealing with El Barrio life and violence dwindled markedly as *salsa romántica* grew to prominence. Violent iconography was replaced by sexy boy/girl images, and song texts turned almost exclusively to topics of love. Regardless, the residue

Figure 3.5 Eddie Palmieri with Christopher Washburne, 2003. *(Photograph by Enid Farber.)*

from this aesthetic of violence, past violent events, and the remaining presence of violence continued to underpin salsa performance practice. And this ambiguous relationship that Manuel highlights, with simultaneous repelling and attracting dynamics at play, remained a consistent force in musicians' lives.

Bandleader Eddie Palmieri provides an illustrative example of how tropes of violence continued to permeate performance practice. In 2003 at the San Francisco Jazz Festival, Palmieri's band was scheduled to perform, alternating on the same stage with several other salsa groups. From his perspective, as well as his musicians', this was an adversarial and competitive opportunity, even though many friendships existed between the various groups. There is a long "battle of the bands" tradition in Latin music, most pronounced during the mambo era of the 1950s between the bands of Tito Puente and Tito Rodríguez, both of whom served as foundational influences on salsa performance.[9] Consequently, that night in San Francisco, Palmieri turned to his musicians just before entering the stage, and, with a devilish grin, exclaimed, "It's battle, men!" Trumpeter Brian Lynch added, "Take no prisoners!" After the first number, Palmieri began introducing the musicians. Emphasizing his competitive stance, he enriched his introductory remarks with bellicosity. For example, he stated, "The capitaine of my percussion section, José Claussell," and, "My secret weapon, on tres, Nelson Gonzalez." After our particularly inspired set, Palmieri turned to the band and victoriously exclaimed, "We smoked them!"—"Them" referring to our "vanquished enemy" (i.e., the other bands). Though there was playfulness in his tone, and "playing up" rivalry is a time-tested dramatic strategy that engages audiences on a deeper level, regardless of the genuine camaraderie displayed between bands offstage, not to be outdone by the competition is a very serious matter in salsa. A musician's job can depend on it. Not rising to the occasion and holding one's own can place a musician's position in jeopardy. During the Palmieri performance, though no violent acts were witnessed or experienced, the competitive nature of the event and the bandleader's proclamation incited musicians to perform with a similar intensity and edge heard at Fuego Fuego (minus the darkness). In this instance, violence was reenacted to provide Palmieri with the effect he was looking for, "playing like there's a gun to your head!" In addition, the discursive tropes and aesthetic choices heard during the performance were informed by past violent experience.[10]

This type of behavior is certainly not limited to Palmieri and his band. For instance, trombonist Orlando Oquendo, just before playing *moñas*, typically turns to his fellow trombonists and exclaims, "lock and load!"—meaning, "arm your weapons (the trombones), we are going in for the fight." Trumpeter John Walsh refers to especially difficult gigs as playing under "combat conditions." And Frankie Figueroa, longtime vocalist with Puente's band, shadowboxes to his *soneos*, punctuating each of his rhythmic vocal attacks with left and right jabs. Knockout punches usually come at the end of each improvised vocal line. The ring and stage are embodied as one in his performative frame.[11]

The intense competition involved in doing salsa business, which extends beyond salseros to club owners, promoters, and bandleaders alike, perpetuates adversity across the salsascape. The financial advantages of commercial success in the salsa scene can be great. With only a limited number of bands, recordings, clubs, and promoters able to enjoy those benefits, a fiercely competitive climate pervades the scene. Competition between clubs can become truculent. Club owners and promoters frequently pay individuals to distribute pamphlets promoting their own events to patrons exiting rival clubs. The windshields of cars parked in the vicinity of salsa clubs are blanketed with similar material. At times even more aggressive tactics are used. For instance, in February 1992 during a performance with Raulín Rosendo at the Manhattan club Las Vegas, the fire alarm began to ring. The full crowd was ushered out onto the street. After the firefighters determined that it was a false alarm and allowed the patrons to return inside, it clearly was evident that only half the audience returned. The cold temperature of the winter night deterred many from waiting in the street for the fifteen minutes the fire investigators required to ensure that the building was safe. As the band returned to the stage, one bouncer commented, "This happens every few months when we have a big night. Another club sees that their crowd is small and they know that everyone is here. So they call the fire department. Once people get out on the street they don't come back in. They either go home or go over to other clubs. Probably to the one who called. It's bad for business because it gives our club a reputation for not being safe. People don't want to come to a place that has fires."

As the number of salsa venues declined throughout the 1990s, competition for gigs amongst bandleaders intensified. A few relied on questionable tactics for obtaining gigs. For instance, Bandleader Z telephoned to ask where I was performing with Ray Sepulveda that evening. I informed him that we were playing at Club Broadway. When the band arrived, we were told that someone had telephoned the club to say that Sepulveda had been in a terrible automobile accident, was in the hospital, and was uncertain to survive. The band members were deeply distressed until Sepulveda entered the club in his normal friendly manner, smiling and greeting everyone. Once the hoax was figured out, it was the consensus among musicians that Bandleader Z was attempting to get the band canceled from the performance. In another instance, this same Bandleader Z called the Copacabana the day after bandleader Louie Ramírez passed away, having learned that Ramírez was scheduled to perform the following weekend. The Copacabana's booking agent Tony G. comments, "Out of the kindness of his heart he humbly offered his services to me if the need arose to find a replacement band. I generously offered this response, 'Fuck no! You'll never play in this club again!'" (T. G., pers. comm.). Though these two examples do not necessarily qualify as violent acts, they demonstrate the intensity of the competition on the salsa scene and amplify the aggressively adversarial domain of salsa performance, something that further supports an aesthetic of violence.

The competitive and adversarial stance both on and off the stage by these musicians, bandleaders, and club owners points to another significant component involved in these performative manifestations of violence: that of being underpinned by the complex web of contradictions associated with notions of masculinity. Palmieri did say "It's battle *men*!" The almost exclusively male, overtly homophobic, and sometimes-misogynistic nature of the New York salsa scene reinforces the engenderment of salsa performance practice in a narrowly conservative male mode. In this case, I am using "gender" in its more narrow sense, referencing its staged and acted-out manifestations accentuated through the competitive modes between males, marked by, for example, exaggeratedly cocky aggressiveness. In some ways, how salsa musicians publicly navigate and work through their violent experiences, and how they subsequently incorporate them into tropes and practice, is guided by prescripted cultural notions of maleness, respect, and dignity. In other words, publicly shrinking away from competition, fear, and violence is not a valid option. And with this in mind, the "We might as well play" attitude, mentioned above, might be better understood as an emboldened and brash statement reading, "No matter what, we are going to play!"

These performative strategies must also be viewed in light of larger macro-level issues. As Frances Aparicio writes, the political economy of El Barrio has inscribed salsa performance practice with "a collective, violent male subjectivity that is clearly articulated in opposition to and in resistance to the forms of colonization and social oppression that dispossessed Puerto Rican men in diaspora [experience] . . ." (Aparcio 2002: 138). In this case, staged hyper-masculinity is the "central tactic in the negotiations of power between racialized subjectivities and dominant institutions" (Aparcio 2002: 138). This hyper-masculinity, then, is constructed in opposition to hegemonic power and a strategic tactic that answers to a societal need for cultural assertiveness and empowerment, as well as serving more localized conceptions of performing masculinity.[12] In this way, as Louise Meintjes writes; "When. . . . aspects of social life are severely repressed, expressive culture becomes a strategic persuasive tool . . . and a means to open up new spaces for the disempowered" (Meintjes 2003: 11).

The Palmieri example presented above illustrates a common type of violent expression in performance. Regardless of its lighter and somewhat playful tone, the seriously personal nature of real violent experience must not be ignored. McDowell writes, "Violence brings about acute suffering to those who are victims, to their next-of-kin, and in attenuated form to those who vicariously experience it. It exposes a flaw in the social contract . . . violence experienced vicariously reaches out to rattle our sense of security and stability in life" (McDowell 2000: 20). Witnessing or experiencing violence is a private matter, as is reacting to it. Reactions can vary broadly: In one instance, violence can act as a deterrent to music-making, but, in another, it can greatly enhance a performance. Not everyone is able to adopt a "we might as well play" attitude. For instance, after a fight broke out at the Palm Tree, trumpeter Chris Rogers (son of Barry) exclaimed, "This is one of the reasons why I quit playing Latin music on a regular basis. This just makes me want to go home. It's just not worth putting yourself at risk like this" (C. Rogers, pers. comm.). And trumpeter Dave Rogers (no relation) says, "I quit playing salsa after I saw a guy get shot in the head in front of the stage. I just couldn't take it anymore" (D. Rogers, pers. comm.). Ruben Blades's reaction to a shooting during a concert in Venezuela provides a contrasting example (see Introduction). Instead of ending his set early, Blades chose to use his popularity to calm the crowd, bringing about peace to squelch further altercations. The incident inspired him to play an even longer set than usual, and he encouraged his musicians to dig into the music and play harder.

What occurs in the aftermath of violent encounters, such as the one described at Fuego Fuego earlier in this chapter, or the Montalvo incident at Boys and Girls Harbor that appears in the Introduction, illustrates the communal nature of violent experience and points to another significant role of violence on the salsa scene: that of community building. Susan Rotker writes, "Violence produces crises in all aspects of life, even in communicating. Individuals search for ways to articulate their experiences, telling their stories again and again. Whether to exorcise their trauma or to explain the political and economic situation that caused it, the complexity of violence can only be fully comprehended when spoken between two people" (Rotker 2002: 8). For instance, within a few days, numerous recountings disseminated the stories of both the Fuego Fuego and Montalvo incidents throughout the salsa community, recountings made by both those present and by those vicariously experiencing the events from afar. The urge to establish a postviolence equilibrium, as well as the inherent pleasure of bearing and sharing extraordinary news, resulted in a dramatic realignment in experience and mental adjustment, a reprocessing of sorts by way of verbalization. Through these postviolent narratives, a shared social arena was activated in which preliminary versions infused with personal commentary and critique were put forth, and then these versions were collectively and collaboratively revised. These stories held real cultural capital. They were something worth sharing, explaining, and arguing about, occasions for communal reflection and reflexivity.

McDowell identifies several phases involved in this communal retelling process in which fresh narrative gives way to a more considered and mediated one. This is where communal issues enter and "when narratives about violence are put forward as collective representations, that is, representations that project, explore, and fortify the common basis of affiliation within a society" (McDowell 2000: 22–24). Ultimately a more stylized discourse, often told in a mode of romance and tinged with humor, emerges, involving commemoration and shared myth. It is at this point that an Arendtean distancing is obtained, enabling catharsis whereby, in a Freudian sense, repressed fears are alleviated.

In the process of this narrativity, social identities are constituted. Margaret Somers writes, "it is through narrativity that we come to know, understand, and make sense of the social world . . . all of us come to be who we are (however ephemeral, multiple, and changing) by being located or locating ourselves (usually unconsciously) in social narratives rarely of our own making" (Somers 1994: 606). Identification with being a salsa musician, then, is partly constructed by placing oneself within and identifying with a repertoire of stories that is made culturally available, many of which have violent encounters as their foci.

For those present at that ill-fated rehearsal with Montalvo, or in the alleyway of Fuego Fuego, the outgrowth of their shared trauma was a strong male-bonding experience (no women were present on either occasion).[13] Michael Taussig writes, "Yet this space of death is preeminently a space of transformation: through the experience of coming close to death there well may be a more vivid sense of life" (Taussig 1987: 7). This heightened sense of living generated communal glue, forever connecting the musicians involved as "comrades in arms." The shared myths became a sacred place that was revisited whenever we gathered. It became a rite of passage, heightening our status and solidifying our place within the community. The myth took on a communal role as well, extending beyond those who experienced the encounters firsthand; established salsa musicians related the stories to newcomers almost as a welcoming ritual, an inclusionary gesture. The myths were shared among musicians in back hallways while waiting between sets. They became part of "salsa education," canonized into the collection of stories behind the music-making. Their bonding power continues to reverberate throughout the salsa community, regardless of the passing of time.

Fernando Coronil and Janet Skurski write, "Aggression becomes inseparable from transgression, the rupture of conceptual and physical boundaries indivisible from the construction of new orders of significance. Violence pushes the limits of the permissible, opening up spaces where customary and unexpected meanings and practices are brought together in unprecedented ways, illuminating hidden landscapes in a flash, and leaving behind the opaque memory of ungraspable territories" (Coronil and Skurski 1991: 289–290). As these writers suggest, despite the human tragedy, violence opens new vistas for interpretive analysis for the ethnographer that remain concealed behind everyday experiences. Encountering violence serves as locus for structural change, incites a realignment of social affiliations, and demands reinscription of cultural meaning. This is emergent social construction in process. For salsa musicians, who routinely encounter myriad violent acts both on the micro- and macrolevels, violence becomes a recurrent crisis that must in someway be navigated and dealt with. Their choices in this difficult process reveal subterranean structures that significantly inform and undergird everyday practices. Narrativity is one such strategy they rely upon, and their subsequent emergent mythologies, as interpreted in the guise of the real and natural, are more influential in the long term than the actual violent acts they encounter. But they also use what they know best to express the unrepresentable: music-making.

I approach violence from a more practice-oriented theoretical perspective, attending to the sundry ways violence informs salsa performance practice in both everyday and within broader historical contexts. I avoid a standard categorization of the effects on sound, an exercise that may prove futile, if not impossible, due to the complex interpersonal processes involved. Regardless, the effects are obviously present and very real for salsa musicians. Music-making on the highest level involves close interpersonal relations. A groove is made collectively, created through negotiation and a willingness to work together. In salsa, this is most often limited to close male contact. Living through a shared violent experience, whether vicariously or not, knits a social fabric of closeness that transcends typical negotiation. It makes for tighter salsa grooves. For trumpeter Hector Colón, "There is nothing like the groove in salsa. It swings the way it is does because of all the violence. All that shit is in there" (H. Colón, pers. comm.).

4

New York Salsa and Drugs

Aesthetics, Performance Practice, Governmental Policy, and the Illicit Drug Trade

In October 1999, I was flying to San Francisco from New York City with Tito Puente's band. Sitting next to me on the plane was Bobby Rodríguez, probably the most significant bassist in Afro Cuban music in New York City over the last fifty years. Bobby defined the modern Latin bass sound and the techniques for playing it. He played with Puente for many years and recorded with just about everyone else. I asked him, after all these years and with such an illustrious career, what was his most memorable experience? He responded candidly and earnestly, "I killed Charlie Parker!" Flustered, but recognizing his serious tone, I asked for an explanation. He replied, "Who do you think used to get him his drugs when he was in New York? I did."

Since its inception, salsa music, its business, and its performance practices have been inextricably linked to the illicit drug trade. Its emergence as a distinct style in the late 1960s and early 1970s coincided with the establishment of an internationally organized narcotics industry for cocaine and its derivatives. Run by two powerful cartels in Colombia, one located in the city of Medellín and the other in Cali, this industry quickly spread to North American cities, especially New York City, due to the increasing U.S. demand for the drugs. In line with a long and sordid history of interconnected relations between the U.S. music industry and criminalized market economies, most often administered by organized crime, individuals associated with these newly formed cartels or drug trafficking organizations (DTOs) quickly asserted influence on salsa, establishing themselves as key partners in the music's production and distribution.[1] Seeking avenues for laundering drug monies, a new demographic of drug dealers/salsa entrepreneurs emerged, producing concerts and recordings as well as opening nightclubs that not only served as drug distribution centers, but featured live music as well. Salsa became the music of choice for many, as it was the voice of a nascent and emboldened movement to assert Puerto Rican and pan-Latino cultural pride. However, as Rodríguez's anecdote suggests, musicians sometimes have been complicit in both the distribution and use of illicit drugs. I argue that the pervasiveness of cocaine and its associated business practices on the salsa scene over the last thirty-five years, as well as the impact of the drug's physical and psychological effects on the body, fundamentally informed salsa aesthetics and performance practice.[2] In particular, I explore the role of "narco-economics" in salsa production, circulation, and consumption; its effects on aesthetic practices; and the role of its transgressive qualities in the social interactions of musicians and dancers.

The influence of the illicit drug trade is by no means limited to salsa or specifically associated with Latino communities. Indeed, as recent publications have documented, its pervasive presence in both the popular music (Yentikoff 2004) and jazz scenes (Davis 1989 and Szwed 2002) demonstrates a widespread use and culturally and ethnically unbiased reach, within the global music industry. Regardless, I feel some trepidation regarding this discussion as I am particularly sensitive to concerns raised by the omnipresent stereotypical and racist depictions of Latinos as drug-dealing, violent thugs in the public media, especially in Hollywood productions. Salsa singers have been particularly prone to this degrading casting practice. Marc Anthony's violent drug-dealer role in Brian De Palma's *Carlito's Way* (1993) serves as a prime example. Due to this complex and problematic association, many scholars have avoided broaching any topic that associates drugs and Latinos in an attempt to compensate for these racist attitudes. As Ronald Glick and Joan Moore note, "there is a strong tendency among middle-class Hispanics who act as spokespersons to decry studies of drug users as stigmatizing and stereotyping of Hispanics in general" (Glick and Moore 1990: 7). I, like others, have no interest in perpetuating such stereotypes and in the past have shied away from exploring the relationship between drugs and salsa in my own research. However, due to the persistent pervasiveness of drugs in the clubs where I routinely played, the numerous occasions when I was offered various drugs at no charge while performing, and the several occasions when I was offered cocaine in lieu of payment for playing, I feel it would be disingenuous to omit such a discussion, or, at the very least, an attempt to address this association.

Launching into such an exploration presents difficulties for the researcher. Drugs, cocaine in particular, often involve real human tragedy. Balancing this dimension of drug abuse with objective analysis is most trying.

Delving solely into the particulars of human suffering and exposing private trauma is not productive in a work dedicated to salsa musicians and music performance. I discuss addiction in connection with musicians who openly have discussed their personal difficulties in prior public forums, but my primary focus is the social conditions that facilitate such rampant drug activity and its subsequent residual effects on performance practice. Another concern is my own personal safety, as well as that of my fellow musicians. Since some of the cartel members and dealers that we worked with in the 1990s remain involved in certain aspects of the music business, I will use pseudonyms in some cases or focus upon individuals who are either incarcerated or deceased.

My discussion here centers on cocaine; however, alcohol, marijuana, ecstasy, crack, and, to a lesser extent, heroin all have a presence on the salsa scene. In fact, because most salsa performances take place in bars that legally serve alcohol, it can be argued that alcohol ultimately has the largest influence on salsa, since many musicians drink while performing and the majority of audience members consumes alcohol while attending salsa performances. Indeed, alcohol-producing companies often underwrite or sponsor concerts and club performances. In 1996, Ray Sepulveda's band auditioned for and won a position as an "Official Bud Band." This was part of an advertising campaign in which bands representing a variety of genres were booked at events where Budweiser products were sold exclusively. We wore Budweiser T-shirts while we played, we received free Budweiser beer during performances (a source of complaint by many musicians who preferred to drink more sophisticated beer products—"Why can't we be a Guinness band?!"), and, in return, we enjoyed a number of high-profile bookings (e.g., pregame performances for the New York Yankees) reserved exclusively for "Bud Bands." However, this relationship to alcohol is not unique to salsa performance, but can be found among numerous other music styles and performance scenes.

Comparatively, cocaine and its associated industry do have a unique relationship to salsa (with maybe only the Mexican *norteño conjunto* style and *banda* music of the *narcocorridos* exhibiting some relational similarities).[3] What sets this relationship apart from other streams of the music industry are salsa's subaltern economic status within that industry at large (Negus 1999), its associations with marginalized Latino communities, and its long-term relationship with criminalized economies. The extremely lucrative cocaine business of the 1970s through the 1990s infused economically marginalized Latino communities with unprecedented amounts of capital, thereby challenging the preexisting political and social power structures as well as transforming the landscape of *barrios* throughout New York City. According to Mary Roldan, narcotics invert societal structures to some extent, allowing the least powerful to distort the political and social status quo from the bottom up, thereby challenging the "political expressions and particulars imposed from above" (Roldan 1999: 174).[4] As such, salsa performance, as archetypal cultural expression emerging from those "nadiral" barrios, has proved the site par excellence for these newly established political and social relations to play themselves out in an overtly public arena, serving as nexus for the underworld and the "legitimate world" to conjoin. At their confluence exists a blurred and opaque space in which salsa musicians inhabit, negotiate, navigate, and, ultimately, make music. It is in this space that my focus lies.

Historical Contextualization

To understand the relationship of salsa and cocaine, it is necessary to first consider the historical factors that mediate such an association. In this effort, I adopt a constructivist perspective informed by the works of Paul Gootenberg (1999) and Wolfgang Schivelbusch (1993). Gootenberg insists that drugs emerge largely from specific cultural and political circumstances (Gootenberg 1999: 7). Schivelbusch discusses how drugs become linked to particular social movements and argues that the psychological and physiological effects of cocaine; its equation with money; and global changes in production, mobility, dissemination, and international relations were all ideal conditions for its rise in the late 1970s: "Each time changes in the taste for drugs occur, they are particular to their respective historical period" (Schivelbusch 1993: 227–228). He documents how drugs, as they become more popular, go through a process of importation, regulation, taxation, and prohibition, depending on the wants and needs of those in power. The strength of such process-oriented and culturally constructed perspectives is that they resist homogeneous hegemonic discourses (i.e., the mass media, governmental agencies, and the like), and therefore are better suited to attend to localized specificities and differences in how drugs are experienced in diverse communities. As I show later, these processes have real and distinct consequences in the communities where rampant drug activity is found.

Cocaine had a presence, albeit a modest one, on the New York music scene throughout the early to mid-twentieth century; however, in the early 1970s it was refashioned as a "glamour drug" and its popularity soared, continuing to increase throughout the 1980s. Extracted from the coca plant, cocaine is a powerful central nervous system stimulant. Its immediate physical and psychological effects produce feelings of euphoria, relief from fatigue, and increased mental alertness. Chronic use can lead to personality disorders, inability to sleep, loss of appetite, emaciation, and an increased tendency to violence and antisocial behavior. It is the largest producer of illicit income among all drugs in the United States. Due to its excessively high price

($2,000 to $4,000 per ounce throughout the 1980s and 1990s), "its very possession conveys status" (Caroll 1885: 176).[5] David Lenson believes that cocaine is the best example of what he labels "pharmacocurrency," due to its "dimelike" packaging, high cost, and its insatiability: "There is no such thing as 'enough cocaine' . . . Yet the act of consuming it . . . permits no satisfaction . . . [cocaine] is more like money than money itself . . . It is mainlined money" (Lenson 1993: 219, 175). Michael Taussig adds, "Like gold, cocaine is imbued with violence and greed, glitter that reeks transgression," having "the unique function of being both symbol and reality of value" (Taussig 2004: xi, 34). For Taussig, cocaine is the quintessence of the commodity fetish, and its value lies in its transgressive potential. It is this transgressive quality, along with the sheer immensity of its economic power, that positions cocaine and its affiliated industry as a dynamic force on the New York salsa scene.

The relationship between salsa and cocaine partially has been facilitated by the synchronous emergence of style (music) and industry (cocaine). According to Roldan (1999), the internationally organized narcotics trading industry for cocaine made its first formal appearance in the United States in 1972. This, of course, coincided with a vibrant period for salsa. The precipitous growth of these newly formed DTOs was subserved by a large immigration wave from Colombia to the United States starting in 1965.[6] This wave, roughly lasting from 1965 to 1975, was prompted by the passing of the Hart-Celler Immigration Bill (or, the Immigration Act of 1965), which significantly loosened the immigratory constraints placed upon Latin American countries. This also coincided with the end of a period of extreme political unrest and turmoil in Colombia, known as "La Violencia," which resulted in much economic hardship. By 1979, roughly two hundred thousand Colombians had settled in New York City, mostly living in the borough of Queens (Sassen-Koob 1979: 316). These new immigrants, who were mostly from the lower classes, provided some of the large labor force necessary to manage the intricacies of drug distribution networks; they also significantly enlarged the local salsa audience.[7] According to the Office of National Drug Control Policy (ONDCP), nearly "75% of the coca cultivated for processing into cocaine is grown in Colombia, and Colombian DTOs are responsible for most of the cocaine production, transportation, and distribution." In addition to Colombians, the U.S. government specifically points to "Bahamian, Dominican, Haitian, Jamaican, and Puerto Rican criminal groups that transport cocaine, usually under the supervision of Colombian DTOs," as well as "Mexican DTOs who are involved in wholesale cocaine distribution in the United States."[8] Identifying DTOs with specific nation-states is a common strategy of the U.S. government. The benefit of this practice is that it identifies a clearly emplaced adversary in its efforts to combat this rogue industry, something useful for swaying public opinion to the government's advantage. However, this strategy inadequately captures the global and transnational nature of the drug trade, and it perpetuates stereotyping based on arbitrary national boundaries, where all people from a particular nation-state are then associated with the criminal activity of a select few. This can have serious ramifications on the implementation of cultural policy and the positionality of marginalized communities within the hegemonic discourse, as well as within the politics of more informal discourse.

The financial statistics for cocaine are stunning. The economic and political power that such large capital yields accounts for the significant influence of DTOs on communities within which they operate. In 1978, the Drug Enforcement Agency (DEA) estimated that the cocaine industry was worth $4 billion, and these figures rapidly increased to peak in 1990 at $69.9 billion (this figure represented nearly 25 percent of Colombia's gross national product at the time). The latest figures available, from 2000, show a decline to $35.3 billion.[9] This decrease is due partly to the intensity of the U.S. government's "War on Drugs," which resulted in the breakup of many of the most powerful DTOs and the incarceration of many *jefes* (DTO bosses).

The "War on Drugs" slogan was first associated with a campaign the Nixon administration initiated in 1973 to address this rapidly burgeoning drug industry. As the numbers demonstrate, though, the campaign's initial efforts had little effect on this thriving business. However, the establishment of a policy that discursively positioned illicit drugs as "enemy," future administrations' reiteration of such rhetoric, and the subsequent implementation of additional governmental policies ultimately had a significant impact on the future of salsa and on the communities from which it emerged. Curtis Marez points out that, even though the "War on Drugs" emerged primarily as a mass-mediated event, it had an immediate impact on the "intimate details of subjectivity and social relations, serving as a formative, structuring context for ideas and practices concerning race, gender, class, sexuality, and nation" (Marez 2004: 2, 4). He believes the government's covert goals for waging the "War"—not the wholesale eradication of drugs, but management of trafficking in ways that supported capitalist efforts—informed this structuring context. Instead of prosecuting corporations that profited from such trafficking, enforcement agencies targeted poor users and dealers from marginal minorities.[10] In other words, the "War" focused on selective eradication, and governmental intervention in marginalized communities emphasized the criminalization of drug use, ignoring the social problems that led to such rampant drug activity in the first place and treating rehabilitation and education initiatives as secondary. This led to significant omissions in the discourse concerning drugs. Marez observes, "The ways in which capitalists and the state have, at the expense of the poor, historically profited from drug traffic; or the ways in which the drug-war activities have often focused on the repression of some of the world's weakest and most vulnerable peoples . . . are a constitutive absence in official representations of the drug war" (Marez 2004: 29). Also absent, I would add, are the ways in which marginalized communities sometimes benefit from the drug trade and how the drug war can result in the eradication of those benefits.

The next official reincarnation of the "War," which reinforced such absences, was the "Just Say No" campaign of 1985, inaugurated by the Reagan administration with Nancy Reagan at the helm. Though this campaign had little overall effect on the exorbitant profits of the drug industry, its significance cannot be dismissed. On a fundamental level, the former First Lady's naive invocation refused to acknowledge or engage with the complex field of societal forces involved with drug use. Further, as Lenson (1993) observes, it explicitly called for an end to any discourse on the subject and imbued words like "drugs" and "drug culture" with excessively pejorative connotations. Nathan Adler adds, these words "make automatic invidious distinctions which connote 'evil,' 'strange,' and 'illegal,' and they invoke a distance" (Lenson 1993: 7). This discursive move served to stigmatize communities, nations, and ethnicities associated with the drug industry as homogenously negative, entrenching their marginalization to a greater extent. The official hegemonic discourse has remained uniformly negative ever since, but for communities that are directly affected by the drug trade, "drug culture" is not lived or experienced in such a homogenous fashion. No drug culture exists "as a unified social body grown up around the use of drugs" (Lenson 1993: 15). As such, the specificities of each social arena in which drugs and its industry have agency must be attended to in any analysis that strives for a deeper understanding of the logic of cause and effect between political and economic discourse and, in this case, aesthetics and performance practice.

Taking office in 1989 at the height of cocaine's profitability, George H. W. Bush's administration proactively implemented new aggressive policies that escalated the "War" and resulted in numerous arrests and seizures. According to the Federal Bureau of Investigation (FBI), there was a significant increase in cocaine-related arrests in 1989 (732,600 total, compared to 239,400 in 1985, the year the "Just Say No" campaign began).[11]

These arrest numbers have remained high ever since, with both Bill Clinton's and George W. Bush's administrations pursuing similarly aggressive tactics. It was precisely in 1989, at the first apex on the chart below, that salsa performance opportunities began to wane in New York City as the DEA shut down a growing number of clubs and busted dealers associated with salsa in drug raids. The steady increase of drug busts since 1989 has prevented the return of

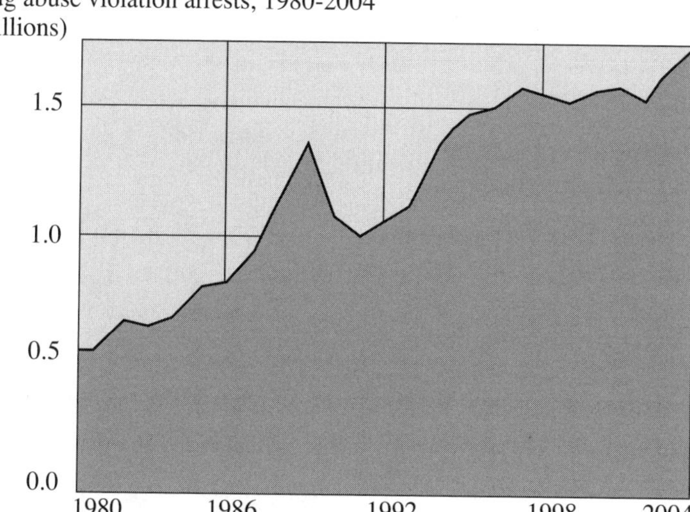

Figure 4.1 Annual report on crime. *(FBI, annual report on crime in the United States, Uniform Crime Reports. http//www.ojp.usdoj.gov/bjs/dcf/tables/drugtype.htm.)*

DTO-run clubs, and their numbers have dwindled considerably. These closures have had a tremendous economic impact on salsa musicians. Less work, fewer working bands, and a dearth of capital investment in the salsa community have driven many away from playing salsa, forcing them to seek work elsewhere. In 2006, trombonist José Davila responded to a question concerning the current salsa scene by exclaiming, "What scene? It's all dried up!" (J. Davila, pers. comm.). Currently, the top bands barely work one or two nights each week, and there are fewer than fifteen clubs in the New York area that regularly program salsa. Governmental policy and drug busts are certainly not the only reason for this change, but they remain central contributing factors in this process.

Salsa and Cocaine

> "Without cocaine, I would not have had a salsa career."
>
> —Trombonist Barry Olsen

To date, the relationship between salsa and cocaine has received little attention in academic literature. One exception is Lise Waxer's ethnographic work on salsa in Colombia, which, undoubtedly, brought her face to face with this issue. However, she, like many others, chooses to veer away from the topic and only briefly mentions that, in the late 1970s, one unnamed promoter/drug dealer "ploughed much of his illicit profits into promoting famous New York salsa orquestas in Cali and nearby Buenaventura" (Waxer 2000: 128).[12] According to Waxer, prior to this promoter's involvement few foreign salsa bands had performed in Colombia, and this individual was solely responsible for bringing in the Fania All-Stars (in 1980), as well as Eddie Palmieri, Hector Lavoe, Willie Colón, Ruben Blades, and many others.[13] According to one longtime member of Lavoe's band, they toured to Colombia twenty-seven times in the 1970s. Considering the vibrant growth of Colombia's salsa scene in the ensuing years, these concerts, providing local exposure to foreign acts, played a significant role in establishing Colombia as an important transnational "outpost" for salsa (Mulholland 1998). Over the years, salsa productions from Colombia exerted considerable influence on salsa at large; bands from Colombia tour regularly, and such cities as Medellín, Cali, Barranquilla, Cartagena, and Bogotá remain popular touring destinations for foreign bands.

The fact that drug monies helped to launch the Colombian salsa scene is significant in itself; moreover, this information is critical in understanding the salsa business in New York. At the time of these pioneering Colombian tours, two individuals based in New York controlled and coordinated all concert touring by the above-mentioned bands: Jerry Masucci for the Fania All-Stars, and Ralph Mercado, who, prior to running RMM Records, was the biggest booking agent/manager/concert promoter in New York and coordinated bookings for many salsa acts of the 1970s and 1980s (both worked closely with Larry Landa, a booking agent who often served as liaison between the Colombian promoters and Masucci and Mercado). Both men established relationships with DTOs in order to arrange these and subsequent tours. Moreover, this symbiotic relationship between the salsa business and DTOs was not confined within Colombia's borders, but extended well beyond into U.S. cities. Throughout the 1970s and into the 1980s, numerous salsa venues opened in New York City that served as money-laundering fronts where drug profits were funneled through the clubs' legitimate business transactions. Both Mercado and Masucci, as well as smaller booking agents, were required to remain in close contact with those establishments, and, in the process, many performance opportunities were created for salsa musicians.

The advantages of having so many performance venues for salsa in one city are obvious (bandleader Larry Harlow, who was one of the first *salseros* to be signed by Fania in 1965, estimates that there were over 100 clubs, ranging from large discos to small neighborhood social clubs, booking salsa at any one time throughout the 1970s). During that time, the most popular bands typically worked five to seven nights every week in the New York area, and much of that work was in DTO-associated clubs. Further, since financing was already secured, these DTO venues were not required to rely solely upon ticket and bar sales for profits. Subsequently, there was less pressure to book only famous acts that would guarantee a large audience draw. Though the most popular bands continued to obtain the majority of bookings, there were sufficient opportunities for newer and lesser-known groups as well. These live performance opportunities were essential for building audiences and developing a band sound. Musicians easily identified DTO-run clubs, because even if only a few people showed up, club owners remained indifferent and paid the bands in full regardless. Trombonist Joe Fiedler related, "I remember we played a New Year's Eve party at Juan Pachanga [a club located in Queens] and only five people showed up. Man, we were worried that the bread would be short! But we played all night and got paid in full in the end. Everybody seemed completely happy!" (J. Fiedler, pers. comm.).

A distinct type of salsa performance venue emerged in the 1970s that was associated with the cocaine industry. Clubs known as "after-hours" were operated exclusively by DTOs and proliferated from the 1970s through the early 1990s.[14] As their name suggests, they catered to the late crowd, often sleepless from the effects of cocaine use (also known among musicians as the "vampire crowd"). Contrary to New York City laws, these clubs remained open during the legally mandated shut-down hours between 4:00 and 8:00 A.M. and continued serving alcohol during that time (an abundance of cocaine also could be obtained easily, usually sold from the bathroom stalls).[15] In one Brooklyn after-hours, the bathroom drug business was so bustling that individuals who were not purchasing drugs were barred and forced to urinate in the parking lot. Patrons typically began arriving after the other clubs closed (between 4:00 and 5:00 A.M.). After-hours that featured live performances scheduled bands to play from 4:00 to 7:00 A.M., and occasionally a second band was booked to play sets between 8:00 and 11:00 A.M. This allowed bands to double, triple, or even quadruple book on some nights, thereby significantly extending their profitability. Saxophonist Mitch Frohman reminisced:

> It's not like it used to be. We used to work so many gigs in a night, sometimes three or four every Saturday night. Now you feel lucky if you have just one gig on a Saturday. On those busy nights, I remember when you went outside to come home, you couldn't see for a while. Your eyes had been in a dark club since 11:00 P.M. the night before. They would always have the windows covered so you wouldn't know it was the daytime. It would be nine or ten in the morning. You would be exhausted from playing all night, walking home in your dark suit, carrying your horn. And then you would see families and old ladies all dressed up, going to church. They would just scowl and look at you all

> cross-eyed like you were doing the devil's work! (M. Frohman, pers. comm.)

By 1996, only one after-hours in New York City (located in the Bronx) featured live salsa performance; all the others had been raided and closed. Frohman lamented, "We all know why the after-hours scene dried up. They all got busted!" (M. Frohman, pers. comm.).

Besides supplying performance venues, the DTOs also provided capital for new bands. A major obstacle for newly established bands was securing a recording contract. This situation has not changed. Throughout most of salsa's history, only two labels—Fania and RMM—dominated and controlled the majority of production. This limited the possibilities for new groups without contracts. Since recording a new project is costly (including arrangements, musicians, rehearsals, and studio fees), and more traditional avenues, such as bank loans, are difficult to obtain for such financially risky projects—and impossible for immigrants without proper legal documentation—DTOs provided an alternative source of support. Some DTO members personally associated themselves with specific bands, establishing a type of patronage system that provided much-needed capital for recording, promotion, and management. In return for their support, musicians often were required to play for DTO members' private parties and events. Like many salsa musicians, I have played at a number of cartel members' private residences, both in the United States and in Colombia, for birthdays, christenings, weddings, and the like. If these new debut recordings grew in popularity, Fania or RMM often would sign the artists for future projects. This often entailed establishing long-term business partnerships with these dealers/producers. Indeed, Fania and RMM relied on these entrepreneurial ventures to acquire new talent for their rosters.

Drug bosses also benefited from these relationships. Besides the obvious financial advantages, their associations with salsa stars elevated their social status. For instance, being able to afford to have someone like Lavoe perform at your private home for a few select friends was a show of power and influence. Harlow related:

> I received a call that the head of the Medellín cartel wanted to meet "La Cartera" [the name of one of Harlow's first big hits]. So he sent a limo for me, and we drove for an hour up into the hills outside Medellín. His driveway was about a mile long, and every twenty feet there was a guy standing holding a machine gun and watching us drive in. He had an enormous estate, and we were led in and given a huge pile of blow [cocaine] and a big bag of pot. We sat there for five hours partying. The

guy never showed up. He was playing pool in another part of the house. So we said "fuck it" and left. (L. Harlow, pers. comm.)

One may surmise from Harlow's story that the jefe's intention may not have been to actually meet the salsa star, but instead to establish bragging rights. He could claim to his pool partners that Harlow was waiting for him in the other room or had been to his house, or that he had stood Harlow up. Harlow was a figure in his power game, not an unfamiliar position for salseros in their relationship with DTOs. In Mark Edberg's work on narcotraffickers and banda, he likewise discusses how musicians "form part of the backdrop of the narcotrafficker identity" (Edberg 2004: 66). The DTO-financed clubs, where salsa is performed and drug deals are made, serve as "theaters of power." As "big men," the dealers perform a "public presentation . . . within a social arena that is a known setting for becoming, displaying, and maintaining a narcotrafficker persona" (Edberg 2004: 100).

My point here is to emphasize that the distinction between legitimate business practice and illegal activity is not so clear-cut. Helena Simonett (2001) documents that within the "narco culture" of Mexico, drug lords are not always viewed as bad people, especially if they become "social bandits" contributing to the social good by supporting local musics and culture. Within the salsa community, DTOs have held this same ambiguous position. They have been integral to business and supplied much needed capital and opportunity, but they also have caused increases in violence and brought human tragedy to the scene, as well as their own set of social inequities. Their association with salsa has forced musicians to operate within circuits of production that bypass dominant routes, thereby perpetuating salsa's marginalization from the mainstream market economies. For instance, since all DTO-associated gigs were paid in cash, musicians were forced into a criminalized economy. There were no pension or health benefits paid on their behalf, and obviously there was no tax-withholding. Musicians were limited in how much money they could deposit in bank accounts, because if they were ever to be audited by the Internal Revenue Service (IRS), they would have to account for these earnings. No one wanted to be the one to identify this money's origins. Trombonist L., who has worked exclusively in salsa for many years, told me that he has never paid taxes; instead, he keeps all his cash—$40,000—in a bedroom safe. He has never had a bank account or credit cards. Bandleader R. adds, "From the perspective of the IRS, I have just slipped through the cracks. I do not exist. I have never paid tax once in my sixty years as a musician. My house and everything I own are in my wife's name."

In many ways the criminalized economy associated with the drug trade set the standard for the business of salsa: cash-based and off the books—that is, until 1989. The "War on Drugs" profoundly changed this. The IRS became one avenue of attack for the U.S. government. When clubs were busted, inquiries soon followed regarding who had been employed there. It was fairly easy to obtain advertisements and performance schedules. Consequently, throughout the early 1990s, the IRS audited a number of bandleaders, including Marc Anthony, Tito Nieves, José Alberto, and manager/promoter David Maldonado. Subsequently, these bandleaders began paying by check and withholding taxes from the musicians' pay.

With the systematic closing of a number of salsa clubs that served as laundering fronts, such as Harlem's Club 2000 and the Palm Tree in Queens, a few new clubs opened in their place that were owned and operated by legitimate business owners. With a new level of scrutiny from governmental agencies, these new venues required bandleaders to provide their social security numbers and to sign for all monies paid out to them. In turn, bandleaders required their sidepersons to do the same.

Further, the capital the DTOs invested into recordings dwindled substantially throughout the 1990s, forcing RMM Records to seek other partners. Mercado began to forge alliances with well-established companies in the music industry. To facilitate and expand record distribution, he turned to Sony Records, which provided access to their extensive global distribution network. In return, Sony acquired a percentage of Mercado's profits. This new relationship required a legitimatization of RMM business activity (i.e., transactions had to be reported to the IRS). In 1996 Sergio George opined, "The old ways of doing business are slowly fading away as the corporate world gets involved. They have to do business 'right' to attract better people" (S. George, pers. comm.). Consequently, RMM Records changed the way musicians were paid for their services by requiring everyone to submit social security numbers and to sign government employment forms before recording sessions and concert performances. The musicians were then paid by check and sent 1099 forms at the end of the year; prior to this point, all business with musicians was paid in cash and not reported to the IRS.

Initially, the changes from these bandleaders and RMM incited protest among salsa musicians who had grown accustomed to receiving cash for their services. In 1994, when Marc Anthony began paying by check, it elicited a temporary breakup of his band. Musicians who held day jobs were faced with being placed in higher tax brackets, and those who had never paid taxes in the past were not only confronted with the daunting task of learning how to fill out tax forms, but possibly faced inquiries from the IRS concerning their employment in previous years. Furthermore, immigrant musicians who did not possess work permits or green cards were compelled to either seek illegal employment elsewhere or refrain from working until their work permit applications were approved. La India sponsored several Venezuelan band members so they could remain in the United States and continue to perform with her band. Since that time, other bands wishing to avoid IRS investigations have adopted similar payment practices. Trumpeter Ray Vega remarked, "The scene has really changed. Let's face it. We were working like crazy because of the 'blow.' When they started to clean up the drugs, much of the scene dried up. Back in the eighties, we worked in all those after-hours joints sometimes until 10:00 A.M. We would play for all those vampires. I mean, they were not regular, hard-working people. They were there for the drugs" (R. Vega, pers. comm.).

Salsa Musicians and Cocaine

Harlow sees drugs as inseparable from the cultural milieu in which salsa operates: "Drugs are just part of the culture. They are everywhere. Some musicians were dealers . . . everybody was using in the seventies and eighties. They were just part of doing business" (L. Harlow, pers. comm.). Walter Yetnikoff's autobiography is instructive in documenting similar trends in the U.S. music industry. He was the president of CBS Records, and his autobiography is a story of excess and how cocaine, in particular, was part and parcel of every aspect of his business day throughout the 1980s. Indeed, this has also been the case with salsa. Cocaine was the currency of choice for exerting influence; with their access to the drug, DTOs held a real advantage. Given to the proper individuals, cocaine bought radio airplay and concert bookings; one reviewer for *El Diario*, the Spanish-language newspaper in New York City, was notorious for demanding blow in return for writing reviews and influencing bookings.[16] Those who possessed cocaine held power. Masucci is quoted as saying, "I used to listen to Symphony Sid on the radio and if by 2:00 A.M. he hadn't played our latest records, I would get out of bed, go and buy him a pastrami sandwich, take it to the studio and wait there until he played them" (Steward 1999: 62). One musician from the Fania All-Stars elaborated on this anecdote, "At 2:00 A.M., Sid was not interested in pastrami! That is for sure. If Jerry were still alive, you should ask him what Sid liked on his pastrami. I'm sure it wasn't mustard!" (Anon., pers. comm.). These practices persisted into the 1990s. Bandleader Tito Rodríguez Jr. stated that, in order for one tune to be placed in radio-play rotation in 1996, programmers from each radio station in New York had to be given $1,000 in payola.[17] Rodríguez remarked that "in Puerto Rico they wanted blow, about $1,000 worth for each station. Pedro Arroyo is the most powerful programmer in P.R. I gave him a copy of the last publicity photo my father [Tito Rodríguez] had posed for before his death. Pedro was so touched that no payola was requested and one of my songs was played once an hour for a number of weeks. Just because of that I sold fifteen thousand units" (T. Rodríguez Jr., pers. comm.). At times, cocaine has even been offered to musicians for payment. The first time it happened to me was in 1990. I asked the bandleader how I was supposed to pay my rent with the drug; he suggested that I sell it. I refused, as did most of my bandmates. Several accepted, though.

Musicians cohabit this contact zone of illegal activity and legitimate music-making and must be able to navigate this tricky, often violent, and hazardous arena.[18] Their associations with DTOs can have positive effects (gigs, tours, recordings, opportunity, etc.), but they also can destroy individual lives and end careers. For instance, Jairo Varela, founding member of Grupo Niche, was convicted of money laundering due to his association with DTOs and spent some time in a Colombian jail in the mid-1990s. This was a great setback for a group that was poised to become one of the most popular salsa bands on the international scene. When working for a band that dealers support, musicians easily can obtain drugs; on occasion, drugs are even distributed gratuitously. A number of musicians who subsequently turned to dealing have spent long stints in jail or have had to leave the country for long periods to avoid incarceration. According to Harlow, Johnny Pacheco was caught dealing at the height of his Fania career. Using Masucci's connections, he was able to avoid jail time by assembling an impressive legal defense team of seasoned lawyers. However, their steep legal fees forced him to sell his partnership in Fania Records back to Masucci, costing Pacheco millions in the end. Pacheco felt that Masucci took advantage of his situation in order to take away his share in Fania. Pacheco exclaims, "I consider myself an idiot. I should have seen what was coming."[19] Due to the more strict Rockefeller drug laws enacted in 1973 as part of the "War on Drugs," musicians caught since then have not been so lucky; many are still serving mandatory long sentences.

Generally, cocaine use and dealing among salsa musicians declined throughout the 1990s, due partly to the drug busts and partly to the changing cultural climate. For younger generations, other drugs, such as ecstasy, would eventually surpass cocaine in popularity. However, cocaine still maintains a strong presence on the salsa scene. For salsa musicians in particular, working late hours and being in continual contact with people using drugs, especially stimulants such as cocaine, present many temptations. Some musicians turn to cocaine to stay awake, to alleviate stage anxiety, to deal with personal issues, for recreation, for the communal benefits of belonging to a group of users, or for a variety of other motives that cannot be reduced to functionalist explanations of the drug's physical and psychological effects. Experienced and seasoned players usually conclude, either through personal experimentation or by witnessing the long-term effects on others, that using drugs only worsens fatigue, and the long-term negative effects far outweigh the short-term recreative and restorative qualities. However, younger, less experienced musicians have fallen prey to the temptations. For instance, in 1994 a twenty-four-year-old trumpeter who had just begun working regularly on the salsa scene died from an overdose during his first tour to Colombia.

Singers and bandleaders are especially prone to drug use because fans or drug-dealing producers offer drugs to show appreciation. "Partying with the star" can elevate a fan's prestige among his or her peers. This "appreciation" has left many salseros struggling with addiction. Tito Nieves, Lalo Rodríguez, and Raulín Rosendo openly have discussed their persistent problems with cocaine addiction. Additionally, Frankie Ruíz's passing and Lavoe's untimely death from AIDS-related complications have been attributed to their drug use.

Even if salsa musicians personally avoid drug use, they are in constant contact with people who are either using or selling. Musicians understand the financial benefits that arise from their association with drug dealers and at times must put aside their misgivings and play potentially hazardous gigs to appease their benefactors. Speaking out against drug use or confronting users or dealers results in loss of work. Musicians privately discuss the issues among themselves, but I have never seen someone berated publicly about drug use or dealing. One cause for concern among musicians is being in the presence of both the dangerous individuals whom the drug trade attracts and drug users, who can behave in irrational and unpredictable ways. Pianist Hector Martignon (who is Colombian) comments, "I never take trips to Colombia with salsa bands anymore, only jazz bands. Because salsa attracts the worse element of society with all those drugs involved. And even in New York, the people that hang out in the scene are not always so cool" (H. Martignon, pers. comm.).

Salsa musicians operate within a subculture of sorts, which is defined in part by cocaine use. For those who use, cocaine becomes a component in the construction of their social fabric, where networks are established based on their communal activity, and nonusers within their community are positioned as facilitators. The seminal work of Howard Becker (1973 [1963]) on drug use and deviance among dance musicians in Chicago in the 1940s is particularly insightful in this discussion: "Where people who engage in deviant activities have the opportunity to interact with one another they are likely to develop a culture built around the problems rising out of the differences between their definition of what they do and the definition held by other members of the society" (Becker 1973: 81). This results in the formation of an "unconventional circle" (Becker 1973: 62) that possesses its own codes that distance the group from mainstream society. Contributing to this distancing is the fact that both the "work" and "workplace" of musicians are discursively and physically removed from mainstream notions of "job" and "office." Through the use of words like "play" and "gig" to refer to "work" and "job," respectively, and because their workplace is the site for others' leisure and pleasure, their daily experiences are, in part, lived outside the confines of the mainstream; in some ways they are "emancipated from the controls of society and become responsive to a smaller group" (Becker 1973: 59–60). What other profession condones drug use on the job?

Cocaine users among musicians range from occasional social users to daily consuming addicts, and from no band members partaking to an entire group participating in immoderate consumption. As long as a musician's use does not interfere with his or her professional duties (i.e., performing competently, arriving for gigs and rehearsals in a punctual manner), his or her cohorts generally support the behavior. Even if a musician displays erratic behavior or becomes unreliable due to drug use, the salsa community rarely ostracizes him or her, and the musician receives multiple opportunities to perform even if the condition worsens, though the quality of the work he or she is called for may decline (i.e., playing with less established bands).[20]

Certain bands develop a reputation for drug use, and musicians may use drugs to obtain work with them. When one trumpeter lost a gig to another less accomplished musician, he explained, "We all know why he was hired, they needed a dealer in the band!" (Anon., pers. comm.). For bands not associated directly with DTOs, securing cocaine can be hazardous and time-consuming for musicians, especially while on tour. Though musicians often take huge risks in transporting drugs for personal use while traveling, there are real advantages to having a well-connected member in the band. Depending on the amounts used, just securing cocaine for one night's work can be difficult. I had the opportunity to tour with the band that the trumpeter refers to above, and it has a reputation for excessive partying. One evening I decided to track consumption closely. Of the ten-member group, eight musicians used drugs regularly (daily on this two-week tour). During one night's performance in California, the resident musician/dealer, with the assistance of the promoter, obtained ten grams of cocaine, one ounce of marijuana, two fifths of rum, and one case of beer for the band. By the end of intermission (within the course of three hours), all substances had been consumed (I drank two of the beers). This was a fairly typical night.

While I toured with the same band in Colorado, two minivans were rented to transport the group through the mountains. The leader asked if I could drive one of the vans, promising to pay extra for my efforts. I accepted. While driving to a gig in Vail, Colorado, several high mountain passes needed to be crossed. When the band members realized that my watch had a built-in altimeter, they kept inquiring about our current altitude, which ranged from seven thousand to twelve thousand feet. Every time we went below eight thousand feet, I could hear much snorting of cocaine from the backseat. When I asked what was up, they said: "Don't you know? You have to be below eight thousand feet to blow, any higher and you can have a heart attack." As I drove past state troopers posted on the side of the road, I realized that, out of the five occupants in the car, I was the only one who was not high (probably why the leader asked me to drive) and that between them they possessed enough cocaine for us all to be sentenced to many years in jail. This was a dream gig for me, but I really had to question whether it was worth such a risk. The seriousness with which they imparted the health risks of consuming cocaine at high altitudes just made my situation seem absurd, let alone deviant. Lenson writes that cocaine affects behavior and perception in unique ways by contracting consciousness and "obsessing over the white physical substance is a large part of the cocaine high" (Lenson 1993: 72). Even as a nonuser, my own behavior was affected (I would frequently glance at my watch). I turned down their next tour, which was in Europe. I could not fathom the risks involved in all those border crossings and customs officers. The band went without me, and only two of them were imprisoned briefly in France for being abusive to an airline steward, behavior brought about by their excessive cocaine use at thirty thousand feet. Remarkably they were able to conceal their stash through the ordeal and rejoined the tour without further incident.

Salsa Music

What does all of this drug use have to do with music sound? I find this question difficult to answer in concrete ways. During the aforementioned gig in California, amidst the consumption of all those mind-altering substances, the performance undoubtedly was affected. The whole vibe changed throughout the evening as musicians became more intoxicated. Tempos rushed, the arrangements were played in a looser fashion, and the leader took excessively indulgent solos (creatively riskier than usual). No one in the band showed concern about the increasingly sloppy playing. From my own fairly sober perspective, I do not believe it was an exceptional performance, nor do I believe, though, that the absence of drugs necessarily would have improved the performance. The musicians appeared to be having a great time and were engaged enthusiastically, and the audience responded well to that. Several audience members did comment to me afterward that the second set seemed more diffused and unfocused. How could it not be? The intensity of the drug use distanced the musicians, experientially, from their audience. The drugs altered their physical and psychological states, informing, impairing, and maybe enhancing their music performances without the knowledge of the audience. The drug use remained concealed. The audience was kept at bay, unable to participate and connect on the same level (unless, of course, they were consuming similar amounts of drugs). This performance was a communal enterprise but within the confines of a closed circle, with the excluded far outnumbering the included. One musician, hiding behind the congas, even snorted cocaine on stage. Other band members looked on, amused, laughing at the fact that no one in the audience noticed. Fooled them again! One musician later commented, "In this band, it's like they are paying us to get high! We do, and the people still dig it." The long-term physical, psychological, emotional, and financial effects of drug abuse; the detrimental effects on personal relationships that this type of use can bring; the pending personal tragedies that some of these musicians will face due to their abuse; and the social circumstances that facilitated this level of consumption were all ignored and left unsaid as the band played on. And they continue to play on in this altered state—often.

Since few salsa song texts deal directly with topics of drugs, a text-based analysis is inappropriate here.[21] Instead, I focus on issues of bodily engagement and the aesthetics involved in salsa performance. Why is cocaine use so prevalent and, thus, compatible with the salsa scene? I believe that one productive approach is to examine the places where salsa is performed and what happens in those spaces: specifically, nightclubs and dancing. A number of scholars conceive of dance clubs as ritualized spaces (Bell 1992, Delgado and Muñoz 1997, Fikentscher 2000, Buckland 2002, Concepcion 2002, Thompson 2002) where "through a series of physical movements, ritual practices spatially and temporally construct an environment organized according to schemes of privileged opposition," set apart from the profanity of daily life (Bell 1992: 98).[22] In salsa, music, dance, and drugs convene and become fundamental in carving out such a space. John Blacking's work is key here. He holds that music's transcendent power is located in its ability to "create another world of virtual time" (Blacking 1973b: 27). For Blacking, the body's role is central to musical performance and this process of transcendence. Both Robert Farris Thompson and Alma Concepcion not only discuss the transcendence of dance, but they specifically implicate ritual as a central trope in mambo and salsa dancing. Thompson identifies *limpieza*, or a self-purification ritual, as a fundamental motivation for dancers (Thompson 2002: 344). Concepcion adds, "salsa dancing reaches a climax in intensity similar to that of a cleansing and renewal ritual" (Concepcion 2002: 173). Writing about drugs, Lenson identifies two transcendental tendencies among users—augmentation and diminution: "The augmenters want to live faster, telescoping the consumerist process of desire into the course of an evening or an hour. And so they shoot speed or snort cocaine. The diminishers want to defeat the process by leisurely patterns of dosing and contemplation" (Lenson 1995: 64). He adds that the augmentative properties of cocaine are particularly desirable because "they do not transform the phenomenal world so much as transcend it" (Lenson 1995: 132). Taussig's work on transgression is also informative here, especially how he positions cocaine as a transgressive form. He writes, "To transgress is to break a rule, and not just any rule but one of such importance we call it taboo because it is a barrier of attraction as much as repulsion . . . To break the rule means to enter into a space . . . in which the rule is suspended and comes to exist in a ghostly, negated form." And these forms are valuable "precisely because [they] cannot be purified of the attraction and repulsion embodied in them . . . What makes a rule a rule is that built into it is the desire to transgress it . . . cocaine [is] the contagion emitted by the breaking of a taboo" (Taussig 2004: 126, 253). Taken together, salsa performances and dancing in nightclubs under the influence of cocaine potentially yield a pointedly transgressive experience for participants.

Stimulants play an important role in the ritualization of many cultures, and the physical and psychological effects of cocaine, in particular, are aligned with the transcendent qualities of highly rhythmic dance music. As Matt Sakakeeny reminds us, more specifically, both the functional and aesthetic aspects of salsa dovetail with the effects of cocaine usage, particularly in performance settings that embody a ritualistic dimension involving euphoria, transcendence, and transgressive behavior, such as in nightclubs.[23] For musicians and dancers, the drug's effects of enhanced stamina, increased mental alertness, and boosted ego are useful in the performance of salsa, especially considering salsa's loud, fast, and repetitively rhythmic musical properties and the intense energy of its "hot" aesthetic, especially in salsa *dura* (the predominant style during the period when cocaine use was most prevalent). Pacheco describes the aesthetic as "[m]usic that would wake up the dead."[24] The intense initial rush of explosive energy, as well as the energy levels that are maintained during a cocaine high, mimic the intensity of the energy salsa musicians must create and maintain during a music set. It is a "high" that does not counteract nor contradict the transformative rituals enacted and embodied late into the night.

However, as drug use among musicians declines, it is obvious that cocaine is not a necessary component in the construction of such an aesthetic, or in the transgressive properties of the dance club experience. Rather, I argue, it is just one factor that contributes to the salsa club experience. More fundamentally, its presence on the scene undergirds performance practice, sets the tone, and affects the vibe. In this way, the influence of cocaine on salsa extends beyond the individual user's experience. Indeed, many participants on the salsa scene never use cocaine or other mind-altering substances. Salsa nightclub rituals involve drug users as well as a number of people who do not use but are associated with drugs in varying ways, such as suppliers, runners, fronts, onlookers, and those who benefit indirectly from the laundering of drug monies. The circle extends way past the actual white powdery substance informing the aesthetic, structuring performance practice, and affecting the daily lives of those who make the music.

The confluence of economic forces, governmental policy, subcultural practices, and deviance that is associated with the illicit drug trade remains a force on the salsa scene. As the U.S. government continues to wage its "War on Drugs," the salsa industry finds itself embattled in its struggle to survive, being forced to legitimize its underground economic structures, to seek new venues for performance, and to invent novel ways to access political and economic power. But the residual effects of cocaine, with its "ruptured traditions, transformed social mores, restructured morality, thought, and expectations" (Roldan 1999: 171), still reverberate from salsa stages and across nightclub dance floors. How salsa is played, heard, danced, made, and talked about is informed by its long relationship with cocaine and the drug's associated industry.

5

La India and the Masquerading of Gender on the Salsa Scene

In March 1995 at a crowded nightclub named Sequoia, located at New York City's South Street Seaport, singer La India entered the stage in front of a packed audience, yelling "What do you want to hear?"[1] The ten rows of mostly women standing directly in front of the stage responded concertedly, "Ese Hombre! Ese Hombre!"[2] By this point in India's career as a rising salsa star, such passionately enthusiastic responses from her female audiences had become the order of the day. India honored their request and began softly singing about "Ese Hombre" ("This Man"), who appears gallant, attentive, proud, divine, likeable, and effusive. She quickly shifted her vocal timbre with ramped up emotional intensity as the song, which begins just like any other *salsa romántica* love song, suddenly took a dramatic turn. She declared that his outward appearance is a lie and the real truth is that he is a "grand fool," "a stupid conceited man," egotistical and capricious. This "payaso vanidoso" ("vain clown") is abusive and the cause of much suffering.

On a semantic level, the scandal of these lyrics arises from the disruption and almost symmetrical reversal of the tropes inherent in salsa romántica, a music style that traditionally has centered on the intimate narrative of amorous heterosexual relations. The image conjured up by the female voice is far from the familiar tales of harmonious love in its exposure of the bleak taboos of oppression and abuse. The man who appears gallant to the eyes of the world is transformed into a sheer plurality of negative epithets, caught up in an ongoing performance of masculine role-playing. Frances Aparicio points out that this enumerative strategy frequently is employed in popular music "as the central structural recourse for singing the gender wars" (Aparicio 1998: 167). She proceeds, "women singers have been inverting the object of men's discursive terrorism as an initial strategy of resistance against misogyny and patriarchy" (Aparicio 1998: 167). But this was something new and unprecedented in salsa.

More significant, though, was India's staging of this song, aggressively delivering (almost shouting) this invective as an anthem for female empowerment while adopting performative gestures most often associated with the type of "cocky," aggressive, misogynistic male behavior that this song purports to expose. In this way, India's performance of "Ese Hombre" transcends the preoccupation with simplistic male/female binaries that fail to articulate multiple modes of gendered subjectivity, offering a displacement of the agency inherent in the gaze from man to woman. At the same time, the staging of "Ese Hombre" functions as a kind of parodic overdubbing of gender stereotypes, producing a doubled perspective that institutes a boundary-crossing dialogue that breaks down the pretense and fixed allotment of precoded social and gendered identities. The true scandal of La India on the salsa scene lies less in her textual explorations than in her gestural manipulations within and across the thresholds of the performance space.[3]

Gender remains a neglected area of inquiry in salsa scholarship. The few exceptions include Lise Waxer's study of all-women bands in Colombia, Aparicio's writings on salsa and gender, and Wilson Valentín-Escobar's work on Hector Lavoe and masculinity, all of which represent a triumvirate of pioneering voices that have begun to address this lacuna. Waxer's and Aparicio's writings are particularly important because both scholars discuss the silencing and marginalization of women in salsa. This chapter aims to contribute to this nascent discussion by using India and her performance practice as a case study. Needless to say, this underexplored area deserves further attention, much more so than is received in this book.

India is a significant figure in the history of salsa because her success, partly due to her staged excessive self-representation and performance practice, represents a rupture from a long-established male-dominated tradition. Prior to 1992 (the year of India's debut salsa recording), a conservative and univocal sexual politic that permeated business, education, and performance practices dictated who was allowed to sing and, thus, was given a voice in salsa; it effectively barred female participation, at least on stage. Celia Cruz, along with a few all-female salsa bands, proved the only exception in this respect. Cruz was such a foundational and formidable force in the development of salsa, even predating the emergence of the genre, that she was able to retain her prominent position as "the Queen of Salsa" throughout her long career.[4] There has been a consistent presence of all-female salsa bands throughout the music's history (e.g., Chicas de la Salsa). However, regardless of their high level of musicianship, they have remained on the periphery, in part due to the attitudes of many male salsa musicians, producers, and promoters who view them more as commercial novelties rather than serious contributors to the scene.[5]

The exclusion of women in salsa music-making can be traced to a number of societal factors. Aparicio's work is instructive here. She writes that "the cultural traditions of Latin American families . . . [which] prohibit young women from inhabiting the male-dominated, public spaces of music making . . . women's lack of access in training . . . all-male networks in production, and the discursive constructions of salsa music as a masculine cultural space" all prevent female participation (Aparicio 2002: 136–137). Indicative of the inherent tensions produced when females do make salsa on stage, and attesting to the inequities in public perception concerning *salseras*, India, like most female salsa singers who have since followed, adopted a stage name and remains publicly known by this alter persona. This strategy discursively distances her private identity (wife, mother), concealing it from public view and, thus, allowing for greater freedom in the construction of her staged identity, freed from the constraints of traditional conceptions of what it means to be Latina. In contrast, adopting a stage name is much less common for male singers; they are most often known by their given names.

The male-dominated tradition found in salsa partly stems from the cultural milieu from which it emerged in the late 1960s. Undergirded by the political economy of El Barrio in New York City, salsa, as previously mentioned, was inscribed with what Aparicio (2002) labels as "a collective, violent male subjectivity" that favored "hypermasculinity" as a performative strategy in countering ethnic discrimination and social marginalization (Aparicio 2002: 138). Indeed, tropes of masculinity continue to serve as the criteria by which to judge and evaluate salsa stylistically. This is evidenced by the use of the term *monga* (limp or flaccid) to describe how salsa romántica differs in aesthetic and sensibility from salsa *dura* (hard), the style most associated with hypermasculinity and the Latino political empowerment movement of the 1970s. This hypermasculinity was constructed, though, not only in opposition to hegemonic power (the U.S. mainstream culture in New York), but also to femininity. By focusing on a male-dominated discourse the crucial roles women fulfill in the construction of "salsa as gendered male" is ignored.[6] For instance, according to singer Ray Sepulveda, the role of women has been fundamental in the emergence of salsa romántica. From his perspective, the genre is marketed solely to women, caters to their consuming trends, is directed toward their desires, and, thus, is created for their pleasure. He states, "To have a successful record, you only need to sell to the young women, and they only buy love songs, so that's what we sing" (R. Sepulveda, pers. comm.). As Sepulveda illumines, even without female salsa music-makers, women have remained central participants as audience members, dancers, and consumers.[7]

The various ways women engage with salsa remains underexplored and absent from most historical narratives. India disrupted these unwritten and unspoken absences by adapting the traditional negotiative tactics of male salsa singers in her salsa music-making, forging new possibilities for the voices of women to be heard in the process, as well as carving out a space for female music-making—with a difference. How she accomplished this proved quite controversial.

On the aforementioned night at Sequoia, as female fans sang along in rapture, a male audience member interfered with the performance. As a provocative response to the abusive language of the text, he threw a balled-up napkin at India, missing her head by inches. Rather than ignoring this disrespectful gesture, India capitalized on the moment as part of her ongoing experimentation with the limits of public performance practice. In the middle of the song's lyric, she cried out a warning to the intruder, thereby engaging her male opponent in a posturing game of attack and counterattack. Responding to her challenge, he hurled a second napkin, which bounced off her head. As the band continued to play, India dramatically picked up her microphone stand, circled it over her head, and threatened to "bash the skull" of the napkin-thrower. The ensuing split second of suspense resulted from the singer's decision to overstep an implicit boundary, pushing the envelope of accepted performance behavior.[8] Acting against all protocols of decorum, she jumped off the stage in order to carry out her threat. At this point, the club bouncers intervened to hold India back, and they expeditiously extricated the man from the club.

India's gesture and sheer willingness to engage in a violent skirmish in this situation clearly pushed against accepted norms of feminine behavior within the mainstream Latino music scene. Despite the fact that an actual altercation most likely would not have occurred (due to the stage division, the high presence of security, and a club full of fans), the risk she took when she proceeded to attack the man was as symbolic as it was physical. Following the explosive fray of engendered combat, she continued with a highly impassioned rendition of "Ese Hombre." The outrageous fact that she suddenly was enacting the message of the song, flipping the direction of abuse (i.e., the physical threat), empowering the female, and not backing down from the challenge ignited enormous enthusiasm amongst her audience.

On this and many other occasions, I suggest, India draws on a complex set of tropes, associated with the poetics of *chusmería*.[9] According to José

Muñoz, chusmería is a "form of behavior . . . linked to stigmatized class identity" and also is associated with deliberately vulgarized representations of the immigrant or minoritarian female body. The prototypical *chusma* embodies sexualized figures of exaggeration and involves critical enactments of " 'inappropriate' and antinormative behavior" (Muñoz 1999: 184). The aesthetics involved in chusmería, in Muñoz's use of the term, grow out of an avant-garde performance tradition with a distinctly homosexual and male agenda (e.g., drag queen performances) and often are employed strategically to challenge the status quo. India's infusion of such codified behavioral representations into the salsa scene are unique insofar as she operates within a relatively conservative mainstream music arena where this type of transgressive poetics is unprecedented. Nevertheless, in her open-ended simulation of gender affiliations as fundamentally unstable and ambiguous, it is possible to locate a similar level of performativity to that of Muñoz's subversive chusma, which feeds off an ostensible commitment to the "live moment" and displaces any simple structuralist notion of binary opposition between the sexes. In the case of India, she adopts an excessive performance practice that employs violence, threats of violence, and gendered role-playing by adopting the role of the "macho,"—not just any macho, but an excessively aggressive and parodically "over-stereotyped" version.[10]

They Say That I Am

Linda Bell Caballero is known professionally as La India (the Indian), a stage name chosen because of her complexion and facial features, which she feels resemble those of the indigenous peoples of Puerto Rico, the *Taíno*. Born in 1970, India is representative of a younger generation of successful salseras. She is a second-generation Nuyorican, and English is her first language. Her musical roots lie primarily in house and soul music, and she draws from these styles, mixing them with salsa romántica and salsa dura. This innovative stylistic cocktail, along with her flamboyant stage behavior (such as smoking cigars, the use of lewd language, and sexually ambiguous impersonations), contributed significantly to the reinvigoration of salsa's popularity in the mid-1990s, but also stirred up controversial feelings within the salsa community. These conflicting images, produced by her multifarious material and symbolic boundary-crossings between public and private discourses, are the subject of the present analysis.

India's musical career began in the house-music scene, working with producers Jellybean Benitez and Little Louie Vega. Despite her success, charting several hits, she soon expressed alienation from something crucial to her self-conception: "He [Benitez] kept seeing me only as what he wanted to invent . . .

[his label] did not understand my being Latina, they wanted me to be white, and that's not who I am."[11] She credits Hector Lavoe, Vega's uncle, with providing the needed encouragement to explore her Latina roots through the performance of salsa. He said to her, "You're wasting your time in the American market. What you should really be doing is focusing on being here with us."[12]

Partly upon her own request, then, India was introduced to the salsa scene by Vega, who produced a house-music track entitled "When the Night Is Over" that featured Marc Anthony and India singing a duet, along with solos by Tito Puente and Eddie Palmieri. Subsequently, Palmieri invited India to sing with his band. Shortly after she joined, he recorded her debut salsa album *Llegó La India via Eddie Palmieri* (India Has Arrived by way of Eddie Palmieri) in 1992.[13] The title track's lyric flamboyantly proclaims India's arrival on the salsa scene and voices her Latino pride: "Y dedicado a mi raza latina, que con orgullo le canto yo" ("I dedicate it to my Latino race, to whom I sing it with pride"). Coupling her with Palmieri was a stylistic stroke of genius for more than one reason. As a musician, Palmieri has been on the innovative edge of Latin music in New York for forty years. His decision to hire India was another opportunity to innovate, providing the opportunity for a female voice to be heard within this male-dominated sonic landscape. Stylistically, his music departs from mainstream salsa romántica and instead features an aggressive, hard-driving sound reminiscent of salsa dura. It is from Palmieri that India acquired the hot fiery aesthetics of old school salsa that eventually infused her own performance practice and that fit well with her house-music sensibilities.

However, it was not until her split with Palmieri in 1993 that India received a high level of critical acclaim. At the same time, she began to fully actualize the possibilities couched in her own self-exploration of what it might mean to be a Latin woman. Sergio George first recognized the commercial potential of her unique mixing of styles and produced her debut solo record in salsa in 1994, *Dicen Que Soy* (They Say That I Am).[14] *Dicen Que Soy*, along with this unprecedented stylistic mix, features lyrics that speak the culturally unspeakable within the salsa community. Her songs tell of women who do not need men and who are disappointed by them, of women who find their male partners' behavior stupid and insolent. Up until India's appearance, few women were represented as productive agents of subjectivity in salsa texts. Aparicio opines, "As a music industry dominated by men, salsa music continues to disseminate lyrics laden with problematic, misogynist, and patriarchal representations of women" (Aparicio 1998: xii). India counters this trend with the song "Ella o Yo" ("Her or Me"), in which she tells a man that he cannot have two women at once and must choose only one; "Qué Ganas De No Verte Nunca Mas" (roughly, "Oh, How I Wish to Never See You Again") is self explanatory; and the title track "Dicen Que Soy" lists various negative critiques of India, to which she retorts "I don't care." Taken together, the lyrics on this record amount to the stubbornly determined message, "I am going to reinvent myself as I am." Her house-music-influenced singing style, in which she shouts and growls what other Latinas have not uttered publicly in salsa before, serves to accentuate the meaning of these texts.

Even more effective than the male-bashing lyrics was her choice to perform them within the traditionally conservative genre of salsa romántica. Prior to India's transformational challenge to the genre, song lyrics, with only a few exceptions, focused almost exclusively on the heterosexual boy-meets-girl scenario of salsa romántica. In comparison, these words would have had little effect in the house-music scene. Instead, India chose to revolutionize a musical format that men had dominated exclusively for thirty years and that promoted a conservative (sexual) politic.

Along with "Ese Hombre," which immediately achieved status as a female anthem of sorts, the song texts of *Dicen Que Soy* lent a voice to many Latinas, especially from younger generations, who embraced their liberating potential. The level of female bonding these songs triggered worked effectively to disrupt the binary distribution of sexual desire to a degree, which conjures up the unsettling interference associated with various forms of transvestitism and drag without amounting to a statement of overt homosexual identity. Indeed, many of those women standing in front of the stage and singing along at Sequoia were holding hands and overtly displaying signs of homoerotic behavior, certainly not a typical scenario on the salsa scene at that time. India, for her part, encouraged such behavior by frequently addressing her love songs to female audience members, and sometimes inviting them up on stage to dance with her.[15] Through such calculated performative gestures, her sheer stage presence served to destabilize fixed notions of desire and blur rigid divides between the sexes by offering alternative notions of sexual orientation.

The Chusma Poetics of Excess

The effects of India's live performance practice were striking. Much of this had to do with her visual self-presentation and incorporation of gender-encoded "stage props." Her busty and curvaceous looks, overtly suggestive dress style, dramatic make-up, and large hair projected a sexualized "loudness" that diverged from the explicitly feminine grande dame image of a singer like Cruz.

Instead, India's embodiment of the "bad street girl" replicated Willie Colón's adoption of the *el malo* (bad street boy) impersonation deployed in the salsa dura scene of the 1970s.[16] Such unnerving co-optation of macho

Figure 5.1 Cover of India's debut recording "Llegó La India" (RMM Records RMD-80864, 1992).

behavioral patterns and their representations by a female artist clearly functioned as a parodic crossbreeding of stereotyped gender images. Even more interesting were the ways in which India drew from the complicitly rebellious chusma tradition of La Lupe, a singer of boleros and Afro Cuban dance music who performed with Tito Puente in the 1960s. India's use of the definite article "La" in front of her name also attests to the consciously staged influence of her predecessor. In discussing the impact of chusmería poetics on the troubled iconicity of Lupe, Muñoz particularly emphasizes her legendary tropes of excess: "The singer was known to shudder and convulse as she sang. Her stage movements often included writhing on the floor. A few witnesses have reported that she concluded her performances by banging her head against the wall . . . If one considers the history of strategic shock effects and theatricalized violence that characterize performance art, La Lupe emerges as an important precursor of that artistic movement" (Muñoz 1999: 192–193).

Figure 5.2 Celia Cruz and Johnny Pacheco performing in Madison Square Garden, 1994. *(Photograph by Enid Farber.)*

In other words, Lupe is positioned as the chusma diva par excellence, one whose aggressive cocktail of vulgarity, overly aggressive behavior, and manipulated stage violence eventually contributed to her ostracism from the Latin dance scene. India picked up on Lupe's ambiguous gender blend and transported it to the salsa arena of the 1990s.[17] Perhaps more revealing than anything, India had a habit of appearing on stage smoking a huge cigar (which might be read as the ultimate avatar of phallic symbolism), handling it smoothly between her lips and fingers as part of a titillating erotic game. More subtly, the cigar conveyed a reference to the Santería religion with which she aligns herself, in which cigar smoke is used for various spiritual cleansing purposes, thus mirroring the symbolic cleansing of patriarchal structures. The belief systems of Santería provide one arena for Latina women, especially priestesses, to wield much power within the community. Often, India's performances explicitly referenced such religious connotations; for instance, she would wear the color red to symbolize *Changó*, the deity of thunder and lightning. In this vein, she recorded a song in praise of two Santería deities, *Yemaya* and *Ochún*, on *Llegó La India via Eddie Palmieri*.

Apart from her staged appearance, a vital component of the total performance picture was the complex ways in which India recontextualized herself within the physical and symbolical boundaries of the stage, using her male band members as "props" to be objectified and formalized as set pieces (I regularly performed in her band from 1994 to 1997). Never employing female musicians in her band was a conscious strategy to exclude competition and focus the performative gaze upon her own sexual masquerade. India explains, "Why would I ever hire a women to play in my band? I don't want any competition on my stage" (L. India, pers. comm.). She frequently tempted her audiences: "Don't I have some fine looking men in my band . . . Ladies, which one would you like?" playfully insinuating, "these are my lackey boys—I'm using them, and you can use them too." This was not a strategy only enacted on stage. Offstage, she did have sexual relationships with several band members, one of which resulted in her marriage to percussionist Luisito Quintero.

A particularly illustrative instance of this objectification of her accompanying male musicians happened during a performance in Orlando, Florida, in August 1995, when a disagreement arose between India and her timbale player (J.D.). India had asked a local *timbalero* to be a guest soloist that night without seeking permission for the guest musician to play J.D.'s drums (a common courtesy gesture). J.D. took offence at what he considered to be an act of disrespectful neglect and left the stage as soon as the guest musician was introduced. Moreover, J.D. refused to return until the concert was over, which meant that the guest had to play the rest of the concert (which consisted of music he didn't know). The moment the concert ended, J.D. returned to the stage to pack up his drums. Before the curtain closed, and in full view of the audience, India threw down her microphone and shouted, "Don't fuck with me, motherfucker!" shoving his drums toward him and throwing violent punches. Two musicians grabbed her, thereby preventing bodily injury.

At first glance, this incident seems to paint a picture of India as nothing but an oppressive, hot-tempered vixen, rather than as a woman working out of (and acting out within) her own conditions of oppression. Yet her comments immediately following this incident dispel this notion. I confronted India with the advice that she should have waited until the curtain went down before attacking her employee in order to avoid the public display of private band disputes. To this criticism she replied, "Hell no, I wanted them to see; can you imagine what kind of press we're gonna get tomorrow?" Her comment, of course, revealed calculation and acuity in the staging of herself, along with a savvy sense of how to manipulate the media. But, more to the point, by purposefully inviting the audience to transgress a private-public boundary, the backstage interaction suddenly was redefined as part of the performance event itself, feeding into the objectification of her band members as mere stage props. What exactly, I am tempted to ask, are the dynamics of gender identity involved in this kind of excessive stage behavior?

As well as drawing extensively from the poetics of chusmería, I suggest that India's performance practice might best be described as a mode of disidentification, in which existing gender stereotypes are engaged and blurred to the point of dissolution and then brought back into play as an open-ended process of restructuring subjectivity. In other words, gender identity is conceived as a dynamic site of struggle where, according to Muñoz, "fixed dispositions clash against socially constituted definitions" (Muñoz 1999: 5). Muñoz's concept of disidentification, developed in his book of the same name, provides an apt methodological framework with which to explore the transformative politics involved in India's performance practice. He defines the term as "a survival strategy [on behalf of the minoritarian subject] that works *within* and *outside* the dominant public sphere simultaneously" (Muñoz 1998: 5; emphasis mine). As such, it begs to be understood as a fundamentally ambiguous position between the more clear-cut strategies of identification and counter-identification, respectively. In the case of India, I propose, the "dominant sphere" is the conservative genre of salsa romantíca, while her "minoritarian position" is defined not by race or ethnicity, but in terms of her marginalized female perspective and the oppressive gender politics inherent in the scene.

Taken in this way, her sexual masquerade draws attention to that ambiguous space, discussed in depth by Judith Butler, between the lived body and its morphological ideal-type, while simultaneously laying bare the dangers of ontologizing such ambiguity. On the one hand, India's playful redistribution of agency within the performance space might be interpreted by some feminists to produce a "third gender," a permanent state of drag that fluctuates between materialist and constructionist images of human sexuality. On the other hand, it could be argued that by her sheer insistence on simultaneously occupying such contradictory enunciative positions, which can neither be identified as solely male or female, India performs a complex process of "transgendering" in a way that moves beyond any such triadic typology of gender.[18]

Yet rather than reaffirming the sexual hierarchy through its negative imprint, her performance practice involves the logic of what might be termed a "double mimesis," an imitation of an imitation.[19] Rosalind Morris points out, "When theorists of gender performativity say that all gender is a form of drag, that means that, like drag, the Western system of compulsory heterosexuality is a set of imitations. What is being imitated is the ideal of binary difference, a difference that not only prescribes social roles but also is supposed to determine sexual desires" (Morris 1995: 580). According to this view, cases of third genders or institutionalized transvestitism must be treated as already framed examples of the performativity that underlies the entire logic of binary sexuality. Throughout the last two decades, feminists have argued that gender is not a fact or an essence, but a series of acts that produce the effect of a coherent, naturalized sexuality. Some feminists have gone even further, arguing that though gender begs to be understood as a "set of acts" (or, as I choose to call it, a "masquerade"), it paradoxically works and derives its compulsive force from the fact that people frequently mistake the act for the essence and, in the process, come to believe they are mandatory and natural. "Performatives are thus both generative and dissimulating" (Morris 1995: 573).

As a consequence, the complacent illusion of "third gender" as an emergent category in India's disidentificatory stage presence might be seen as a logical extension of this "drift" toward naturalization involved in the double mimesis; however, it is misleading insofar as it reaffirms the self-same categories it sets out to extricate. For this reason, Muñoz's notion of disidentification seems more apt here, since it playfully imagines the potential empowerment of reversals while acknowledging the inextricability of gender from the material inscription of the body within its localized cultural context. India's hard-boiled chusma image situates itself exactly within such a precarious space "between" well-known stereotypes of male and female essences, rather than "beyond" categories of gender per se. Moreover, her strategic oscillation between (visual) feminizing and (gestural) defeminizing images of the Latina body through the aggressive reenactment of clichéd patterns of sexist behavior is driven by an almost Brechtian thrust, one that reads as an ideologically subversive device of "complicit alienation." By making gender fabulously artificial, these performances illuminate the artifice of gender.

An illustrative example occurred during a performance in September 1995 at Studio 84, a Latin dance club in Harlem, when a few of India's musicians arrived late for the gig. In a tirade at the beginning of the set, over the club's sound system, she berated the musicians for their tardiness. She then modulated her voice into a provocative monologue concerning men and her only use for them: sexual pleasure (once again objectifying her musicians, this time as part of their punishment for their tardiness). She proceeded to graphically describe her systematized exploitative behavior. Her narrative began with a scenario in which she ventured to a club to seek out the "finest-looking man." As soon as the objectified target of desire was chosen, her goals included seducing and luring him to her house. Once there, he was stripped, mounted (India remaining on top), and forced to fornicate without achieving orgasm (a sexual act just for her pleasure). Once India was gratified sexually, she dismounted and kicked the man out of her house, symbolically raping him, thus mimicking the most brutal act of misogyny.

Again, on a semantic level, India's narrative apparently is generated through mere role-reversal, where a woman replaces the male rapist and a man replaces the female victim. In a feat to strategically overcome the essentialist link of sexuality to the male body, India correctly recognized the impossibility of physically taking up the position of the "female rapist," and (by way of a sophisticated strategy) chose to act out her drama of sexual power and ambiguity on the level of narration. At Studio 84, storytelling was put to work as a substitute for real-life sexual domination, contrary to what transpired at South Street Seaport and in Orlando, Florida. Narrative conquest was manipulated to achieve what her bodily stage image could never procure because of an uncanny material residue inherent in the game of masquerading gender. Whether her tantalizing tale of abuse was truthful or contrived matters little in this context. What matters is that this particular instance of performativity took her strategy of disidentification one step further, by capitalizing on the symbolical potential intrinsic to the originary moment of gender inscription. However, the full repercussions of this transgression only become apparent when viewed in light of what happened in the wake of this incident.

India was unaware that Studio 84 had a policy of videotaping all performances, including her own. As a result, her fiercely provocative monologue soon was disseminated widely throughout the salsa industry, and the appalled responses from the salsa community were instantaneous. In 1995 she had sold more records than any other new Latina artist, and thus was positioned as the obvious candidate for the prestigious Lo Nuestro Award (Latin music industry award) in the "best new female artist" category. Despite this fact, the award that year went to a lesser-known artist. Sony executives and others who controlled the awards distribution felt they could not trust India to go on national television, fearing obscene language and violent behavior. Here, for the first time, she had overstepped a boundary that was not to be crossed. The sheer crudity of the monologue pushed the limits of subversive behavior in the salsa scene. As a direct result, she lost performance opportunities; eventually, this temporary ostracism led to a self-imposed revamping of her image. India tempered her staged behavior, stopped smoking cigars, and generally toned down her use of lewd language. Ironically, the storytelling incident turned out to be the one that got India into real trouble, rather than the other episodes that included physical violence.

India's Politics of Parody

On a very basic level, India's musical innovation and nontraditional stage image has had a profound effect on the salsa scene because she has opened doors to other female singers/bandleaders. *Dicen Que Soy* was particularly significant in this respect because it launched the first commercially successful salsa career of a female singer since Cruz and Lupe, which in turn paved the way for a number of upcoming female artists to create names for themselves as salseras (e.g., Brenda K. Star, Alexa, Miosotis, and Corinne, among others). The growing presence of these women changed the climate of the salsa scene by providing female voices and perspectives in a traditionally male-dominated environment. For example, the fact that a song like "Ese Hombre" attained such quick and sweeping success indicates that its lyrics spoke to a real need in Latino culture (especially in New York City) to challenge the role of patriarchy, speaking against misogyny and abuse from men. Meanwhile, India remains active on the scene, though in a less controversial, more amenable version of herself. As far as musical influence is concerned, her bold incorporation of house and soul styles into salsa greatly revitalized the scene, attracting a younger generation of Latinos and contributing to a resurgence of salsa's popularity in the mid-1990s.

Yet India's unusual career also has had wider ramifications beyond the mere logistics of the mainstream music market. With her unique strategy of infusing chusmería into her performance practice, India effectively colonized one of the most conservative popular Latin dance scenes, salsa, as an arena for challenging established norms of gender roles. Her complex process of disidentification was manipulated consciously to the extent that it became a means of self-empowerment, yet one that notoriously threatened to subvert her own range of control precisely because of its fundamentally transpersonal mode of operation. The ultimate effect was to orchestrate a virtual theater of social identity, in which sexual differences beg to be considered less as stable institutions than as parodic forms of double mimesis, allowing for a sustained critique of society's naturalized representations of ideal gender.

6

"They are going to hear this in Puerto Rico. It has got to be good!"

The Sound and Style of Salsa

"It's not a rhythm, or a melody, or even a style. Salsa was, and still is, a Caribbean musical movement."[1]

—Johnny Pacheco

"To many displaced young Latinos all over the world—it is home, a flag, a grandma . . . it is a cultural place where they can belong, a socio-political movement, a platform to tell our stories . . . Salsa was the force that unified diverse Latino and other non-Latino racial and ethnic groups . . . It is a concept. An open, ever-evolving musical, cultural, socio-political concept."[2]

—Willie Colón

Attempts to define salsa abound in both the popular and scholarly press. Indeed, the metadiscourse concerning salsa seems obsessed with formulating definitions that both accentuate specific affiliations and affirm genealogies, while avoiding any limiting or binding stipulations. Remarkably, even labeling salsa as a type of "music" is often omitted from such efforts (too limiting!). This fluidly evasive discursive dance is readily apparent in the words of the bandleaders quoted above; salsa is portrayed as a "movement" and a "concept," among other things. Scholars engage in similar strategic positionings. Such writers as Angel Quintero Rivera, Luis Manuel Alvarez, and Jorge Duany posit salsa as a "mixture of mixtures," preferring to accentuate the intercultural exchange involved in the music's production and consumption (Rivera and Alvarez 1990, Duany 1996). Duany further states, "Salsa is neither a musical style nor a particular rhythm, but a hybrid performed mostly by Puerto Ricans in New York and on the island . . . an amalgamation of Afro-Caribbean traditions centered around the Cuban *son*" (Duany 1984: 187). Roberta Singer counters, salsa is a "particular style of playing and instrumentation that is based on a variety of older musics that have been redefined and reinterpreted in the salsa format" (Singer 1983: 139). Juan Carlos Quintero Herencia prefers to read salsa as revolution and resistance, a practice of interdicted nationality, thus engaging a discourse of oppositional politics: "Salsa not only crosses borders, but corrodes them, convocating listeners not as citizens but as friends engaged in the 'open conspiracy' of forging an 'auditory free territory in the Americans'" (Quintero Herencia 1997: 28). Lise Waxer aptly points out that the global reach of salsa extends beyond the "Americas," operating in cultural milieus that are constructed in opposition to the places and cultures most often associated with the music (the Caribbean and Latin America): "Salsa is also a gateway to the cultural Other, a fascinating and often exotic world where new selves find liberation from cultural strictures" (Waxer 2002: 3). These representatively broad statements strategically favor vagueness and cultural hybridity, remaining open and unsedimented for future reinscriptions and imaginings. However, for music that often is linked to specific cultural identification and nationalistic agendas, the opaqueness of the discourse surrounding this music is striking. In some ways, it is a normal response for musicians, fans, and advocates to resist bounded definitions and stipulations; on the other hand, it is indicative of the modern cultural milieu from which the music emerged. This consciously constructed unlocatability serves utilitarian needs that facilitate the very pliable cultural and national affiliations that are part and parcel to salsa performance.

In recent anthropological work on the Caribbean, "transnational circulation" and "hybridization" have become central tropes of inquiry, where creative blending, the flow of people and cultural artifacts, and the layered inscriptions of meaning with which these result are accentuated (García-Canclini 1990; Basch, Schiller, and Blanc 1994; Benítez-Rojo 1996; Hall 2003b). It is at the nexus of these movements and flows that Duany urges scholars to locate their studies of popular music in the Caribbean, following "the lead of many of their informants, whose lives, identities, and musics are increasingly transnational in form and content" (Duany 1996: 189). Following that lead, we must acknowledge that the "mixture of mixtures" in salsa occurs on the local, regional, national, and international levels, and that these distinct levels are not disparately bounded entities, but rather engaged in a dialectical relationship—thus, the nature of transnational flows and circulations. Furthermore, the range with which people generically bind and unbind salsa and the diversity of interpretation and signification involved in salsa performance, along with the discourse around that performance, are indicative of salsa's fundamental relationship with such global processes.

Undoubtedly, salsa inhabits a contested space marked by increased identity fragmentation and migratory relationships. The salsascape is mapped with boundaries that are not solid (were they ever?), but rather smudged and porous (Feld and Basso 1996). Waxer notes, "Salsa's rapid spread through Latin America during the 1970s, followed by its adoption in Europe, Japan, and Africa during the 1980s and '90s, has similarly posed the need for considering this genre in terms of multiples sites of production and reception . . . style and meaning are contingent to local historical processes" (Waxer 2002: 6, 8). This is certainly the case even within the various communities of New York City, Puerto Rico, and other "originary" locations, as each performance setting is inflected and shaded by the unique social dynamics at play in any given circumambient space of music-making. Though salsa is undoubtedly a combination of styles, what I feel to be most significant are the particularities that are privileged in any given performance and how groups choose to bind or unbind the music. This chapter concerns itself with such issues, particularly how sound structure, *clave*, and music style are implicated in these identificatory processes.

From a musician's perspective, structurally and stylistically salsa seems fairly easy to delineate. Its unique rhythmic structure serves as its most identifiable feature. Salsa performance practice in New York City is fairly standardized and rather stable, and it has been so since the 1970s. When ownership, ethnicity, and nationhood get drawn into the discussion, however, things become blurred. Then again, as soon as any delineation of structure and style is attempted, these seemingly marginal issues already operate at the core of any such analysis. Though many have attempted through the analysis of song texts to show how this discourse functions (Rodríguez 1988; Manuel 1995; Waxer 2002; among others), I choose to take a different approach, attending to the more broadly understood dialectical relationship between sound and cultural forces. Through an analysis of various elements of salsa's sound structure, I explore how salsa's rich intercultural production reverberates sonically in ways that microcosmically play out larger cultural processes. I argue that the fundamental intercultural historical undergirding of the music enables a wide range for interpretation and inscription, making it pliable to serve as ethnic code, nationalistic pride, and essence for a wide variety of people. Specifically, the following discussion explores elements of salsa's sound structure by examining performance practices associated with the predominant style of the late 1980s and 1990s—*salsa romántica*. The role of clave in salsa performance, as well as the relationship between New York and Puerto Rican salsa, are central to this discussion.

Before addressing deeper analytical issues, some preliminary descriptive remarks concerning salsa's formal structure, instrumentation, playing techniques, and performance practice are in order. Throughout the 1940s and into the early 1950s, a definitive and distinct New York City–based, Latin dance music performance practice emerged, forged primarily by the orchestras of Machito, Tito Rodríguez, Tito Puente, and, to a lesser extent, Arsenio Rodríguez.[3] These groups combined older Cuban genres (e.g., son, *guaracha*, mambo) with big band jazz, developing norms of performance practice, composing, and arranging that remain fundamental to New York salsa performance. The intercultural exchange central to their performance practice, fostered by the unique ethnic mix of the city, certainly is key to understanding the foundational sounds of salsa. Indeed, the collaborative efforts of newly arrived Latino immigrant groups with older established African American and European American communities throughout the twentieth century have been well documented (Roberts 1979; Glasser 1995; Loza 1999; Flores 2000; Fernandez 2005).

Salsa Form

One characteristic that the above-mentioned bands developed in the 1940s that has remained relatively standardized and unchanged over time is the basic formal structure used in salsa arrangements. Almost all arrangements employ some close variation of the bipartite form most prominent in *son*, a Cuban genre popular among New York bands throughout the middle of the twentieth century. In a traditional setting, *sones* consist of main themes or tunes, which have predetermined lengths and often are in a variety of standardized song forms, such as AABA or verse-refrain. This is followed by an open-ended improvisatory section known as the *montuno*. Montunos employ call and response structures in which a lead singer alternates with a chorus. Standard salsa arrangements build upon this structure (see Figure 6.1, below). Usually a salsa song will open with some type of instrumental introduction, which is then followed by the statement of the main theme. An improvisatory section, called by the same name as its antecedent—the montuno—will then follow the theme. The montuno's most identifiable feature is a repetitive harmonic and rhythmic vamp (two, four, or eight measures in length) played by the rhythm section. The harmonic structure of montunos is generally a simplified derivation of the chordal structure established in the main theme. Over this rhythm vamp, as in sones, vocalists perform in a call and response fashion, alternating between a precomposed chorus and lead vocal improvisations. Several contrasting instrumental sections that feature the horn section will interrupt this open-ended section. The first, derived from one of salsa's stylistic antecedents, is a precomposed instrumental section called the mambo.[4] The mambo is often characterized by a heightened intensity in energy and sound, where intricate and virtuosic

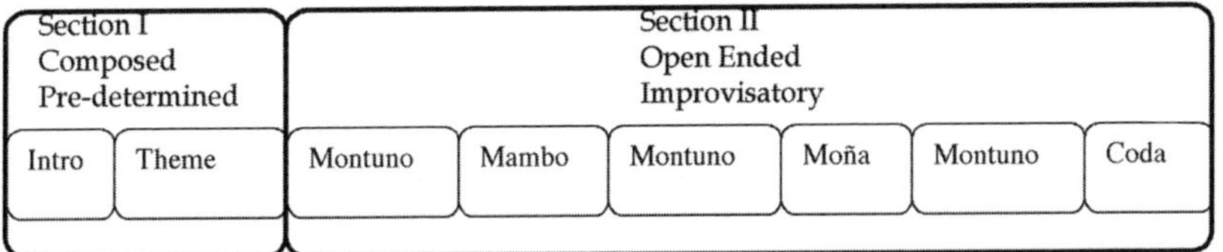

Figure 6.1 Standard form of a salsa arrangement.

horn-writing is featured, and it often incorporates rhythmic breaks played homophonically by the entire group. The mambo serves as an occasion for the arranger to introduce new material, often including a brief harmonic shift for contrastive effect. At the completion of the mambo, the montuno returns either in its original state or in a slightly abbreviated form (i.e., a shortened chorus statement). Additional instrumental sections called *moñas* (literally, hair curls)[5] are often included. Moñas either can be precomposed or spontaneously and collectively improvised by the horn section. Due to their improvisatory nature, moñas tend to be shorter rifflike vamps in which the horn section layers contrasting melodic lines that result in a buildup of energy and excitement. The montuno returns after each one of these sections. Instrumental solos featuring one or several instruments can occur over moñas or during montuno sections. Most arrangements include a closing section, known as the "coda," which often revisits material from the main theme.

The instrumentation of salsa bands is derived from earlier Cuban ensembles, such as *conjuntos* of the 1920s (small groups that played son). These bands typically included *tres*, guitar, bass, bongos, trumpet, maracas, and vocals. During the 1940s and 1950s, bands based both in Cuba and New York gradually changed this traditional lineup, often dropping the tres and guitar, and adding congas, *timbales*, piano, larger horn sections, and more vocalists. The particular roles each of these instruments assumes within an ensemble are also adapted from salsa's musical antecedents.

The Rhythm Section

A typical salsa rhythm section includes three to four percussionists (playing congas, bongos, timbales, a variety of cowbells, and hand percussion), a bass player, and a pianist/keyboardist. A full drum set or parts from it, such as a snare and bass drum, occasionally are added and played by the timbale player (*timbalero*). The percussionists provide the underlying rhythmic pulse and drive upon which the other instrumental and vocal parts are layered. The rhythmic interlocking that results from three or four percussionists working together as a unit provides one of the most identifiable features of salsa. The basic patterns the percussionists play are notated in Figure 6.2, below.[6]

Typically two congas (*tumbadoras*) are used and played by one musician (the *conguero*).[7] The lower-pitched drum (the *tumba*) most frequently is tuned to a G (below middle C), and the higher-pitched drum (the conga) is tuned to middle C. The conga pattern (the *tumbao*) is two measures in length and serves as the basic pattern throughout a performance (see Figure 6.2). Players often vary this pattern according to the context of the composition, often mixing in *bomba*, *plena*, and *rumba* patterns as well as solo flourishes. Striking the drums with their hands, congueros produce a variety of sounds, including open tones, muted tones, and slaps.

The bongo player (*bongocero*) alternates between playing the bongo drums—a pair of small, double-headed drums (the higher-pitched drum is referred to as the *macho*, or male, and the lower-pitched drum is called the *hembra*, or female)—and a large cowbell (*cencerro*). The bongos are tuned in octaves at a higher pitch level than the congas (tuning varies from player to player). Similar to the congas, the bongos are struck by the hands to produce a variety of sounds. During the statement of the main theme and during piano solos, bongoceros play the *martillo* (literally, hammer) pattern. The martillo serves as the rhythmic foundation upon which the bongocero spontaneously invents embellishments that are meant to dialogue with (or *repicar*) and musically support the vocal melody or piano soloist (see Figure 6.2).[8] During the brass and woodwind solos, and during the montuno, mambo, and moña

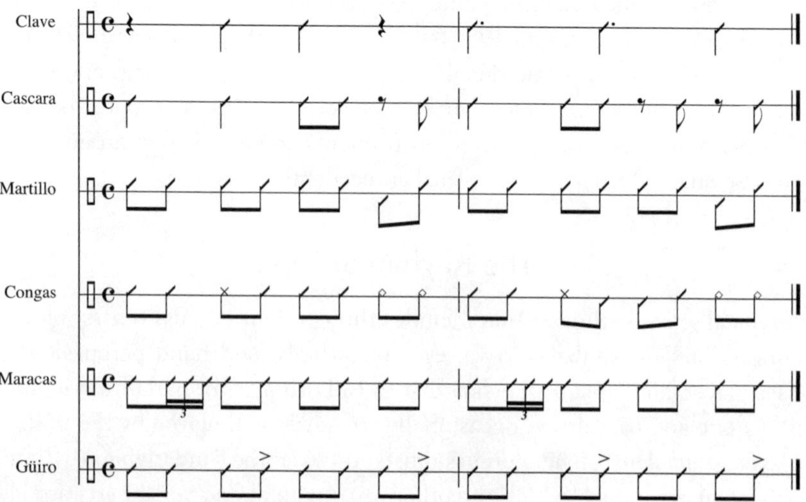

Figure 6.2 Basic percussion patterns played during the verse.

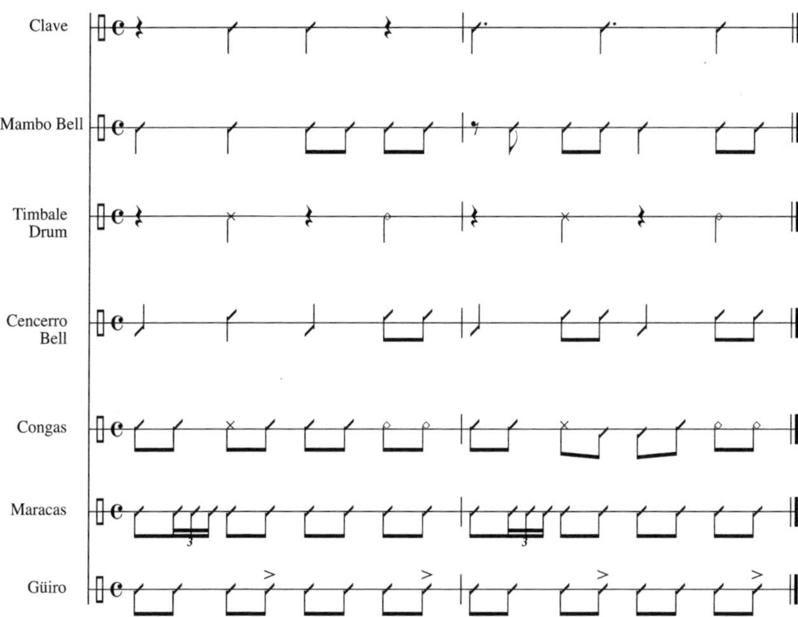

Figure 6.3 Basic percussion patterns played during montunos.

sections, the bongocero switches to the cencerro bell, on which the *campana* pattern is played (see Figure 6.3). The bell is held in one hand and struck by a short thick wooden stick held in the other. By manipulating the handheld bell, open ringing and closed muted sounds are produced.

The timbales (*pailas*) consist of two drums mounted together on a stand (they are often tuned with the same intervallic and pitch relationship as the conga drums), two cowbells (the mambo bell and the smaller cha-cha bell), one or two cymbals, a clave block, and occasionally a high-pitched snare drum. The timbalero strikes these instruments with two thin, dowel-shaped wooden sticks. During the statement of the main theme and during piano solos, the timbalero plays the two-measure *cáscara* pattern (see Figure 6.2). Cáscara (literally, shell) refers to the physical location on the drums—the outer surface of the body of the drums—where the pattern is played. During the montuno, mambo, moña, and wind solos, the timbalero begins striking the mambo bell with one stick, playing the "mambo montuno ride pattern," and the lower timbale drum is struck with the bare hand, alternating between a muted stopped sound and a ringing open tone (see Figure 6.3).[9] This pattern change coincides with the bongocero's shift to the cencerro bell. The result of two bells sounding concurrently is dynamically louder and, thus, used for the more energetic sections of the arrangement. Often a simultaneous slight hastening of the tempo—what percussionist Johnny Rodríguez calls "agitating the ride"—occurs with the introduction of the bell patterns, enhancing the effects of the increased energy level. At times the clave pattern will be played on the clave block in lieu of having the bare hand strike the timbale drum. Each timbalero varies these basic patterns in unique ways, responding to accents in the vocal melody, the precomposed horn parts, or to an instrumental soloist's improvisation. Rhythmic punctuations and fills (brief percussion solos) often are improvised using a combination of cymbal hits and strikes on the drumheads with sticks. Each percussionist is expected to improvise in a similar fashion by individually adding variations to these basic patterns and by collectively creating "rhythmic breaks" (rhythmic punctuations that demarcate the ending and beginning of the various sections within an arrangement). Extended percussion solos routinely are included during salsa performances. Additional hand percussion, which include maracas, guiro,[10] or claves, most often are played by vocalists (their basic patterns are notated in Figure 6.3).[11]

The preferred keyboard instrument used in salsa recording is the acoustic piano. Since most performance venues do not own pianos, however, synthesizers or electric pianos are the norm in live performances.[12] An auxiliary synthesizer player may be added to provide effects and to enrich timbres. The basic repeating rhythmic pattern played by the pianist is referred to as a *guajeo* (and sometimes montuno). These figures are typically two to four measures in length and outline the harmonic structure (see Figure 6.4). Each salsa arrangement has its own unique guajeo, and each pianist personalizes these patterns by adding notes and varying the rhythm to various degrees. The main function of the piano is to contribute to the rhythmic drive of the percussion section by playing these repetitive rhythmic figures that interlock with the various percussion parts. This rhythmic style of playing may be preempted with chordal accompaniment figures during the statement of the theme if the arranger calls for a more subdued and sparse texture. During extended improvised solos, pianists are free to play in a more melodic fashion.

Drawing upon the Cuban son, the harmonic structure of salsa traditionally has favored a single tonal center, primarily using unaltered diatonic chords (i.e., I, ii7, iii7, IV, V7, vi7, and vii°), with particular emphasis on I, IV, and V7 chords (as in Figure 6.4). At times, chordal movement that rapidly oscillates between the tonic and dominant, or between the tonic, subdominant, and dominant, will account for all of the harmonic content used throughout an arrangement (another borrowing from son). However, the influence of jazz and popular music styles, especially on more recent salsa styles, is evidenced by the now common practice of using ii7–V7 chord progressions, tritone substitutions, inverted chords, and the upper chordal

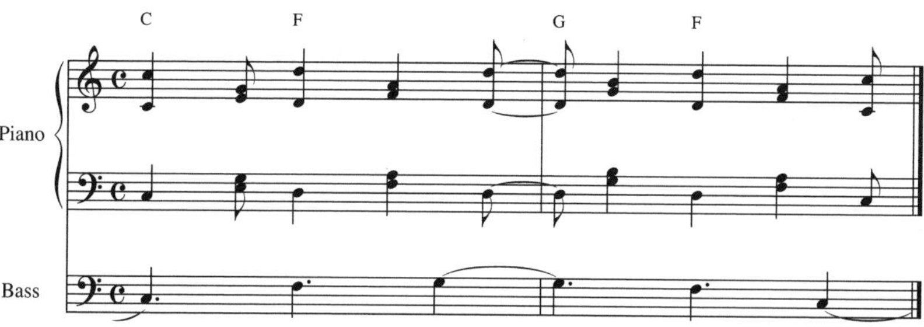

Figure 6.4 Piano guajeo with bass tumbao.

extensions and alterations. Generally speaking, one distinguishing characteristic of *salsa romántica* is the frequent incorporation of complex harmonic progressions.

Salsa bassists use either an electric bass guitar or an upright solid body baby bass, both played with amplifiers.[13] Live performance mixes are bass heavy, and meeting those needs requires substantial amplification equipment. The bass's primary function in salsa is rhythmic. Indeed, its standard repeating pattern shares the same name as the conga pattern, the tumbao (see Figure 6.4). In a variety of Cuban traditions this bass pattern was played on a percussion instrument—the *marímbula*, a large low-pitched *mbira-* or *sanza-*like instrument of Congolese origin. This pattern serves as the foundation upon which bassists add personalized embellishments, though they never stray far from this basic rhythmic configuration. The pattern's most identifiable feature is an emphasis on the fourth beat of each measure and the avoidance of articulating downbeats. This creates a unique vertical alignment within the harmonic structure, because the bass tumbao pattern anticipates any harmonic change that is notated on the downbeat. In Figure 6.4, notice how the bass consistently anticipates the chord change before the piano guajeo changes. Peter Manuel contends that this "anticipated bass" is "perhaps the single most distinctive feature in Afro-Cuban popular music" (Manuel 1985: 249).[14] Further, the anticipated eighth-note tie into the third beat of each measure also anticipates harmonic changes that are notated on the third beat.

Piano guajeos tend to alternate between anticipating the harmonic change by one eighth-note before the downbeat and then firmly changing chords on the downbeat every other measure. This alternating pattern coincides with the clave rhythm (which I discuss later in this chapter), where the downbeat attack occurs in the two-stroke measure and the anticipated bar occurs just before the downbeat of the three-stroke measure. This results in a degree of momentary harmonic tension and release within each measure of music, contributing to a "driving motion" within the salsa groove that propels the music forward. The degree of harmonic tension between the bass and piano parts also alternates in each measure from one-quarter note to one-eighth note of difference. This continual and alternating harmonic tension creates what Manuel describes as "a desire for the corresponding harmony of the next bar. At the same time, the weak stressing of the downbeat, when it does arrive, undermines its potentially cadential effect, such that the rhythm in effect 'rides over' the downbeat . . . the deliberate avoidance of the downbeat also lends to the rhythm a unique flow and momentum which make it ideal for the supple and fluid salsa dance style" (Manuel 1985: 255). Basic salsa dance steps do indeed correspond to this by often initiating steps on beats two and four, deemphasizing downbeats.

Additional rhythm section instruments in salsa bands, though found with less frequency, include the tres, violin, electric guitar, and the *cuatro*. The tres is a guitarlike instrument with three double courses of strings that is played primarily in conjuntos, an older and smaller instrumental format. The function of the tres is comparable to that of the piano—that is, playing guajeos and being featured as a solo instrument. Violins are integral to salsa bands that favor the *charanga* style, which employs a more subdued, less brass-heavy sound.[15] Like the tres, violins play guajeo-type repeating figures and are featured soloists. Electric guitars and the Puerto Rican cuatro (a small-bodied guitarlike instrument) occasionally are featured solo instruments as well.

Vocals

Most salsa songs are sung in Spanish. The lyrics are clearly enunciated and mixed by sound engineers in a forward and present manner in both live performance and recorded mediums. Typically, there is one lead vocalist per group; occasionally, two or more will share the duties, especially if the bandleader is an instrumentalist who does not sing. During the 1990s, most bandleaders were vocalists and, subsequently, the focus of arrangements remained centered upon featuring them. The duties of a lead vocalist include singing the melody of the composition (the verse) and creating *soneos*. The soneo, sometimes referred to as the *inspiración* (inspiration), is a textual and melodic improvisation that occurs during the montuno. These improvisatory phrases usually alternate with the *coro* (chorus), an unvaried repeated precomposed phrase, in a "call and response" fashion.

Though love and romance typically are the lyrical topics of salsa romántica, other topics include incitations of cultural pride, social commentary, and allegoric stories. Salsa lyricists have considerable freedom in their poetic choices (rhyme schemes and topical construction). Songwriter Lino Iglesias commented, "There is no standard format that we use in salsa. For me, and I think it is the same with many other composers, my choices have to do with the feeling, the emotion of the song. Sometimes I use rhymes, sometimes nothing rhymes in the lyrics. Sometimes I write in stanzas, sometimes not. Every song is different" (L. Iglesias, pers. comm.). Likewise, there are few restrictions on the subject matter of the improvised soneos. These often include comments derived from the coro, statements concerning the topic of the song, commentary on events taking place during the performance, limericks and rhyming jokes, or political commentary and social criticism. During soneos, I have heard singers (*soneros*) improvising texts that admonished musicians who were drunk and played poorly, and even texts that arranged a date with a woman in the audience. The melodic content often is derived from the melodic construction of the coro, or main theme, though introducing new and unrelated melodic material is acceptable. The soneo is the place where singers can show off their creativity, displaying their musical and textual improvisatory prowess. Commenting on the content of soneos, singer Ismael Rivera explains, "The *sonero* is like a poet of the common people/masses. A *sonero* must make a history of the chorus presented, without losing the theme. You must know the language of the populace, because you have to interweave things from our daily life. You have to be part of the common people, so that you may reach the common people. You have to use the words that are being used in street corners" (Flores 1997: 9).[16]

There is no "typical" vocal type or quality preferred in salsa. However, stemming from older Cuban styles that featured high, tenor-range male voices with a nasal timbre, singers who sing in this fashion still predominate. As singer Johnny Rivera explains, this style serves utilitarian needs as well as aesthetic concerns: "Singing salsa, especially in New York, you need to sing loud with a lot of high notes all night. And that's not easy. So when I was young and first trying to have my voice make it through the night, singing all those high notes, and having it cut over loud bands, I figured out a trick where I would sing through my nose . . . It made singing higher easier and my throat didn't get as tired. I could hear myself a lot better, too" (J. Rivera, pers. comm.). With the growing influence of popular music styles among younger salsa singers in the 1990s, many emerged with a smoother, less nasal, pop-oriented crooning style, such as Marc Anthony, as well as singers influenced by soul and R&B, such as Huey Dunbar from Dark Latin Grooves (DLG).

The coro is sung by at least two, but preferably three, vocalists. Extra vocalists are hired to fill these positions, or instrumentalists will double as coro singers (*coristas*). These vocalists provide backup vocal effects during the verse and also sing the harmonized precomposed responses (the *coros*) to the soneos during the montuno. Salsa coro harmonies tend to outline diatonic triads. In addition to singing, coristas often play hand percussion and supply improvisatory choreography to enhance the show.

The Horn Section

The horn section usually consists of a combination of three to five players playing trumpets, trombones, and occasionally saxophones (the baritone saxophone is the most common), but this varies greatly from group to group. When flautists are included, they provide improvisatory fills throughout performances and are featured as soloists. The horn section plays mostly precomposed parts, some improvised horn riffs known as moñas, and improvised solos. Like the coro, the horn section often is encouraged to supply improvisatory choreography. When the horn section plays the precomposed parts during the main body of the composition, their function is primarily to provide musical support for the lead vocals. Arrangers accomplish this by writing background melodic and chordal figures or rhythmic figures, sometimes referred to as "punches," that accentuate key points in the text or melody, or by writing instrumental interludes that provide transitional material between vocal sections (e.g., between the verse and refrains or between the main theme and montuno sections). The horn section shifts from a supportive role to a primary one during the mambo, precomposed or improvisatory moña sections, and improvised solos. These sections often include the most intricate horn writing in which both the arranger's prowess as well as the horn section's competence can be featured. These instrumental sections provide a respite from the demanding vocal parts, a means for extending the arrangement (a necessity in live performance to accommodate dancers), and contrasting shapes and textures to the performance. The horn section manipulates the energy shifts so integral in the dynamics of live performance. Often, moments of energy buildup occur during the instrumental sections of an arrangement.

Stage Setup

The stage setup (shown below in Scheme 6-1) during a performance reinforces the tripartite structure of the salsa band. Each section occupies a row across the stage: vocalists in front, rhythm section in the middle, and horns in the back (see also Figure I.1 in the Introduction).

This utilitarian setup promotes musical coherence by enabling musicians within each section to hear one another clearly and to maintain visual contact. Sonic coordination is a persistent concern in salsa due to the excessively loud stage volumes and inadequate sound systems used in most clubs. The rhythm section's centrality in establishing the groove is reflected in its centralized location. The essential relationship of the bass and conga tumbao patterns, with both instruments emphasizing the fourth beat, requires that they be placed next to each other. Similarly, the piano and bass, which jointly

Scheme 6.1 Typical stage setup for a salsa band.

supply the harmonic material, are placed side by side. The timbales and bongos are in close proximity to one another to facilitate the interlocking and synchronization of their bell patterns.

Their predominantly supportive role places the horn section at the back of the stage. However, some bandleaders invite horn players to the front during solos to spatially highlight their temporary functional shift. In a horn section that includes two trumpets and two trombones, the lead trumpet player establishes the phrasing for the entire section (when only trombones are playing, the lead trombonist will assume those duties). Their respective leading roles place them together. This facilitates expedient transmission of musical decisions made by the first trumpeter to the first trombonist, who will then pass the information to the second trombonist. A highly competent horn section follows this chain of communication within a split second to achieve the desired result: a unified body of sound where intonation, timbre, attacks, sustains, and releases are executed in a synchronized fashion. A commonly heard compliment paid to highly competent horn sections is, "That horn section is tight. They play like one player!"

The foregrounding of vocalists in salsa performance is reflected by their physical position at the front of the stage. Because they are most visible to audience members, they commonly execute intricate choreography. Ray Sepulveda comments, "The singers are in front, in full view of everyone, and it doesn't look good if they are just standing there, especially when they are not singing. People come to see a show, so you have to give them one" (R. Sepulveda, pers. comm.). Often bandleaders who are not vocalists, such as percussionists Ray Barretto and Johnny Zumont, place themselves in the front line and move vocalists off to one side to emphasize their significance. Remarks by bandleader Tito Puente, who established the present-day stage set, shed light on the functionalities of his decision:

> I was the first to move the horns to the back of the band and the percussion forward. It was really just by accident that it happened. After I started my own band in the '50s, my partner, trumpeter Jimmy Frisaura, said that every time I gave a cue the entire band had to look back at me. Musicians would miss my cues. He suggested that I stand in front so they could see me better, and, besides, it was my band! I moved the other percussionists up close to me as well so we could hear each other better. After that, everyone started to copy my setup. It made sense because there were so many bandleaders who were percussionists, such as Mongo Santamaria and Ray Barretto. (T. Puente, pers. comm.)

As Puente's comments illumine, considerations concerning the staged presentation as well as highlighting the hierarchy within the band structure are involved in the stage setup; however, musical considerations are also central. The large membership of salsa bands requires intricate coordination and execution of musical parts over a relatively large space, and the setup described above facilitates musical negotiations that result in what salsa musicians refer to as playing with "*sabor*" (taste or flavor, meaning "playing with the right feel and sentiment") and "*afinque*" (a musical state that refers to playing rhythmically, precisely, solidly, virtuosically, locked together, and grooving hard).

Clave: What to Listen for and What to Comment On

Key to playing with sabor and afinque is clave, the fundamental rhythmic structure of salsa that has been inherited from the Cuban son.[17] Clave is a rhythmic concept found in a variety of Latin American musical styles, though it is predominantly associated with Afro Cuban musical traditions. In Spanish, "clave" literally means key, clef, code, wooden peg, or keystone. Claves are two wooden sticks struck together to produce a high, piercing sound.[18] In Latin music terminology, the word "clave" refers not only to these instruments, but also to specific rhythmic patterns associated with them and the underlying rules that govern these patterns. All musical and dance components in salsa performance are governed, to varying degrees, by the clave rhythm.

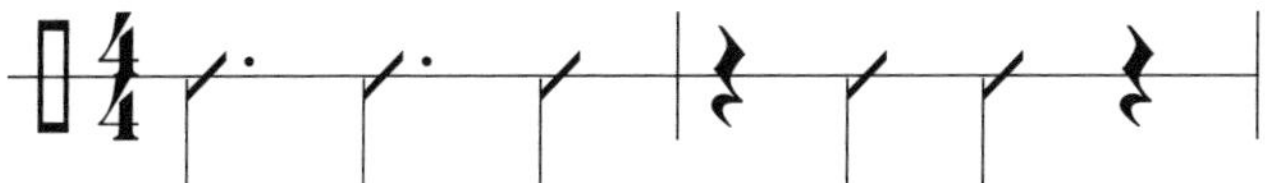

Figure 6.5 Son Clave (3-2).

The clave rhythm most often found in salsa is known more specifically as the "son clave," denoting its central role in the Cuban son tradition.[19] In performance, the clave may be stated overtly by someone playing the claves, or implied by the other instrumental parts without the actual playing of the sticks or block. Competent salsa musicians develop a "clave sense" that is reminiscent of what Richard Waterman labels a "metronome sense," whereby a subjective pulse serving as an ordering principle is felt by the participants in a musical event (Waterman 1952). Each participant must maintain this clave sense throughout a performance for the proper (i.e., acceptable to *salseros*) execution of the music. I have observed bassist Johnny Torres tapping his foot on beats one and three while simultaneously chewing gum to the clave beat. Steve Cornelius observes that the clave pattern is two measures in length "in which each measure is diametrically opposed. The two measures are not at odds, but rather, they are balanced opposites like positive and negative, expansive and contractive, or the poles of a magnet. As the full pattern is repeated, an alteration from one polarity to the other takes place creating pulse and rhythmic drive" (Cornelius 1992: 23). If adhered to in a competent fashion, the clave provides the rhythmic momentum, drive, and swing in salsa.

In a salsa composition, adherence to certain rhythmic placement criteria insures the piece to be "in clave." Ignoring those criteria will produce rhythmic passages that clash with the clave framework; such passages are said to be *cruzao* (crossed) and disruptive to the flow of the music. Cuban composer and musicologist Emilio Grenet succinctly states the importance of clave adherence:

> Going into the rhythmic structure of our music we find that all its melodic design is constructed on a rhythmic pattern of two measures, as though both were only one, the first is antecedent, strong, and the second is consequent, weak . . . This adaptation of the melodic concept to the rhythmic pattern is manifested in such a manner that the change of a measure in the percussion produces such a notorious discrepancy between the melody and the rhythm that it becomes unbearable to the ears accustomed to our music. This is what Cubans, employing a very graphic term, call getting in the way (*atravesarse*) . . .

> The alteration of the rhythmical order is of absolute anti-musicality. (Grenet 1939: xv–xvii)

A more contemporary perspective is offered by arranger/trumpeter Willie Ruíz: "You know if it is in clave by how it feels . . . if the phrase makes the tune swing and groove and the music drive, then it is. If it feels awkward, then it isn't" (W. Ruíz, pers. comm.).

The following are general guidelines to determine if a music phrase is in clave and to which measure of the clave it corresponds:

1. Accented notes correspond with one or all of the clave strokes.
2. No strong accents are played on nonclave stroke beats unless they are balanced by equally strong accents on clave stroke beats.
3. The measures of the music alternate between an "on the beat" and a "syncopated beat" phrase or vice versa. The last eighth note of the two-stroke measure is often tied to the first beat of the three-stroke measure to accentuate the syncopated clave measure.
4. A phrase still may be considered in clave if the rhythm starts out clashing but eventually resolves strongly on a clave beat, creating rhythmic tension and resolution.

The phrasing of the melody determines which measure of the clave will be played first (e.g., where the accented rhythms of melody occur). This is referred to as either 2-3 or 3-2, meaning either the measure with the three-strokes is played first with the two-stroke measure following, or vice versa. Once a song begins, the clave does not change its measure order (e.g., a 3-2-2-3 clave sequence is rare and was considered inappropriate by salsa performers in the 1990s). Its function, similar to that of bell patterns found in West African musical traditions, is to provide a rhythmic formula that serves as the foundation for the performance.[20] As Singer states, "clave is a rhythmic time line that . . . functions as a rhythmic organizing principle for the entire ensemble" (Singer 1982: 168).

Clave Analysis

In order to demonstrate how the clave affects the musical components in salsa performance, an excerpt from a José Febles arrangement of "Vamonos de Rumba," performed by Conjunto Clásico (Lo Mejor Records LMR 817), has been transcribed. This arrangement was chosen for its adherence to the clave rhythm and because of Febles's prominence as an arranger. The transcription

Figure 6.6 Excerpt from "Vamonos de Rumba."

is copied directly from Febles's original score, which included the trumpet, piano, bass, and percussion parts. In addition, I have notated the corresponding clave rhythm on the bottom staff. In this example, the clave is not actually played, but rather implied from the instrumental parts. To an informed listener, a 2-3 clave pattern is distinguished easily by the rhythmic structure of the opening two measures.

Notice that in the first measure, the trumpet phrase accents the third beat. This corresponds with the second stroke of the two-stroke measure. The motive played by the rhythm section in the second measure resolves firmly on beat four, corresponding to the third stroke in the three-stroke measure. The second stroke of the three-stroke measure, the "and" of beat two, is also played. Notice how the brass and rhythm section parts interlock with the clave strokes. Each measure includes one to two corresponding rhythms; an "x" denotes each concurrence. It is evident that the clave serves as a skeletal structure upon which the various instrumental parts are constructed. "Vamonos de Rumba" is in clave.

Figure 6.7 Interlude from "Cali Pachanguero."

Another example, one that is demonstrably cruzao, is provided for contrast. This is an arrangement of "Cali Pachanguero" performed by the Colombian salsa band Grupo Niche (Globo Records 9878-1-RL). Though there are several discrepancies, the most blatant crossing occurs in the interlude notated in Figure 6.7. The transcription includes the vocal melodic line, the clave rhythm, and "x" notations demarcating clave correspondence.

Up to this point, the arrangement has remained in 3-2 clave, with the exception of a short ambiguous introduction. Abruptly, this interlude begins strongly in 2-3, creating the crossed clave. Notice the lack of clave correspondence in measures 1 and 3. Measures 4 through 11 return to a 3-2 configuration, only to be crossed once again in measure 12. This situation is disruptive for dancers who are aware of the tradition. Just as an arranger writes each note in relation to clave, a skilled dancer measures each dance step in relation to the clave rhythm. Commonly, older dancers and musicians, who tend to be more aware of traditional dance steps, will not dance to this song. Moreover, I have often witnessed these same older dancers and musicians alike "getting down" with ease to the arrangement of "Vamonos de Rumba." In the Febles arrangement, at least one stroke of the clave corresponded with an accented note in the instrumental parts in each measure. In "Cali Pachanguero," three of the twelve measures notated do not have any correlation to the clave strokes.

The reasons for the crossing of clave in "Cali Pachanguero" are unclear. Coming from Colombia, the arranger may not have understood the use of clave as well as the New York–based Puerto Rican Febles. Perhaps the arranger viewed other musical factors as taking precedence over adherence to the clave and made a conscious decision to depart from conventional practice. Whether it was the result of a shrewd artistic decision or serendipity, "Cali Pachanguero" became 1989's biggest salsa hit. Its popularity, in spite of its "musical discrepancies," is indicative of striking stylistic changes that marked the salsa of the late 1980s and 1990s.

I now turn to examine those changes by focusing on issues of musical style and performance practice associated with salsa in the 1990s. These practices, like form and instrumentation, are rooted in older traditions, but, as with clave, they also differ in that they encompass particularities that are illustrative of more recent trends and cultural processes.

Style and Practice of Salsa Romántica

Salsa of the late 1980s and 1990s incorporated significant stylistic changes that differentiated it from earlier styles.[21] The processes that brought on those changes were complex and both musical (music structure) and extramusical (contextual). Some include the dynamically interdependent relationship between the New York and Puerto Rican salsa scenes; the rapid globalization of salsa's popularity and production; economic pressures, such as the drive to sell records and RMM Record's monopoly on salsa-recording and concert-promoting; the influence of other popular music forms; immigration patterns in New York City and in Puerto Rico; the cultural and linguistic "Americanization" of Latino youth in New York City; and attempts to reestablish or reaffirm cultural roots through salsa performance. The diversity and dynamic nature of such processes demonstrate that style and performance practice encompass so much more than bounded, static, and purely musical considerations and must be seen in this light. The work of Steven Feld is particularly instructive here for conceptualizing style within a larger social framework. He writes:

> [S]tyle is more than the statistical core reflection of the place or time, or patterned choices made within constraints. It is the very human resources that are enacted to constitute the reality of social life in sound. Style is itself the accomplishment, the crystallization of personal and social participation; it is the way the performance and engagement endows humanly meaningful shape upon sonic form. Style is an emergence, the

> means by which newly creative knowledge is developed from playful, rote, or ordinary participatory experience. Style is the way an internalization and naturalization of felt thoughts and thought feelings guide experience. (Feld 1988: 107)

The social factors so integral in determining the means with which participants negotiate and navigate stylistic possibilities must be included in any conceptualization of style and practice.

What emerged from the confluence of these processes was a new salsa style and aesthetic, known as salsa romántica, that remained dominant through the late 1990s. This newer style and aesthetic distanced itself from the preferred "hot" and hard-driving dura sound of the 1970s and early 1980s ("playing like you have a gun to your head"), and instead embraced a milder, more subdued attitude. The differentiating features of salsa romántica were highly polished and slick studio productions, smooth vocal quality (i.e., less of a nasal or harsh quality that was so prominent in salsa dura), a controlled and refined brass sound, subdued percussion playing in a laid-back fashion, a looser adherence to clave, much less improvisation, the predominance of song texts featuring romantic themes, and often "pretty boy" crooners who were chosen as bandleaders/sex symbols. Along with salsa romántica came a homogenization of style as performance practices became more standardized and the variation in stylistic possibilities limited. The standardization of practices was caused, in part, by the centralization of the salsa recording industry.

Beginning in the late 1980s, RMM Records controlled the majority of recording activity and its production preferences resulted in fewer stylistic possibilities and less variation in sound. RMM established two main production centers, New York City and Puerto Rico, and the producers in both locales favored using a select group of studio musicians along with a limited number of arrangers. These practices differed from the established recording techniques used by Fania Records in the 1970s, where musicians who regularly performed as group members recorded on band albums. After the late 1980s, band members rarely participated in the recording of their respective groups' commercial releases. With virtually the same group of musicians and arrangers in each locale backing every new singer/bandleader, diversity in sound between recordings was limited, which resulted in a standardization of style for both New York and Puerto Rican salsa. Often one studio musician's personal style of playing or one arranger's writing preferences quickly became common practice after appearing on numerous recordings. With two main centers of production that each had its own group of studio musicians, however, two distinct sounds developed within salsa romántica that distinguished the New York and Puerto

Rican productions. Additionally, a unique dynamic emerged between both locales as each competed for work and sonic dominance.

Newer recording techniques borrowed from pop music recordings were adopted in both places. The highly polished studio production techniques included overdubbing and layering each instrumental and vocal part individually (where only one musician records at a time), incorporating synthesizers for orchestrational enhancement, using advanced digital technology to provide reverberation and ambience, and using digital computer-editing tools to manipulate pitch and temporal discrepancies. These techniques rendered the final products virtually impossible to reproduce in a live performance due to monetary and technical constraints. The sound quality, including such aspects as ambience and reverberation effects, was impossible to emulate without a sophisticated sound system and an engineer who knew how to operate it, both of which were too costly for most salsa clubs. This departed from traditional salsa-recording contexts wherein musicians could interact spontaneously with one another as they recorded all their respective parts simultaneously, simulating live performance (a common practice in Fania productions). In the view of some critics, this led to the deadening of the recorded medium's performance quality.[22] Producer Sergio George comments on the newer recording trends: "Music is not as free as in the '70s because society is not as free. So there is less improvisation in the music . . . plus people listen to pop music on the radio, that sound is what they are used to. In order to sell records, I record with the guys that will give me that sound, though I try to leave some looseness in the music to keep it fresh. If it is too clean, it sounds sterile" (S. George, pers. comm.). This points to the significant role that sound quality and mass mediation play in structuring music genres, determining what is heard and listened for and informing the various cultural affiliations associated with those sounds (e.g., musical improvisation equaling or mirroring societal freedom).[23] George's comments demonstrate that decisions made in the production of salsa are complex affairs that simultaneously must attend to market forces; artistic sensibility; and the local, national, and transnational trends of the music industry. In line with the work of Louise Meintjes, who has pointed out that timbre is an essential ingredient in the process of linking politics to aesthetics and key in the production of feeling (Meintjes 2003: 13), it is through the micromanipulations of sound in their studio productions that salsa producers work to achieve their artistic and commercial goals.

George's comments indicate that commercial pressures were central in determining his sonic choices. The performance and sonic standards he, as well as others, adopted were set by formulaic Top 40 productions heard on the radio (a real departure from the gritty street sound of salsa dura). As salsa began to recover from its commercial lull of the early 1980s, and its popularity grew, producers increasingly became wary of taking the financial risks involved in attempting something new. Instead, they preferred to rely on the proven successful formula of the salsa romántica style. Variations in style, tempo, instrumentation, artist's image, and topics of song texts from band to band were greatly reduced. In 1992, bassist Johnny Torres commented, "It is difficult, if not impossible, to be different or original in the music today, it doesn't matter what musicians think or how good the music is—the only thing that counts is if it sells" (J. Torres, pers. comm.).

The importance placed on vocalists and their extramusical sexualized images was also adopted from pop music practices. As a result, fewer instrumentalists were signed as bandleaders in the 1990s; instead, RMM sought singers who had images they could market. Recording contracts sometimes were awarded based on marketability rather than on musical merit. Inexperienced, amateur singers frequently were placed in positions that historically had been held by well-seasoned salseros. No longer were accomplished musicians leading bands. Instead, singers who often had little technical knowledge of music and conventional salsa performance practice found themselves fronting the orchestras. This affected the music structure in several dramatic ways. The first aspect of the music that changed was the ability of lead vocalists to *sonear* (to improvise soneos). Percussionist/bandleader Barretto commented, "Gilberto Santa Rosa, because he came from Willie Rosario's band, is one of the few new singers who can really improvise—most of them have lost that art form."[24]

Historically, spontaneously improvised solos and moñas by horn players provided a means for extending selections, yielding longer music sets to accommodate dancers. Their spontaneity also brought a freshness and excitement to the shows. However, additional solos and moñas required more soneos per song. The inexperienced singers of salsa romántica tended to cling to the original formats of their recordings (by singing the same soneos as on the record) and were unable to invent new ones. Because of the lead vocalist's inability to improvise, song structures in live performance were predetermined, strictly limiting improvisation and the spontaneous invention of moñas, and, thus, lasting a radio-friendly four minutes (not ideal for dancing in clubs). The virtuosic instrumental solos featured by the salsa groups of the 1970s and early 1980s were phased out, and the role of the salsa band became more focused on supporting and featuring the lead vocalist. Eddie Palmieri comments on these newer trends:

> We still have good singers like Gilberto Santa Rosa and Tony Vega, and orchestras that are quite well structured, but the era of the highly exciting dance orchestra has disappeared . . . in the last 15 years, the salsa *sensual* and salsa *erotica* [these names are at times used interchangeably

> with *salsa romántica*] has been completely destructive to the health of the orchestras, because the orchestrations are being superimposed by a recording company that is completely unqualified . . . the orchestrations are that way because they are being dictated to: either you record this way, or you don't sell a record . . . but now they suppress the orchestra, and here comes this unprepared talent . . . now you have got a Jerry Rivera that's popular, and Frankie Ruíz. These young artists are not musicians, and there are very few of them who are even interested in learning how to sing. All they can do is lead to more destruction of our music. (Birnbaum 1994: 17)

Timbalero and bandleader Manny Oquendo adds:

> Let me say something first about today's singers. In my opinion they cannot be compared with the real soneros such as Machito and Tito Rodríguez. These people today memorize a couple of inspiraciónes and they develop a set singing routine and that's it. They are not the *soneros bravos de verdad* [real soneros]. Some of the music I hear is real Mickey Mouse. I guess it's all right for people to accept it. Maybe it's only the lyrics that they like. The fact is that there is no one around like Tito Rodríguez . . . Besides that, if you watch the bands play, it's really monotonous. No one takes a real solo, it's always the same routine. (Figueroa 1997: 23)

These comments represent the pervasive attitudes held by the older generation of salseros concerning the stylistic changes of salsa romántica. They viewed these developments as a move toward the routinization of performance practice and loss of artistic adventurousness, individuality, and spontaneity, and a move away from long-established traditions. However, for the next generation of salseros, this move to align salsa with pop music practices revitalized the salsa scene, opened new commercial avenues and opportunities, and created an original voice for the next generation of Latino youth. Salsa dura was the music of their parents; romántica was something they could claim as their own. Romántica revived salsa in New York and Puerto Rico during the 1990s and led the way for a third generation of salseros who would eventually rediscover the grittiness of dura through their interest in hip-hop and rap.

Clave as Concept

The generational and cultural tensions that are part and parcel of the stylistic evolution from dura to romántica are often played out through contestations concerning clave. Along with the stylistic changes associated with salsa romántica, clave similarly has undergone some significant changes, which in turn have sparked heated contestations and revealed a dynamic picture of the conceptual framework in which it operates. Rather than a static musical attribute dictating style and performance practice, clave emerges as a dynamic and socially charged concept. As a concept, clave encapsulates a continuum of ideas, beliefs, meanings, understandings, and interpretations held by, in this case, participants in the New York salsa scene. The concept reaches far beyond the music structure, as demonstrated by the following excerpt from the inside cover of the first issue of New York's *Clave* magazine, published throughout the 1970s:

> Clave . . . To us the word goes beyond explanations and definitions. It means life, salsa, the food of our leisure time, the motion of intense rhythm, the emotion of 20,000 people simultaneously grooving to the natural sounds of life. It's being in beat, on key, on clave . . . It means to be on top of things, to be playing it right, no matter what it is.
>
> To have clave means to really have something. Having a clue, a direction, the key to the solution. Clave is in our blood, in our minds and hearts. It runs in the streets in syncopated beat with our children as they let it loose upon the top of cars, the sides of bottles, on their kneecaps. To have it is to be happy, to share it is to give love and to keep it for a lifetime is to die in peace.
>
> Clave is history, it's culture. African drums from far off places like Nigeria, Dahomey, and Ghana married the Spanish guitar to bring us clave. The seeds were planted in the Caribbean and now their grandchild is Salsa.
>
> Our parents, and their parents before them, understood clave. They lived with it, made love with it and held it close in times of despair. They kept clave in their hearts and passed it down to us. (Anon., ca. 1977)

This declaration effectively illustrates how clave, within the salsa context, is a negotiated, multilayered symbol that embodies ethnicity and issues of identity, and functions as a gauge for judging authenticity. It also serves as an apt lens through which to explore generational differences, intercultural tensions, and stylistic changes. Mirasol Berrios-Miranda points out that "*ritmo* [rhythm] . . . is an important marker of difference and distinctiveness in salsa" (Berrios-Miranda 2000: 148), and it is rhythm, especially relating to clave, that often functions as the point of contention between musicians, criteria for evaluating the ability of other musicians, and a means for asserting philosophical and cultural ideas through musical expression. However, unlike the generalized and all-encompassing view presented in the quote from the *Clave* magazine, participants in the New York salsa scene paint a more subtle picture. The relationship of clave to each participant is at times uniquely individualistic. As the excerpt above suggests, though, the performance of clave is a living and breathing tradition shaped by the performance practice of individuals. Each musician contributes to the proliferation and evolution of that tradition by his or her own subtle variations of feel and nuance. These differences are often motivated by economic, political, and other cultural factors.

Some changes in the role of clave in salsa performance are tied to the advent of salsa romántica style and were prompted, in part, by the younger and culturally more diverse audience of the late 1980s and 1990s. This was the result of RMM's expansion into new markets throughout Latin America, Europe, and Asia; the growing populations of non–Puerto Rican Latino immigrants in New York City bringing their own musical traditions (e.g., Dominican merengue and *bachata*); and the prominence of rap and hip-hop among inner-city youths, particularly second- and third-generation Nuyoricans. With this new generation of dancers, listeners, and consumers, new criteria arose for judging the music that diverged from traditional ones, and these criteria did not always include considerations of clave. As a result, dance traditions loosened; clave-based dance steps slowly were replaced with other more stylistically generic ones, which often drew inspiration from specific cultural dance traditions that were not clave-based.[25] These new consumers did not always have access to formal lessons or to older family members to learn the traditions (for instance, the intricate salsa dance steps) of their newfound music. As they participated on the dance floor, their new inventions of bodily movement slowly and surreptitiously transformed those traditions in the process. For instance, performing in the predominantly Colombian salsa clubs in Queens, one noticed striking differences in dancing styles from those dancers who drew upon their rich *cumbia* traditions, which are not dictated by the clave pattern. Similarly, differences could be observed in predominantly Dominican clubs where merengue served as the foundation for many of the dancers' moves. The clave discrepancies in "Cali Pachanguero" often were viewed as insignificant by this expanded audience.

Interviews with musicians concerning clave reveal a wide diversity in definitions and ideas, rooted in a continuum between two divergent points of view that I label "traditionalist" and "innovationist."[26] The traditionalist stance concerns the adherence to established practices; each innovation in style is judged in terms of its relationship with past models. The conformity of newer practices to established norms is the goal of traditionalists, which, in some respects, limits the parameters of change in performance practices. I am using "tradition" here in the sense that Richard Handler and Jocelyn Linnekin describe: "We must understand tradition as a symbolic process that both presupposes past symbolisms and creatively reinterprets them. In other words, tradition is not a bounded entity made up of bounded constituent parts, but a process of interpretation, attributing meaning in the present through reference to the past" (Handler and Linnekin 1984: 287). In this way "tradition," with continual reinvention at its core, remains an emergent process, rather than a cemented structure (Ricoeur 1988: 221). The innovationist stance, on the other hand, privileges experimentation that pushes the envelope of acceptability. Crosscultural borrowing is often the preferred mode for musical innovation; along with it comes new criteria for judging the validity of those particular innovations. This judgment does not always include comparison with past models; rather, it often is judged solely on economic factors (specifically, how many records were sold).

In New York, the traditionalist approach most often is associated with Puerto Rican and Nuyorican musicians. Singer quotes an informant: "In the ensemble *clave* is the most important thing . . . If something doesn't fall into *clave* it doesn't work. If you don't have *clave* in a Latin rhythm section, then you don't have Latin rhythm—you have something else" (Singer 1982: 168). The quotation illustrates the centrality of clave that the traditionalist stance maintains. Note the all-encompassing use of "Latin," though her informants were primarily Puerto Rican and Nuyorican salsa and Latin jazz musicians. Referring to the tenacity of some Puerto Rican musicians adhering to Cuban music traditions, bandleader Frank "Machito" Grillo was widely quoted as saying, "Puerto Ricans are best at understanding and performing Cuban music." The "truth" may lie closer to the notion that traditionalist Puerto Ricans uphold a Cuban tradition reinvented by Puerto Ricans. Reinterpreting the Cuban traditions, the Nuyorican and Puerto Rican musicians transformed originally more fluid practices into stricter forms dictated by austere guidelines. Cuban percussionist Mongo Santamaria, responding to a question about clave, corroborates, "Don't tell me about 3-2 or 2-3! In Cuba we just play. We feel it, we don't talk about such things."[27]

Along with salsa romántica came the incorporation of a variety of non-clave-based musical styles, such as pop, hip-hop, R&B, and soul. As arrangers struggled to "fit" these music styles into the salsa format, a variety of "clave discrepancies," or clashes, like in "Cali Pachanguero," often resulted. As the salsa style became more culturally diverse, Nuyorican and Puerto Rican traditionalists often reacted by emphatically positing clave as representative of, or essential to, Puerto Rican cultural identity, affixing an unprecedented amount of cultural significance to the rhythm. This enabled them to appeal to cultural preservationists concerning the urgency of preserving and upholding "the clave tradition" as something essentially Puerto Rican in order to combat what they viewed as the proliferation of newer, less culturally specific, and, for some, culturally threatening practices. According to Panamanian bassist Guillermo Edgehil, this traditionalist stance among New York musicians was a relatively new phenomenon: "In the 1950s and '60s, nobody cared like they do now. In the mambo days the clave, at times, changed in the middle of the song. The systematization of the percussion parts comes from Puerto Rico, not Cuba. Playing the same clave from beginning to end of an arrangement is a Puerto Rican practice" (G. Edgehil, pers. comm.). Arranger Ray Santos confirms this notion: "Clave always played a role, but it was not as strict as some people think today" (R. Santos, pers. comm.).

The contrast between traditionalist and innovationist stances caused a contentious and revealing debate during a rehearsal of the Tito Rodríguez Jr. Orchestra in 1993. Santos had reorchestrated Harold Weigbright's 1960 arrangement of "El Moldo de las Locas," originally written for and recorded by the orchestra of Tito Rodríguez Sr. (*Live at the Palladium*; West Side Latino L31067). The coda contained a phrase with a 3-2-2-3 clave configuration. It sounded wrong to the ears of the younger musicians. An argument ensued as to whether a measure should be added to compensate. The older musicians who had played for Rodríguez Sr. stated that this was not abnormal and the rhythm section used to just switch and play the 3-2-2-3-2-3 combination. The younger musicians, accustomed to strict clave guidelines, were uncomfortable with the configuration. Outnumbering the older musicians (forty-plus years of age), they insisted that the arrangement be changed. Santos returned to the next rehearsal with the additional measure included. In this case, the traditionalist stance upheld the strict clave adherence by not performing the composition in its original form, but by alternating the structure to adhere to the "newer traditional" constructs, replacing the older established performance practice in the process.

Sergio George, the A&R (Artists and Repertoire) representative of RMM Records and the busiest and most influential arranger in salsa from the mid-1980s to mid-1990s, embraced an innovationist stance. He opined:

> Though clave is considered, it is not always the most important thing in my music. The foremost issue in mind is its marketability. If the song hits, that is what matters. I don't write music for musicians. When I stopped trying to impress musicians and started getting in touch with what the people on the street were listening to, I started writing hits . . . Some songs, especially English ones originating in the United States, are at times impossible to place into clave. This makes some sections of the tunes ambiguous in their relationship to the clave. (S. George, pers. comm.)

He also added that his favorite group in salsa was Grupo Niche because of its "originality," and that the crossing of clave in "Cali Pachanguero" did not really bother him.

Many traditionally minded musicians frequently complained about George's arrangements because of their clave discrepancies. Percussionist and arranger Louie Ramírez said that the last time he saw George, he condescendingly asked, "Hey Sergio, what do you think clave is? Probably just two sticks, right?" Ramírez claims he personally banned George from producing his last record because of his "disregard for the tradition" (L. Ramírez, pers. comm.). Regardless, George's productions and arrangements were the most popular through the late 1980s and into the 1990s. He was responsible for most of the crossover attempts to reach the English-speaking market, arranging popular songs with English lyrics in the salsa style. His efforts culminated in the 1991 release of the successful *Salsa in English* recording (RMM Records, RMIC 80553). He also produced and developed the sounds of Tito Nieves, La India, and Marc Anthony by mixing pop, R&B, soul, and hip-hop music into the salsa format. As his arranging style became prominent, the studio musicians he hired had to practice tolerance and to adjust when necessary, prompted more out of financial necessity than from an ideological stance. When faced with playing something cruzao, percussionist Marc Quiñones commented, "Yeah it's messed up, but that's what he wrote and that's what he wants, he's paying, so we just play it" (M. Quiñones, pers. comm.).

Marc Anthony is a product of George's innovationist approach. As a novice to Latin music, he was propelled into a bandleader position with little knowledge of how the music was structured. One revealing moment came during a performance in 1994, just after he had launched his salsa career. During a piano solo, he approached the timbales, picked up a stick, and attempted to play clave on the clave block along with the band. It became apparent that he had no idea where to place the rhythm. The timbalero quickly demonstrated where to place the strokes and played along to assist Anthony. Shortly thereafter during a radio interview in San Juan, Puerto Rico, he exclaimed that his commercial success proved that you did not need to know about clave to make it in Latin music. This comment caused an uproar among musicians and critics alike, both in Puerto Rico and in New York. Bassist Abiúd Troche reacted by stating, "[T]here are still a lot of people in Puerto Rico who still believe in clave" (A. Troche, pers. comm.). After receiving the bad press, Anthony refrained from discussing the subject in public, and he did not attempt to play clave on stage until he had received some private lessons.

Ricky Gonzalez, who in 1995 replaced George as one of the most active arrangers after George left RMM Records, holds a traditionalist stance

(Ramírez chose Gonzalez over George for his last production). Clave is so central to his writing and performing that, while playing at an Orchard Beach concert in New York with Sepulveda's band, an audience member began playing clave sticks cruzao directly behind him. Shortly after the audience member began, Gonzalez became so distracted that he forgot the chord changes of the tune and had to quit playing piano to tell him to stop. He has also earned the nickname "the clave police" among horn players and percussionists whom he admonishes when they play crossed. As an outspoken critic of George's discrepancies, he maintains that clave is a central concern in his arranging style:

> I have too much respect for the music's history. You can trace clave and the rhythms back to Africa. It is bigger than any one of us. Who is anyone to ignore this tradition? All the percussion parts are built from those fundamental rhythms. To change what is played on top of them is changing the rules. Ignoring the established tradition disrupts everything. They disregard and dismiss the clave because they lack the humility to admit that they do not really understand its complexity. Even with all my experience and accomplishments, I slave over every note I write and keep expanding my knowledge of clave and writing in its tradition . . . The commercial success of arrangers who ignore these traditions is deceiving. It is not their ability to write in clave that brings them success. (R. Gonzalez, pers. comm.)

Unlike George, Gonzalez incorporates many musical styles in his arrangements while maintaining a strong sense of clave. As his commercial success grew in the late 1990s, so did his influence among other New York arrangers, such as Willie Ruíz and Pablo "Chino" Nuñez. Many of the top Puerto Rican arrangers, such as Humberto Ramírez and Tommy Villarini, wrote and arranged with similar clave perspectives during the same period; thus, an equally vital traditionalist approach was sustained during George's successes. Arranger Carlos Jimenez commented, "Everyone is concerned about clave. The clave police are out! You have to be concerned about everything you write" (C. Jimenez, pers. comm.). During a rehearsal for trumpeter Ray Vega's debut Latin jazz recording, the band noticed a cruzao section in one arrangement. The conguero remarked, "You know this is your first recording. People are going to hear that and start to talk!" Reacting to that criticism Vega stated sardonically, "Let them talk. I don't believe in clave anymore, I quit it!" (R. Vega, pers. comm.). He then proceeded to rewrite the chart, bending under the pressures stemming from this heightened concern for clave amongst musicians and arrangers.

Clave as Identity

Writers such as Adelaida Reyes Schramm (1975), Roberta Singer (1982), Laurie Sommers (1991), and Vernon Boggs (1992), among others, have written about the various ways clave serves as a cultural "boundary marker" in music and how it can play a central role in the identity politics involved in music-making. For salsa musicians, this manifests in myriad ways. For example, Singer writes, "As an objective feature it marks off Afro-Caribbean music from other musics, while as a boundary marker its execution allows performers to define and evaluate the performance of others who are playing the music which is so central . . . The mere performance of music played . . . in clave is a symbolic communication of some kind of Latino identity or affiliation and identification with, at the very least, Latino musical culture (Singer 1982: 169, 214). Singer is correct that salsa musicians and informed listeners alike use the adherence to clave, and the originality of that adherence, as a means for appreciation and evaluation of performances. The issue of boundary marker, however, may not be so clear considering that there are many Afro Caribbean traditions that do not incorporate clave. A serendipitous interchange I had with several salsa musicians during a set break suggests that a rethinking of "boundary" may be in order. As I read an article concerning universals in music, the musicians inquired about the text. After briefly explaining the issues involved in the articles, they unanimously concluded that the only universal in music was clave. They were not exclusively referring to Afro Caribbean music, but to all genres of music. As examples they mentioned "Magic Bus" by the rock group The Who, and Bo Diddley's trademark groove, both of which use the son clave rhythm. They also cited African and Middle Eastern music traditions, and numerous North American pop tunes that are conducive to being performed in the salsa style (some of which George had arranged). Determining if this claim of universality is viable is not pertinent to this discussion. What is significant, though, is that these musicians had acquired a "clave sense" that stretched far beyond Afro Caribbean traditions and functioned as a way of hearing. The "boundary marker" quality of clave must in some way include its function in the perception of music. Salsa musicians can, in some respects, be identified by how clave functions in their perception of music. It is what they are listening for.

The clave rhythm also can be used for communicative and identificatory means. When my doorbell rings with the clave pattern, I know a salsa musician is at my door. Walking down Eighth Avenue in New York City and hearing a car horn beep clave, I know it is directed at me (bandleader Barretto was at the wheel). Their use of the rhythm reinforces the common connection to the clave tradition of both parties (knocker/beeper and receiver), each identifying with and through the rhythm. During a performance event, audience members will clap the clave rhythm to communicate with performers. This most often occurs when requesting an encore, desiring the concert to begin, or as a spontaneous participatory gesture communicating enthusiasm and appreciation. One example occurred during a performance by Isidro Infante's band at an outdoor festival in Brooklyn in July 1996. The band was delayed, causing the audience to grow restless. As the musicians began setting up, audience members shouted lewd comments concerning the band's tardiness. To diffuse tensions, the emcee responded by asking everyone to clap clave to demonstrate their readiness for the show to begin. Meanwhile, band members expeditiously readied themselves. The comments were drowned out by the clapping, and the performance began without further incident. During the first composition, Infante invited the audience to clap clave to accompany his piano solo. In this case, clave served several purposes. First, it channeled energy that swiftly was becoming negative into a positive outlet, hastening the musicians' setup and drowning out the negative comments. Infante then used the rhythm to include listeners in the music-making process. This built enthusiasm and transformed those negative jeers into positive hollers of appreciation. Clapping clave at a concert in sync with the performing musicians provides for group participation in music-making even to a novice. However, the messages transmitted can be, and often are, imbued with more meaning than simply, "Let's all participate!" A newcomer to salsa, whether performer, dancer, listener, or consumer, must acquire some level of clave competence before engaging in these "clave dialogues" in a deeper, more significant way.

Clave as Cultural Weapon

Frances Aparicio maintains that "expressive cultures have offered Latinos in the United States a space for collective identification and self-recognition in the larger context of their invisibility within the dominant society," and that salsa functions as "a cohesive force among Latinos" in the United States (Aparicio 2004: 356). This is true in many situations, but not all, and this type of observation ignores the often-hostile clashes between Latino communities that can be so prominent in salsa performance. The force with which clave can elicit communal feelings in performance settings, such as the one described above, can be used equally for divisive and exclusionary purposes. One revealing incident occurred during a performance with Sepulveda's band in a Peruvian bingo hall dance in Washington, D.C., when the Peruvian emcee disrupted our set by coming on stage to make a long announcement. In order to rile up audience enthusiasm, he encouraged them to clap clave. He started in 3-2. However, the band's road trip from New York to Washington had been arduous. The promoters had hired a bus that was in disrepair, with many broken seats and a putrid smell coming from the bathroom. The normally four-hour trip lasted almost seven because of continual traffic jams and the driver's getting lost. Once we arrived at the venue, we were made to wait four hours before performing because the promoters had informed us of an incorrect starting time to ensure our punctual arrival. The morale of the group was low. The emcee's interruption was viewed as disrespectful, and one of the percussionists had reached the limits of his patience. In a fit of anger, he began playing 2-3 clave extremely loudly on the clave block. The entire audience became confused, and the emcee was dismayed as this action immediately disrupted the clapping. The result was a lull in enthusiasm, the opposite of the emcee's intentions. I do not believe he realized why the percussionist had acted in that fashion. Regardless, in this instance clave was a weapon. When I questioned the percussionist about his action, he replied, "These people don't have a clue about our music!!!" Assuming an air of superiority, he said that "they stopped clapping because they thought they were doing something wrong." From his perspective and as a Puerto Rican, he was asserting his musical dominance over what he perceived to be a less "clave-informed" Peruvian audience.

Using clave to assert cultural dominance for exclusionary purposes is not such an unusual occurrence. In fact, clave typically serves as a marker between "insider" and "outsider," meaning those who "have clave" and those who do not. But it is not limited to this binary; it also is used to differentiate various levels of competency achieved by those posited as insiders. These distinctions are not only tied to musical ability, but also to the assertion of racial, cultural, national, and ethnic differences. For instance, during a recording session for Raulín Rosendo, Puerto Rican composer Ramon Rodríguez complained about the arrangement of one of his compositions. From his perspective the brass figures did not correspond with clave. Rodríguez said, "This arranger is Venezuelan. They don't understand the Puerto Rican style. These guys think they understand our music, but they write all cruzao and think they can get away with it" (R. Rodríguez, pers. comm.). He rewrote the arrangement. Another illustrative incident happened when Cuban conguero Daniel Ponce rebuked his entire band, which consisted of seasoned Puerto Rican and North American musicians, unhappy with how we were performing one night. He yelled, "You have to be black and Cuban to be able to play Cuban music. To understand it. To play in clave. You guys don't play shit!" Shortly thereafter we all quit his band (but that is another matter).

Panamanian flautist Mauricio Smith offers another perspective. Smith claims that he never allowed the clave rhythm to be played overtly in his band because he does not believe in it. He observes, "It is not something that you should talk about. It is just something that Latinos invented to keep North

Americans out of the music. In my day we never discussed clave" (M. Smith, pers. comm.). In line with this perspective and suggestive of how essentialized notions of cultural difference are very much operative in such contestations, often when non–Puerto Rican musicians lack clave competence, their deficiency is attributed to their otherness, but when Puerto Rican musicians lack competence, it is due to inexperience. For example, during a performance with Sepulveda, the musical director called for an improvised moña. The Puerto Rican trombonist next to me created one and taught the line to me moments before we played it. After several measures, it was clear there was a discrepancy with the clave. The timbalero threw up his hands and stopped playing. He proceeded to turn to the trombone section and cross his fingers (the cruzao sign). After the song ended, he exclaimed, "Leave it to the white boy to get crossed up!" (referring to me). When he was informed that the Puerto Rican trombonist was responsible for the crossing, he remarked, "Man, he needs to do his homework!"[28] It is widely held that clave is "in the blood" of Cubans and Puerto Ricans as a learned cultural behavior introduced through music during the formative years of childhood. Regardless, to actively participate in the salsa scene, both Puerto Rican and non–Puerto Rican salseros must contend with the issues of the clave concept in their "minds" and assimilate clave, to varying degrees, into their "hearts."

In summation, clave serves many diverse purposes within the salsa context. First, musicians use clave to construct musical compositions and improvisations, whereby its structural components serve as basic building blocks for the rhythmic content of a composition or solo. Second, the African-derived rhythms and concepts connect the music with past traditions by establishing a lineage of musical heritage from Africa to New York City, by way of the Caribbean basin. Further, clave serves as a gauge within that tradition for distinguishing between music that is aligned with traditional performance practice and music that wanders from established custom by the incorporation of innovative elements. It becomes a vehicle for evaluating salsa composition, arrangement, and performance, and, as documented above, it serves as a way to approach the music of others as well. Clave is what to listen for and what to comment on.

The New York/Puerto Rico Dynamic

I now examine the symbiotic relationship between the two main salsa production centers of the 1990s—New York and Puerto Rico. Historically, music produced in Cuba and played by Cuban musicians exerted the most dominant influence in Latin music performance in New York. As I have discussed above, much of contemporary salsa practice is modeled on older Cuban forms. After the U.S. government's 1962 establishment of the embargo against

Cuba, however, that influence slowly began to wane. Cuban shortwave radio programs still could be received in Puerto Rico, and Latin music radio programs in New York City, such as WBAI's Sunday afternoon broadcasts, often aired smuggled tapes of Cuban bands throughout the 1980s and 1990s; but live performance, touring, and collaborative musical interchange were reduced greatly. This is central to understanding how salsa of the 1990s is distinguished from its antecedents. Few salseros active in salsa romántica were old enough to have seen Cuban bands perform live, nor did they have access to musicians living in Cuba. The "roots" and "models" for this younger generation were not the Cuban bands from which the Fania-era salseros took inspiration; rather, they were the salsa dura bands of the 1970s, whose membership consisted of mostly Nuyoricans and Puerto Ricans. In this regard, Puerto Rico supplanted Cuba in terms of its influential thrust in the daily lives of salsa's music-makers.

Further, throughout salsa's history musicians from Puerto Rico and New York have maintained close relationships that were (and continue to be) interdependent and crossfertilizing, with each locale exercising influence over the other—so much so, that New York and Puerto Rican salsa should not be seen as separate entities, but as engaged in a dynamic and dialectic relation. This has been facilitated by the persistent interchange of arrangers and producers who worked on both New York and Puerto Rican productions simultaneously, and by bandleaders and musicians who traveled frequently between both locales for performances and to visit family and friends. Indeed, the close association of both places contributed to the uniformity of stylistic change in salsa performance practice throughout the late 1980s and 1990s. However, these interchanges exemplify what Ulf Hannerz (1989) labels "asymmetrical culture sharing" in that their relationship was complicated by a turbulent history of Puerto Rican and U.S. relations, perennial tensions between Nuyorican and Puerto Rican communities, and continual struggles to assert dominance of influence.

New York salsa in the 1990s shared a sort of duel citizenship between New York City and Puerto Rico. Even though salsa as a genre emerged from the cultural milieu of New York City, its business infrastructure remained centered there, and many of its subsequent stylistic developments were spawned in the city, salsa often was marked as representative of something essentially and authentically Puerto Rican. As such, Puerto Rico served as a marker for authenticity in salsa. For instance, since the 1970s, many Puerto Rican singers have relocated to New York to pursue their singing careers. Hector Lavoe serves as a prime example. Regardless of Lavoe's permanent residence in New York City, he routinely was introduced at performances as "coming directly from Puerto Rico." Since this certainly could not refer to the route he physically took to the gig (which in his case would have been the Long Island Expressway), it is indicative of what Aparicio discusses as "an ambiguous self-location on the part of the singing subject" (Aparicio 1998: 72) and for the other salsa performance participants as well. In other words, the economic and geographic realities of the salsa business and New York's role in the production of an "authentically" Puerto Rican music style were deemphasized; instead, the Puerto Rican-ness of the music and its performers were accentuated in the performance context. This Puerto Rican emphasis served as a marketing tool where audience members were told that they bought tickets for not just any salsa performance, but for a particularly authentic event because the singer came "directly" from Puerto Rico, not by way of the New York salsa business infrastructure. This advertising strategy reflected the desire of many Nuyoricans to reaffirm cultural ties with the Island and position salsa as a viable way to assert a shared cultural pride in an overtly public manner. It also mirrored the movement and flow between Puerto Rico and New York City and the bilocationality that is so fundamental to the experiences of Nuyoricans. As Wilson Valentín-Escobar points out, in this way Lavoe acted as a "floating trans-*Boricua*" embodying a "diaspo-Rican alterity" that embodies a "doubleness" that simultaneously conjures an authentic Puerto Rican identity along with a cosmopolitan diaspo-Rican New York presence (Valentín-Escobar 2002: 163).

Many of the most innovative salsa recordings of the late 1980s and 1990s were produced in New York City. At the same time, though, Puerto Rico played the role of gauge for, or judge of, those innovations. For instance, as George's productions grew looser in the mid-1990s, in his attempt to keep the music "fresh" (for example, leaving in slightly out-of-tune notes and rhythmically ambiguous passages instead of editing them to perfection) and in some ways musically more simplistic (having, his horn-writing began incorporating simpler rhythms and unison lines, as opposed to the rich harmonies and contrapuntal writing traditionally part of salsa), criticism came fast from Puerto Rican producers. Disregarding George's ability to produce numerous commercially successful recordings and motivated by the financial benefits of recording salsa productions in Puerto Rico, Puerto Rican producers, arrangers, and studio musicians collectively criticized his New York productions. Comparatively, the Puerto Rican productions favored a higher level of studio perfectionism and a more refined, mellow timbre than the New York ones. In some ways, these performance preferences can be traced to the influence of pianist Rafael Ithier, leader of El Gran Combo, one of the oldest and most established salsa bands based in Puerto Rico. Ithier's perfectionism in performance, and his polished, well-rehearsed, and conservative arrangements set the standard for many Puerto Rican salseros in the 1990s.[29]

New York–based bandleader Sepulveda remarked, "I am going to record in Puerto Rico for my next record because my producer Julito Alvarado said that he couldn't get that right sound with the New York players. He thinks that guys up here just don't care about the final product. Down in P.R. they take pride in the music and you can hear it in how tight they play" (R. Sepulveda, pers. comm.). The Puerto Rican producers equated pride and an elevated state of music-making with a cleaner, tighter, and highly perfected product. To George, this was a move toward homogeneity and "sterility," which was a criticism that ironically had been directed repeatedly toward him by older salseros. Responding to the criticism from Puerto Rico, George said, "The P.R. productions all sound the same, they're too clean. I'm interested in selling records, not in a perfect sound. They don't do anything for me, they sound dead" (S. George, pers. comm.).

Nevertheless, the result was that New York musicians acquired a reputation for not being as precise as their Puerto Rican counterparts, and in the mid-1990s some record producers, including those associated with RMM, began sending more productions to Puerto Rico, causing great financial loss for musicians, arrangers, and producers based in New York. For complex social and economic reasons, including issues of authenticity, identity politics, and the like, eventually the studio perfectionism and refined mellow timbre of the Puerto Rican productions became a standard for New York productions, especially after George left RMM in 1995 to form his own record company, Sir George Records. He claimed that his departure was due partly to the fact that he was tired of the salsa romántica style, especially with more and more artists demanding a Puerto Rican sound. He wanted to be free to pursue other stylistic possibilities in Latin music.[30] With George no longer controlling the New York production scene, New York arrangers and musicians were forced to adopt the Puerto Rican sound or suffer the loss of work.

New York–based producer and arranger Ricky Gonzalez adopted such a strategy, attempting to counteract the trend of recording in Puerto Rico and preferring instead to record with musicians he regularly performed with in the New York area. For instance, during a production for Danny Rojo, he explained that the record company wanted a Puerto Rican sound. Consequently, several Puerto Rican arrangers were hired to contribute arrangements, and the mixing session was scheduled in a studio in Puerto Rico. Gonzalez claimed that it was only after some difficult negotiation, promising that he could provide the sound they desired, that he received permission to record in New York. When I arrived for the recording, he stressed the importance of playing with the Puerto Rican trombone sound (in a mellow and refined way) and that the production needed to be of the highest quality. He exclaimed, "They are going to hear this in Puerto Rico. It has got to be good." The two trombone parts that I normally would have recorded in one eight-hour session took a grueling twenty-three hours over the course of three days. Each phrase was played several times and then polished so that the attack, sustain, and release of every note was executed to perfection. He approached each instrumental part in the same fashion. Upon his return from Puerto Rico, Gonzalez exclaimed, "We did it! They could not believe that this production was recorded in New York with New York musicians." After achieving the refined quality of the Rojo production, Gonzalez acquired numerous contracts for arranging and producing from Puerto Rican bands, and he was partly responsible for an increase in New York recording activity in the late 1990s.

The influence that Puerto Rico exerted on New York salsa, which extended beyond timbre concerns and recording quality to various other aspects of performance practice, produced conflicts and ambivalence among New York musicians. One illuminating example occurred in Sepulveda's band over a discussion concerning the band's uniform. Sepulveda had requested his band to wear suits and ties for a particular gig. Percussionist George Delgado complained, "This band needs a uniform. You never see a band in P.R. dressed like this, all different colored suits. It looks very unprofessional." Trumpeter Hector Colón responded sharply, "I hate this uniform shit, have you ever seen those bands from P.R.? They look like they bought their clothes at Kmart. This is New York. We are not in P.R." Delgado tried to persuade the band members that the common Puerto Rican practice of bands requiring all members to don the same clothing was a standard worth attaining. Colón's retort demonstrated the strong feelings that are spawned when Puerto Rican viewpoints clash with New York attitudes. Band uniforms are a contentious issue for New York musicians who often are forced to purchase clothing they dislike and clearly will not wear on any other occasion than when performing with the band that forced them to buy it. Vocalist Claudette Sierra responded to the interchange, "To hear George and Hector argue just reminds me that here in New York we talk, walk, and live differently, and this is reflected in the way we perform. In Puerto Rico there is more homogeneity, it's more conservative, and as a result there is less influence from other styles" (C. Sierra, pers. comm.).

The stylistic changes brought on by Puerto Rican performance practice also proved contentious. Historically salsa brass-playing favored a loud, full-bodied sound due partly to the necessity of horn players to project their sounds over large rhythm sections without sufficient electronic amplification. Not only did this serve the utilitarian need of being heard, but the fiery tones were in line with the "hot" aesthetic associated with the salsa of the 1970s. Comparatively, Puerto Rican salsa musicians, many of whom have been trained classically, preferred to play with a softer, more refined sound. As the Puerto Rican influence gained strength in the 1990s, timbre changes in the brass sound began to take place in New York salsa. Most recordings, such as the Rojo session, required a mellower refined tone instead of the older loud and strong approach. New York–based Robert Rodríguez, a Cuban American trumpet player, reacted to these changes: "This music [salsa] is dirty music. The guys in New York play it that way with a lot of strength and fire. In Puerto Rico they play too soft and gentle. That is not what this music is about. It's dirty" (R. Rodríguez, pers. comm.). These timbre differences also could be heard in the percussion parts to some extent. Timbalero Jeffrey Lopez observed, "You can always tell when guys from New York are playing percussion. There is that edge, a lot of fire" (J. Lopez, pers. comm.).

Further, ambivalent feelings were fostered between musicians from both locales due to the work lost when Puerto Rican bands toured New York and vice versa. When Puerto Rican–based bands visited New York City, bookings of New York–based bands often were preempted. In November 1995, for instance, Sepulveda's band had only eight scheduled gigs, five of which were canceled. When I inquired about the band's infrequent work schedule, Sepulveda responded, "Just look in the paper. There are at least five bands from Puerto Rico visiting this month. The promoters think they can sell more tickets with P.R. bands." The top Puerto Rican salsa bands traveled to New York several times throughout the year, staying up to two weeks at a time. Reciprocally, the relationship was seen as asymmetrical. New York bands rarely were invited down to Puerto Rico, with monetary factors usually given as the reason. Often New York–based singers traveled by themselves on promotional tours (i.e., radio interviews and lip-synch television performances) or performed with a pickup orchestra instead of bringing their New York musicians. My first tour to Puerto Rico came only after seven years of performing salsa in New York. I had been a regular member of India's band for nine months, and during that time she had three one-week tours to Puerto Rico, using a pickup orchestra while leaving her New York musicians behind. Only after repeated protests from her New York musicians was a tour organized. Of the five scheduled gigs, we played only three. The Puerto Rican promoters claimed that two were canceled because they were losing too much money, having to pay for her entire band to come down. They underpaid us for the tour and sent us home early. During that trip we alternated sets with Puerto Rican bands. Often there was little social interaction between the New York and Puerto Rican musicians in those clubs. Percussionist Bobby Allende observed, "They are not talking to us because they are jealous. They want to protect their scene. We are a threat. Many of them played in India's P.R. band, but now that we are here, they don't have that job anymore" (B. Allende, pers. comm.).

Despite the appearance of animosity, however, the salseros of both locales shared a mutual respect. Their relationship remained dynamically interdependent; each community carefully monitored the other, feeding and influencing the direction of salsa performance practice both in New York and Puerto Rico. During India's Puerto Rican tour, even though direct social interaction was lacking, both groups of musicians, Puerto Rican and New Yorker, remained near the stage and attentively listened to the others' performance. This intercultural monitoring played a key role in the evolution of performance practice, especially for New York salsa musicians since they often turned to Puerto Rico as a cultural symbol, geographic location, or musical ideal to reestablish or reaffirm the cultural roots of New York salsa. This often was accomplished by incorporating elements or gestures that were perceived as unique to Puerto Rican performers. I observed and unwittingly participated in one such intercultural exchange, inspired by a Puerto Rican practice that resulted in a change, albeit a rather limited one. I performed in Miami in March 1993 with Sepulveda; during the show, a Puerto Rican salsa band alternated sets with us. I noticed two peculiar embellishments that the trombonists in the Puerto Rican band, Rafi Torres and Tonito Vasquez, interjected throughout their performance. Maintaining the original melodic contour, they rhythmically reconfigured melodic motives that incorporated syncopation in the three-stroke measure of the clave. This was done by substituting staccato triplet figures in place of the precomposed rhythm. These embellishments most often occurred at the end of a repeated phrase. The first time a passage was played as the arranger intended, and the second time through, the passage was embellished. The two forms of the rhythmic change are notated in Figure 6.8, below.

The top staff provides the original prearranged melodic line. The second staff demonstrates the first type of variation. The syncopated rhythm in the

Figure 6.8 Tripletization.

second half of the first measure is changed to a quarter-note triplet figure beginning on the third beat. The third staff presents the second type of variation in which the quarter-note triplet figure is displaced by one eighth-note, beginning on the second half of beat three. I later discussed the technique with Rafi Torres. He commented, "I never played in salsa bands. I went straight from playing in hotel gigs to recording. So I approached salsa not from live performing but from just records. We play the way we do because it fits the lyrics better. More mellow . . . Tonito is a conga player and he plays very rhythmically. So we would discuss changing the parts to make them more rhythmically interesting, especially if we had to play a repeating figure several times. We alternate between what the arranger wrote and our version."

During the next Sepulveda set, I began incorporating the same embellishments. The rhythmic change was received with immediate enthusiasm from the other musicians in Sepulveda's band. They recognized the source of the embellishments (Torres and Vasquez were the two busiest studio trombonists in Puerto Rico and well known among musicians). It seemed the more I incorporated the embellishments, the better. The changes I included that evening and during the subsequent month, as I perfected the technique, remained a permanent part of Sepulveda's arrangements and were expected by the other musicians in subsequent performances. In November 1993 a new trombonist, Jose Davila, joined the Sepulveda band. Upon hearing the embellishments he exclaimed, "Man, you guys sound like a Puerto Rican band!" Being familiar with the technique, he found even more possibilities for the changes, and eventually the embellishments were included two or three times in each of Sepulveda's arrangements. In praise, percussionist Delgado commented, "This is the only trombone section in New York that has that Puerto Rico sound!" In January 1994 Davila left the Sepulveda band, and a slew of substitute trombonists played with the band until a permanent replacement could be found. As each one played, I was forced to teach him or her the technique to keep the arrangements sounding the same. In late January 1994, Davila and I were contracted to record for one of Gonzalez's productions. During a repeating moña figure, Davila suggested that we use one of the embellishments. We changed the figure to Gonzalez's surprise and ultimate approval. At Gonzalez's next recording session in February 1994, the embellishments had been notated into his arrangements. When I inquired about their presence, he commented, "I had to put them in because I know you would play them anyway. This way I decide where they go!" Arranger Willie Ruíz, trumpeter for the Sepulveda band, and Pablo "Chino" Nuñez, percussionist for Sepulveda, both began writing the figures into their arrangements as well. By July 1994, Gonzalez complained that everyone in New York was using the embellishments: "It is so overused. It's a cliché. Everyone has it on their records now. I have to write those triplet things in all of my arrangements" (R. Gonzalez, pers. comm.).

The incorporation of the embellishment into the Sepulveda repertoire was perceived as bringing the band more in line with Puerto Rican practice, something that was viewed as worthwhile, and, to some extent, prized. To my knowledge, no musician in Sepulveda's band ever discussed the embellishments with Torres or Vasquez; instead, they based their interpretations on their own perspectives and those shared by the other band members. Whether Torres and Vasquez intended the embellishments to be something uniquely Puerto Rican, serving as an identity marker for the Puerto Rican style, or if they viewed them simply as a means to add personal flavor to the music, asserting their own musical sensibilities onto others' music, was not considered. Their personal preference to embellish the music in that way, regardless of their motivation, was reinterpreted by the New York musicians as something authentically Puerto Rican. George M. Foster reminds us that "[t]wo components figure in this complex design (intercultural communication) namely, the range of presented fact and the cross-cultural interpretation of it. That is, no culture presents its full face to the other, and to the facade that is presented cross-cultural meanings are attached which may have little or no relation to their intracultural significance" (Foster 1960: 9). Margaret Kartomi concurs, "the use of foreign musical traits in a new context automatically implies that new musical and extra-musical meanings are attached to them, and innovative composers or other individuals in question do not necessarily understand these meanings in their native context, nor do they, of course, need to" (Kartomi 1981: 236). Indeed as the use of these embellishments spread to other New York salsa bands, they became marked as something specific to the Puerto Rican style of playing. For instance, when I began performing with India's band I attempted to add an embellishment in one of the arrangements. New York–based trombonist Jimmy Bosch was quick to reprimand me: "This is not a Puerto Rican band. We don't play that Puerto Rican way in this band. This is a New York band with a New York sound, so play it that way!" The "Puerto Rican-ness" of the embellishments was an unwelcome addition in the band of a singer who was attempting to foster a "bad girl from the Bronx" image accompanied by a hard-driving salsa sound reminiscent of the 1970s.

Navigating stylistic change in New York salsa throughout the 1990s has provoked many dynamic exchanges within the salsa community. Producers, arrangers, and performers align themselves either with older New York practices, the newer ones associated with George, or Puerto Rican–influenced ones. For instance, when Johnny Rivera telephoned to hire me, he said, "On my band we play the Puerto Rican way, ok? None of the loud Willie Colón playing." In contrast, during a hiring call by Johnny Colón, he said, "I need a trombone player who can play strong and make up moñas. Can you do that? These days I got to ask before I hire someone" (J. Rivera, pers. comm., mid-1990s). Others choose to locate themselves somewhere between the hot aesthetic of the 1970s and the milder style of the 1980s and 1990s, drawing from both. This can be seen in George's efforts to leave some looseness in his recordings, polished pop but with some of the "dirtiness," or Sepulveda's preference to label his brand of salsa "salsa *gorda*" (fat salsa)—that is, salsa romántica mixed with some of the hot aesthetic heard on the streets of Brooklyn, where Sepulveda grew up. Some of the newer New York–based bandleaders, such as Marc Anthony, attempt to find a balance within their music, using the two styles not as separate or opposing entities, but rather as two ends of a continuum consisting of numerous possibilities to be combined and explored. On mixing the dura style with salsa romántica, Marc Anthony comments:

> We do that on purpose, it's something that I love . . . I love listening to that music. But I'm romantic at the same time, so what happens? You combine those two elements and you get a "Nadie Como Ella." I think that marriage is possible, and I can combine both because that's where it is at for me. It's extremely fulfilling to play hard and fast, you know, that fat sound. That appeals to me and for the next one [recording] I'm planning to do more, but without losing the essence of what I feel and what I want to say, which is the sappy part of me. (Alvarado 1996: 10)

I began this chapter by documenting the wide range of interpretive definitions that attempt to bind and unbind salsa. For salseros, these contestations take place in their daily negotiations concerning style, clave, and performance practice. Through these everyday interchanges, one can witness the rich intercultural production that is so fundamental to the music. Salsa emerged from a long relationship with Cuban music, owing much of its initial stylistic parameters to Cuban performance practice. However this relationship was facilitated and colored by the rich cultural interchange within various Latino groups living and working side by side in New York City that, as diasporic communities, remain in dialogue with their respective homelands. For it is not only Puerto Rican and New York voices in the mix, but Colombian, Venezuelan, Dominican, Cuban, and every other group that claims a stake in the production of salsa that imbues it with a wide range for interpretation and inscription, making it pliable to serve as ethnic code, nationalistic pride, and essence for a wide variety of peoples. As such, salsa remains emergent and a productively contested space through which salseros assert, define, affirm, and explore who they are.

Appendix I

The following is a list of New York–based salsa bands or Latin music artists with whom I performed during the research and writing of this book, from 1990 to 2006 (listed alphabetically):

José Alberto, Tito Allen, Marc Anthony, Apocalypses, Ray Barretto, Mario Bauzá Orchestra, Ruben Blades, Wichy Camacho, Charlie Cardona, Milton Cardona, Antonio Cartagena, Orlando "Watussi" Castillo y Cartel de la Salsa, Santiago Cerón, Johnny Colón, Willie Colón, Anthony Cruz, Celia Cruz, Cruz Control, Dark Latin Grooves (DLG), Grupo Dinamita Internacional, Oscar D'Leon, Yorman D'Leon, Cheo Feliciano, Oscar Figueroa, Eddie Garcia, Sergio George and the Ralph Mercado Music All-Stars, Giro, Tito Gomez, Junior Gonzalez, Guianko, Paquito Guzman, Larry Harlow, La India, Isidro Infante, Joe King, Hector Lavoe, Lebron Brothers, Van Lester, Orquestra de la Luz, Manhattan Latin All-Stars, Victor Manuelle, Ismael Miranda, Tito Nieves, Louis Ogando, Luis "Perico" Ortiz, Grupo Oriza, Johnny Pacheco, Manny Pacheco Band, Palenque, Eddie Palmieri, Ray De La Paz, Miles Peña, Papo Pepin, Orquestra Porteño, Los Primos, Tito Puente, Domingo Quiñones, Louie Ramírez, Hector Ramos, Johnny Rey, Ricoson All-Stars, Johnny Rivera, Toby Rivera, Willie Rivera, Harry Rodríguez, Pete "El Conde" Rodríguez, Ramon Rodríguez, Tito Rodríguez Jr., Danny Rojo, Raulín Rosendo, Frankie Ruíz, Viti Ruíz, Ivan Sanchez, Victor Sanchez, Adalberto Santiago, Eddie Santiago, Pupy Santiago, Ray Sepulveda, Eddie Torres and his Mambo Kings Orchestra, Natalie Toro, Yomo Toro, Los Tremendos, Cuco Valoy, Xavier Vasquez, and Tony Vega.

During the years 1990 to 2006, my performance schedule included extensive touring with salsa bands throughout Central and South America, the Caribbean, Europe, the Canary Islands, and the United States.

Appendix 2

Compiled below is a list of salsa dance clubs (listed alphabetically), located in, within, or near the greater New York metropolitan area that programmed professional salsa bands at least once a week during the 1990s. Of the five boroughs, Staten Island has been omitted because of the lack of performance activity in that region.

BRONX

Astromundo
Cacique
Circle
El Baturro
Garden of Roses
Mon Ami
P.C.'s
Riddlers
Sidestreet
Tapestry
Voices
Yesterdays

BROOKLYN

Casa Borinque
Ernie Barry Nightdreams
Red Plum
Sports Lounge

MANHATTAN

Club Broadway (later renamed the Latin Quarter)
Copacabana
El Morocco Palace
Fuego Fuego
Las Vegas
MK's
Palladium
Pulse
Roseland
Sports Lounge
Studio 84
Sweetwaters
Taller Latino Americano
Village Gate

QUEENS

Aguacatala
Añoranzas
Asmeraldo
Chibcha
Ecstasies
El Abuelo Pachanguero
El Padrino
Golden Palace
Hillside Casino
Ilusiones
Juan Pachanga
Palm Tree/Club 40
Recordando el Ayer
Rincondelos
30 30 Club

NEW JERSEY

Dynasty (Elizabeth)
Foxes (Elizabeth)
Galaxy (Union City)
Palace (Elizabeth)
Shanghai Reds (Union)

Listed below are the results of a survey taken in 1994 to illustrate the performance activity in New York's most prominent salsa clubs: the Copacabana, Les Poulets, Club Broadway (later renamed the Latin Quarter), Broadway Too, and Sidestreet. These clubs were chosen because they primarily programmed salsa and featured the most popular and well-established professional salsa bands. The objective of this survey was to document who was performing in the salsa scene. Listed below are band names, the nationality of the bandleaders, and the country or city of residence for both bandleaders and musicians. Two hundred thirty-four club engagements were surveyed, which included fifty-four different salsa bands. Also listed below is a schedule from Les Poulets from September 1994 that was included in the survey. It is representative of other clubs' schedules, where a different lineup of bands was featured each week, and weekend nights frequently included performances from two or more bands. Bands seldom appeared more than once a month at each club. A booking agent for Les Poulets remarked, "I always try to include as many groups as possible in my schedule. But if one group, like Ray Sepulveda, brings in a crowd, then I keep having them return to play once a month" (pers. comm.). Sepulveda performed monthly at Les Poulets from 1994 to 1997.

SAMPLE SCHEDULE OF ARTISTS/BANDS, LES POULETS, SEPTEMBER 1994

Wed (8/31): Los Hermanos Morenos
Fri (9/2): Tito Rodríguez Jr.
Sat (9/3): Jesús Enriquez
Wed (9/7): Conjunto Imagen
Fri (9/9): Rey Reyes
Sat (9/10): Johnny Ray and Anthony Cruz
Wed (9/14): Gilberto Santa Rosa
Fri (9/16): Ray Sepulveda
Sat (9/17): Edwin Rivera
Wed (9/21): Tito Nieves
Fri (9/23): José Alberto
Sat (9/24): Los Hermanos Morenos and Conjunto Clássico
Wed (9/28): Oscar D'Leon
Fri (9/30): Raulín Rosendo

SAMPLE LIST OF BANDS PERFORMING IN NEW YORK CLUBS

The numbers following each category and name are the total number of club engagements of the 234 surveyed. Percentages following the total number of engagements represent market share.

NEW YORK–BASED PUERTO RICAN OR NUYORICAN LEADERS AND NEW YORK MUSICIANS 155 (69.4%)

Ray De La Paz 19
Ray Sepulveda 17
Hermanos Moreno 15
Tito Nieves 13
Conjunto Clásico 9
Frankie Ruíz 8
Tito Rodríguez Jr. 8

Miles Peña 8
Johnny Rey 7
La India 6
Marc Anthony 6
Isidro Infante 6
Junior Gonzalez 6
Conjunto Imagen 6
Eddie Torres 5
Tito Puente 4
Fascinación 4
Sarabanda 3
Richie Cabo 2
Los Hermanos Colón 2
Manhattan Latin All-Stars 2
Oscar Figueroa 1
Joe Cuba 1
Bobby Rodríguez 1
Willie Colón 1
Billy Carillón 1
Eddie Montalvo 1
Madera Fina 1

NEW YORK–BASED DOMINICAN LEADERS WITH NEW YORK MUSICIANS 23 (9.8%)

José Alberto 8
Raulín Rosendo 6
Rey Reyes 5
Johnny Pacheco 3
Santiago Cerón 1

NEW YORK–BASED COLOMBIAN LEADERS WITH NEW YORK MUSICIANS 2 (0.8%)

Jerry Galante 1
Alberto Barros 1

PUERTO RICO–BASED LEADERS WITH NEW YORK MUSICIANS 16 (6.8%)

Hector Tricoche 7
Ismael Miranda 2
Victor Manuelle 2
Wichy Camacho 2
Eddie Santiago 1
Guianko 1
Alex D'Castro 1

PUERTO RICO–BASED LEADERS WITH PUERTO RICAN MUSICIANS 14 (5.9%)

Tito Rojas 5
Gilberto Santarosa 2
Nino Segarra 1
Johnny Rivera 1

Jerry Rivera 1
Ray Ruíz 1
Puerto Rican Power 1
Edwin Rivera 1
Tony Vega 1

NEW JERSEY–BASED LEADERS WITH NEW JERSEY MUSICIANS 6 (2.5%)
Elemento 10 3
David Cedeño 2
Manny Pacheco 1

PHILADELPHIA-BASED LEADERS WITH PHILADELPHIA MUSICIANS 4 (1.7%)
Edgar Joel 3
Anthony Cruz 1

CHICAGO-BASED LEADERS WITH CHICAGO MUSICIANS 1 (.04%)
Jesús Enrique 1

VENEZUELA-BASED LEADERS WITH VENEZUELAN MUSICIANS 4 (1.7%)
Oscar D'Leon 4

ITALY-BASED LEADERS WITH ITALIAN MUSICIANS 1 (.04%)
Salsa Bella (Italy) 1

NEW YORK–BASED BANDS (80%)
New York–Based Puerto Rican or Nuyorican Leaders and New York Musicians 155 (69.4%)
New York–Based Dominican Leaders with New York Musicians 23 (9.8%)
New York–Based Colombian Leaders with New York Musicians 2 (0.8%)
Bands Using New York Musicians (86.8%)
New York–Based Puerto Rican or Nuyorican Leaders and New York Musicians 155 (69.4%)
New York–Based Dominican Leaders with New York Musicians 23 (9.8%)
New York–Based Colombian Leaders with New York Musicians 2 (0.8%)
Puerto Rico–Based Leaders with New York Musicians 16 (6.8%)
U.S.-Based (Other Than New York) (4.24%)
New Jersey–Based Leaders with New Jersey Musicians 6 (2.5%)
Philadelphia-Based Leaders with Philadelphia Musicians 4 (1.7%)
Chicago-Based Leaders with Chicago Musicians 1 (.04%)
Puerto Rico–Based Bands (5.9%)
Puerto Rico–Based Leaders with Puerto Rican Musicians 14 (5.9%)
Other International Bands (1.74%)
Venezuela-Based Leaders with Venezuelan Musicians 4 (1.7%)
Italy-Based Leaders with Italian Musicians 1 (.04%)

Notes

INTRODUCTION

1. Hector Lavoe died on June 29, 1993.

2. *Nuyorican* or *Newyorican* are terms that New York–born individuals of Puerto Rican descent use when referring to their own ethnicity or when making a distinction between those living in Puerto Rico and those living in New York City.

3. All quotes in this volume, unless otherwise stipulated, are from personal communications with the author. All interviews and conversations took place between 1992 and 2006. In some cases, musicians preferred to remain anonymous, especially when discussing sensitive topics. In those instances, I have respected their confidentiality and withheld their names.

4. These lyrics are from "Mi Gente," one of Lavoe's biggest salsa hits. Because of its popularity and lyrical praise of Puerto Rico, it has been called the "Nuyorican national anthem" or, as Valentín-Escobar labels it, the "diaspo-Rican national anthem" (Valentín-Escobar 2002: 176).

5. The terms *Latino* and *Hispanic* often are used interchangeably within the New York Puerto Rican community, but there are subtle differences in meaning that should be acknowledged. As Edward Murguia writes, Latino and Hispanic "are similar in denotation, [however] they differ in connotation, with Latino suggesting pluralism and Hispanic suggesting integration" (Murguia 1991: 8). Considering how salsa expression is often tied to cultural particularities and specific ethnic identifications, I use *Latino* exclusively in this volume. That said, and turning to the work of De Genova and Ramos-Zayas, I acknowledge the inherent inconsistencies and incoherence of socially constructed categories, such as Hispanic and Latino, and conceive of them rather as "ongoing reconfigurations" of "Latinos" as a racial formation in the United States (De Genova and Ramos-Zayas 2003: 16).

6. Lipsitz makes the distinction between *collusion* and *collision*, differing in the kinds of crosscultural identification, one which "advances emancipatory ends and one which reinforces existing structures of power and domination" (Lipsitz 1994: 56).

7. Even the notion of a physically bounded El Barrio as an ethnic enclave of Latinos is problematic and has been effectively challenged by Adelia Reyes-Schramm (Schramm 1979).

8. This was the title of a film released in 1971 that featured a live performance of the newly formed Fania All-Stars band at the Cheetah club in New York City.

9. Padura-Fuentes 2003: 120.

10. Casey 1996: 14.

11. For historical studies that explore the stylistic antecedents of salsa, see Acosta (1983), Feijóo (1986), Galán (1983), León (1974), Linares (1974), Milkowsky (1988), Sublette (2004), and the works of Fernando Ortiz.

12. Jorge Duany argues that Cuban son was popular and influential in Puerto Rico because, in some sense, it is a pan-Caribbean form, having a wide range of influences that are not exclusively Cuban. This is why Puerto Ricans can relate and recognize a part of themselves in that tradition (Duany 1984).

13. Obtaining exact sales figures is nearly impossible since Fania was never forthcoming about their bookkeeping, nor were there structures in place to accurately track Latin music sales in the 1970s. According to Keith Negus, in 1975 Fania accounted for over 80 percent of all record sales in the United States and Puerto Rico (Negus 1999: 135; figures originally published in Flores 1987: 1). And in the *Daily News*, Ruby Garcia wrote that Fania had 70 percent of market share of $8 million in 1976, though it is unclear how these writers obtained this information.

14. See Keith Negus (1999) for further comments on the salsa recording industry.

15. Attendance estimate from the Fania website (http://www.faniarecords.com/Fania/site/About.aspx).

16. For a discussion concerning the tension between pan-Latin identity and nationalism in the United States, see David G. Gutiérrez's introduction, "Demography and the Shifting Boundaries of 'Community': Reflections on 'U.S. Latinos' and the Evolution of Latino Studies." In *The Columbia History of Latinos in the United States Since 1960*, 17–19. New York: Columbia University Press, 2004.

17. Miami-based Emusica.com has bought the distribution rights and is re-releasing the Fania catalogue on CD. Masucci died in Argentina a very wealthy man in 1997. Pacheco remained in New York City, leading his own band and occasionally leading reunion concerts of the Fania All-Stars.

18. Two more *Noche Caliente* productions followed and were produced by Fania stalwart Larry Harlow. Harlow used Menique and Tito Allen to sing on his first production, and the other featured "Los Tres," referring to the three vocalists he included (Orlando Watussi, Doris Eugenio, and Ray Perez).

19. Although predominant, salsa romántica was not the only style heard in the 1980s and 1990s. Groups firmly rooted in the fiery sounds of the 1970s, such as Oscar D'Leon, José Alberto, Raulín Rosendo, and Grupo Niche, as well as bands that were popular in the 1970s, such as Ray Baretto, Eddie Palmieri, and Johnny Pacheco, continued to perform.

20. The interview was originally printed in *El Diario*, September 24, 1993: 32.

21. I performed with the RMM All-Stars from 1994 until 1998 and recorded on a number of productions for Mercado and George.

22. The tour featured duet performances of RMM's best singers, which is why they chose to label the release "the perfect combination."

23. Abu-Lughod 1986: 10.

24. Salsa is a popular dance music and, as such, movement plays a significant role in performance settings. As Delgado and Muñoz have written: "Dance sets politics in motion, bringing people together in rhythmic affinity where identification takes the form of histories written on the body through gesture" (Delgado and Muñoz 1997: 9). This study, however, is musician based and biased, reflecting my own expertise and interests. I acknowledge that an indepth exploration of dance and movement is greatly needed here. I am unqualified to embark upon such a study in any theoretically significant way and I must leave that work to others more qualified.

25. See Appendix 1 for a list of my performance and recording activities during the researching and writing of this book.

26. Gerhard Kubik has discussed this fluctuation between inside and outside status: "Due to the universal learnability of culture any so-called outsider to any culture can eventually become an insider. Likewise an original insider might well cross cultural borders that first separated his small world from the outside world, until he or she eventually becomes an outsider to the culture into which he or she was first enculturated. In practice, nobody is ever a 100% insider, and nobody is ever a 100% outsider to anything that exists" (Kubik 1996: 7).

27. Readers less familiar with the sound of salsa may want to first refer to Chapter Six, which begins by explaining the basic mechanics of salsa music-making.

CHAPTER 1: SALSA BANDS AND THE PERFORMANCE OF PUEBLE

1. Jairo Moreno (forthcoming) takes issue with Santos-Febres's seemingly reductive populist frame because he feels that she "dismisses all too quickly the persistence of national space in the imagination of cultural practices across Latin America." Moreno is less inclined to separate "people" from "nation" as grounds for a cultural practice, stating that both can act as surrogates for naturalized forms of identity. He turns instead to Nestor García-Canclini's (2002) conception of "polylocalization," which considers national space as an indispensable prism for a Latin American analysis. In my consideration of pueble, I aim not to dismiss nation, but rather attend to how national affiliations, along with their frequent erasure (or deemphasization), are central in the sociopolitical self-positionings of salseros.

2. *Salsascapes* is a play on the various *-scapes* ("ethnoscapes," "mediascapes," etc.) of Arjun Appadurai, which he invented for conceiving the interconnectedness and often disjunctive flows found in the global circulation of cultures.

3. When a cover band makes the transition to a professional original one, that change is initiated by the release of a commercial recording.

4. The majority of salsa recording in the 1990s took place at Skylight Studios, located in Belleville, New Jersey. Initially, Skylight's popularity stemmed from its ability to offer lower hourly rates because of its location outside of New York City. Moreover, this Cuban American–owned and –operated business provided a "user-friendly" environment for Spanish speakers. Specializing in Latin popular music styles since 1986, it developed a studio sound that rapidly grew in popularity, setting a standard that smaller studios emulated.

5. "Singer/Songwriter Elizabeth 'Mimi' Ibarra Meets Nestor Louis," http://www.palosalsero.com/mimi.htm.

6. The rates salsa musicians receive for recording and performing are comparable to other freelancer musicians working in New York City, such as in Broadway pit orchestras, in society bands, or in freelance classical groups. However, the main difference is that salsa musicians lack union representation and therefore do not qualify for pension and health benefits, and additional royalty payments for recording and television appearances.

7. The edited volume assembled by Paul Greene and Thomas Porcello (2005) explores how recording studios serve as the arena where the very nature of sound is negotiated. Using case studies from various cultures, the contributing authors trace how the micro decisions made in the recording process play out in many socially significant ways.

8. In order to gain a clear picture of the nightclub scene—that is, which bands were performing and their geographic and national affiliation—I conducted a survey of club activity in the mid-1990s, the results of which can also be found in Appendix 2. These results clearly demonstrate that salsa performance in the New York club scene was dominated by New York–based musicians (87 percent) and Puerto Rican and Nuyorican bandleaders (70 percent). New York performances of Puerto Rican bands using Puerto Rican musicians greatly dropped in frequency throughout the 1990s because promoters preferred to pay for bandleaders to travel alone and to assemble a group of New York–based musicians to perform with those bandleaders, thus reducing travel and lodging expenses. Puerto Rican promoters who brought New York–based singers to Puerto Rico reciprocated with the same practice. Some bandleaders who frequently traveled between Puerto Rico and New York, such as Johnny Rivera, Domingo Quiñones, and Hector Tricoche, opted to maintain two bands simultaneously, a New York band and a Puerto Rican one. The growth of Dominican-led bands throughout the 1990s (roughly 10 percent of salsa bands) reflected the growing Dominican immigrant population living in New York City. Performance opportunities were greatly increased as more Dominican-owed clubs opened. Conversely, the decrease of Colombian participation (less than 1 percent), which was more prominent in the 1980s, reflected the numerous closings of Colombian-owned clubs that were associated with the drug trade. Since the budgets of nightclubs tended to be smaller than concert and festival productions, New York–based groups primarily were featured.

9. Direct boxes allow electric piano, keyboard, and bass players to send signals directly from their amplifiers to the sound system, omitting the use of microphones. The advantage is that their sounds are sonically isolated in the system, providing engineers the ability to control their volumes with less feedback problems.

10. http://www.littlejudy.com.

11. Paul Berliner (1994: 459) offers an insightful discussion of audience feedback loops as they relate to jazz performance settings.

12. http://www.palosalsero.com.

13. For instance, Puerto Rican and Nuyorican musicians can harbor considerable animosity toward Dominican musicians, a dynamic fueled, no doubt, by the rapidly growing Dominican communities in Washington Heights. As their numbers increased, so did the popularity of merengue. This resulted in greater performance opportunities for merengue bands, often at the expense of salsa groups.

14. Also see Sommers (1991), Padilla (1985), and Trottier (1981) for further discussion. See Aguirre and Saenz (1991) article for a critique of Latinismo.

15. According to Javier León, this expression originated in the port city of El Callao by soccer fans who used this call and response phrase as a chant to support their professional teams. "Chimpún," the call, is thought to be an onomatopoeic imitation of the cymbal crash and bass drum hit that are used by musicians to cue the cheering section during a soccer game. This call is immediately followed by a resounding responsorial "Callao" by the crowd. Over time, this context-specific call and response phrase has been adopted in almost any kind of setting where a group of Peruvians is present, especially salsa concerts, and has been used to incite a broader nationalistic pride.

16. Excerpts of the text are included below and have been translated by the author. Original lyrics are in quotation marks, and translations follow in parentheses.

17. See Manuel (1998) in *Island Sounds in the Global City*, Ray Allen and Lois Wilken, editors (New York: ISAMNYFS), for a discussion of other salsa lyrics that include experiences or locations associated with New York City.

CHAPTER 2: "THE MUSIC IS SO GOOD, BUT THE SCENE IS PURE DUES!"

1. Will Straw offers the following definitions for "scene" and "community": A musical community presumes a "group whose composition is relatively stable—according to a wide range of sociological variables—and whose involvement in music takes the form of an ongoing exploration of one or more musical idioms said to be rooted within a geographically specific historical heritage. A musical scene . . . is that cultural space in which a range of musical practices coexist, interacting with each other within a variety of processes of differentiation, and according to widely varying trajectories of change and cross-fertilization . . . Within a musical scene, that same sense of purpose is articulated within those forms of communication through which the building of musical alliances and the drawing of musical boundaries takes place" (Straw 2004 [1991]: 84–85).

2. The almost exclusively male makeup of this group is reflected in the language. I choose to use the more neutral "sideperson" in this book out of deference to the select few women musicians with whom I worked and who provided valuable insight for this study; however, this word choice does not reflect the male-centric practices of most salsa musicians.

3. In this case, "top salsa bands" refers to New York City–based groups that have recorded and performed original material and worked regularly in the most prestigious salsa venues. See Chapter One for further discussion of salsa bands.

4. My work with the bands of Tito Nieves, Raulín Rosendo, Marc Anthony, and La India was also instructive in the writing of this chapter.

5. Statistics are based on my own observations of New York salsa bands from 1989 to 1999.

6. As a regular member, I include myself (the "Anglo") in this cultural breakdown. My position was not unusual for New York City salsa bands, since most typically have one to three Anglos as regular band members.

7. It should be noted that the lack of female musicians in other New York music styles points to larger crosscultural issues rooted in a complex of sexist and prejudicial practices that also affect salsa performance.

8. Cover bands play the repertoire of the top salsa bands, offering audiences a variety of hit songs at a much lower price.

9. The number fluctuates between ten and twenty players on each instrument that is found in the majority of New York salsa bands (piano, bass, percussion, trumpet, trombone, and vocals). Many perform other music styles to supplement their salsa income.

10. Compadrazgo does involve women, as godmothers for instance, as well as relationships between couples, but these relationships exhibited among salsa musicians remain exclusively shared by men. See Wolf (1956) and Bourgois (1996: 82) for further discussions of compadrazgo relations.

11. The Harbor Performing Arts Program was founded in 1970. The music instructional program was founded in 1973. The school also houses the Raíces Latin Music Collection, compiled in 1979, which contains a large "collection of materials tracing and documenting the Afro-Caribbean roots and the subsequent evolution of salsa and Latin jazz," and also the Latin Music Museum, a "multi-media collection documenting the history of Afro-Caribbean Latin music in New York City"; http://www.boysandgirlsharbor.net.

12. Instrumentalists schooled in Latin America and in the Caribbean most often receive training in classical music from music conservatories in their respective countries.

13. I performed regularly with Rosendo's band throughout this period.

14. New York state law requires bars to stop serving alcoholic beverages at 4:00 A.M. The twelve times I performed at Elegante throughout the 1990s, alcohol continually was served throughout the morning hours.

15. A "club-date" refers to a gig with a band that plays primarily jazz and pop covers for weddings, private parties, and other social occasions (see MacLeod 1993).

16. See Singer (1982) for further discussion.

CHAPTER 3: "PLAY LIKE THERE'S A GUN TO YOUR HEAD!"

1. One rich historical source that documents the relationship of musicians and violence, though mostly descriptive in nature, is the *costumbrista* writings from the Caribbean and Latin America. One example is R. Emilio Jimenez's *Al Amor Del Bohio: Tradiciones y Costumbres Dominicanas* (1929), which floridly (and humorously) describes how musicians in the Dominican Republic dealt with violent encounters during performances. Additionally, Marshall Sterns offers an account of violence and Latin music performance in New York City from a dance at the Manhattan Center in 1946: "By eight o'clock—seven hours after opening—the heavily stocked bar manned by ten bartenders was bone dry. 'Various parties on the balcony,' recalls Gabriel Oller [the promoter of the dance] . . .'were bouncing bottles down among the dancers, and service men in uniform were firing small arms at the ceiling.' Keeping the music going was the only solution to these irregularities; 'When the music stop, everyone punch everyone; when the music start, everyone dance,' adds Oller. In spite of eight professional bouncers and fourteen policemen, four customers were hospitalized at St. Vincent's, and one police lieutenant had his scalp lifted by a flying chair" (Sterns 1956: 176). The valuable perspectives offered in these types of works remind us that violence and musical performance have a long shared history. This is not something new or specific to salsa. What is unique, though, is how salsa musicians choose to navigate through such encounters.

2. Mary Jackman (2002) offers a useful critique by normalizing violence as "part of the human repertoire of strategic social behaviors" rather than something beyond daily

experience. She also points out that what is often missing in discussions on violence is the recognition of the conditions and dispositions that lead people to tolerate it, and, at times, to seek it out.

3. Stephen Diamond points out that violence potentially can be considered constructive or destructive; the latter engenders evil (Diamond 1996: 18). I prefer not to delineate such a simple binary, acknowledging a large gray zone that lies between these two extremes. Positing an act as either constructive or destructive is often a matter dependent on individual perspective and context. Many acts of violence can possess both constructive and destructive dimensions.

4. Raymond Williams also points out this additional sense of the word as it relates to the meaning-making process of act and response, as in the expression "violently in love," for example, which summons the sudden eruption of passion and sheer emotional intensity triggered by tropes of confrontational interaction (Williams 1976: 329–330).

5. See also William Rowe and Vivian Schelling, who discuss the enormous amount of destruction that has accompanied movements throughout Latin America in the form of "both genocidal and symbolic violence; of the eradication of social groupings and of 'the gentle, hidden form which takes shape when overt violence is impossible'" (Rowe and Schelling 1991: 3).

6. See Barbara Wittmer's *The Violence Mythos* (Albany: State University of New York Press, 1997: 119–120) for an in-depth discussion of Ricoeur's work on language and violence.

7. David Lenson classifies alcohol and cocaine as the two drugs most associated with violent crime (Lenson 1993: 171). See Chapter Four for further comment.

8. Ramiro Martinez Jr. documents that low income and lack of education correspond with higher homicide rates and violence. As of 1996, Latinos living in urban areas in the United States have a substantial 19 percent poverty rate, and less than half (45 percent) have graduated from high school. The homicide rate for this demographic is 20:100,000, twice that of the overall rate in the United States. Though this study problematically treats all Latinos as a homogeneous group, it does indicate troubling overarching trends (Martinez 1996).

9. Competition to receive top billing and to outperform other bands intensified during the mambo era (1950s). Its attendant discourse, which served as an effective marketing tool, was exploited and dramatized in advertisements and in the press. The competition was especially heated between the bands of Tito Puente and Tito Rodríguez. Such songs as Puente's "El Cayuco" ("The Hick with No Musical Time"), written about Rodríguez, and Rodríguez's musical answer "Avisale a Mi Contrario" ("Warn My Adversary") attest to the intensity of the competition.

10. Cesar Miguel Rondón writes that Palmieri's sound significantly differed from the mambo and cha-cha bands of the previous era precisely because he adopted a sound characterized by "violence": "The music stopped being ostentatious . . . there was no pomp but violence" (Rondón 1980: 25).

11. This type of rhetoric is not limited to salsa performance, but can be found in many diverse musical and cultural settings. However, the specific ways salsa musicians incorporate this discourse in their performances and express stylized enactments of violence through music performance are unique to the genre.

12. For a more in-depth discussion of gender dynamics in salsa, see Chapter Five.

13. Refer to Chapter Five for a discussion concerning women and salsa.

CHAPTER 4: NEW YORK SALSA AND DRUGS

1. The extensive nature of questionable business practices in the U.S. music industry has been well documented by Fredric Dannen (1991), and the Latin music industry both in the United States and in Puerto Rico is no exception.

2. I wish to gratefully acknowledge the contribution of my research assistant Matt Sakakeeny, whose insightful comments and diligent research greatly enhanced this chapter.

3. *Banda* music is a musical style from Mexico that has as its most identifiable feature a narrative song form that historically documents and glorifies the lives of social bandits and drug traffickers. See Helena Simonett's *Banda: Mexican Musical Life Across Borders* (Middletown, Conn: Wesleyan University Press, 2001), and Mark Edberg's *El Narcotraficante: Narcocorridos and the Construction of a Cultural Persona on the U.S.-Mexico Border* (Austin: University of Texas Press, 2004).

4. Of course, this perspective is a bit oversimplified in that it does not take into consideration how powerful institutions are often quick to join in, aligning with the newly established order, and ultimately benefiting in some way. The least powerful—in this case, musicians who are not bandleaders—rarely have an opportunity to challenge the hegemonic order.

5. "In 2001, the wholesale price for cocaine ranged from $10,000 to $36,000 per kilogram, $400 to $1,800 per ounce, and $20 to $200 per gram. Prices for crack cocaine ranged from $3 to $50 per rock, with prices usually ranging from $10 to $20"; http://www.whitehousedrugpolicy.gov/drugfact/cocaine/index.html.

6. For further discussion on the role of immigrants in the drug trade see Franscisco Thoumi (1994), and Luis Eduardo Guarnizo and Luz Marina Díaz (1999).

7. It is important to note that the numbers of Colombian immigrants involved in the illicit drug trade represent only a small fraction of the population. Nonetheless, the high visibility of the drug wars in the mass media unfairly has stigmatized the entire community. For further discussion, see Luis Eduardo Guarnizo, Arturo Ignacio Sánchez, and Elizabeth M. Roach (1999).

8. http://www.whitehousedrugpolicy.gov/drugfact/cocaine/index.html.

9. Ibid.

10. The statistics on the ONDCP website seem to support his view. Notice the racial breakdown of arrests listed for 2001: "5,356 Federal drug offenders were convicted of committing an offense involving powder cocaine and 4,999 were convicted of committing a crack cocaine offense. Of those convicted for powder cocaine, 50.2% were Hispanic, 30.5% were black, 18.1% were white, and 1.2% were of another race. Of those convicted for crack cocaine, 82.8% were black, 9.3% were Hispanic, 7% were white, and 0.9% fell into another race category" (http://www.whitehousedrugpolicy.gov/drugfact/cocaine/index.html). These statistics do not reflect drug use in the United States, but instead speak to the racial inequities of the judicial system and highlight underlying strategies employed by governmental institutions. However, these types of statistics do have an impact on generalized societal impressions.

11. "Enforcement," U.S. Department of Justice, http://www.ojp.usdoj.gov/bjs/dcf/enforce.htm.

12. Though not specifically focused on salsa, Mary Roldan's work documents how nightlife in Medellín was transformed and invigorated in the mid-1970s after the cocaine

industry was established. Hernando Calvo-Ospina briefly mentions how young gangsters working in the Colombian drug trade "find their philosophical identity in salsa," adopting songs like "Siempre Alegre" by Raphy Leavit, which purports living in the moment because death is always looming, as an anthem of sorts (Calvo-Ospina 1995 [1992]: 124–125). However, he does not explain this relationship of salsa and the drug trade in any detail.

13. It is important to note that during the 1960s, the city of Calí had its own nascent salsa scene that was grounded in a well-established and passionate relationship with Cuban dance music. The drug monies of the 1970s and touring of New York–based acts in the 1980s greatly invigorated this scene.

14. Illegal clubs operating past curfews have been part of the New York music scene throughout the twentieth century, and obviously not all have been associated with DTOs. However, through my research I have found no examples of after-hours that programmed salsa bands that were not owned exclusively by DTOs.

15. According to the New York City Administrative Code, Chapter 2, Subchapter 20, § 20-367, all bars must be closed between the hours of 4:00 and 8:00 A.M. The statute reads: "Places closed to public within certain hours. Premises licensed hereunder shall not be kept open for business, nor shall the public be permitted to enter or to remain therein, between four ante meridian and eight ante meridian; and if the occupant is a membership corporation, club, association, or society, its members or their guests shall not be permitted to enter or to remain therein between such hours."

16. Attesting to the influence of this journalist, one bandleader commented, "Every time I played at the Copacabana, 'R' would come up to me and say, 'did you see the piece I wrote about you in the paper? How about hooking me up?' After two years of that shit I refused to give him anything. Now we don't play at the Copacabana anymore" (Anon., pers. comm.).

17. According to Dannen, the word "payola" is a contraction of "pay" and "Victrola" and refers to illegal payments made for radio airplay (Dannen 1992: 13).

18. See Chapter Three for a more in-depth discussion of violence.

19. Johnny Pacheco, interviewed by Felix Contreras, "Seminal Latin Label's Music Resurrected," *Morning Edition*, National Public Radio, June 1, 2006.

20. Joseph Fitzpatrick suggests that the ethnic character of the population makes a difference in determining how drug users are treated within their respective communities. In his work he finds that Puerto Rican families from lower economic classes are less likely to reject addicts and heavy users than other ethnic groups and classes (Fitzpatrick 1990: 119–120). This may provide a partial explanation for the acceptance of drug use in the salsa community, since the majority of New York salsa musicians have lower-economic-class backgrounds and are of Puerto Rican descent. More study is undoubtedly needed in this area.

21. Waxer provides rare examples where "narcojargon" has been used in Colombian salsa lyrics (Waxer 2000: 158).

22. Catherine Bell writes, "The purpose of ritualization is to ritualize persons, who deploy schemes of ritualization in order to dominate (shift or nuance) other, nonritualized situations to render them more coherent with the values of ritualizing schemes and capable of molding perceptions . . . The effectiveness of ritualization as a strategic practice lies precisely in this circularity and deferral" (Bell 1992: 106–108).

23. Matt Sakakeeny, Unpublished manuscript (2005).

24. Johnny Pacheco, interviewed by Felix Contreras, "Seminal Latin Label's Music Resurrected," *Morning Edition*, National Public Radio, June 1, 2006.

CHAPTER 5: LA INDIA AND THE MASQUERADING OF GENDER ON THE SALSA SCENE

1. Portions of this chapter were coauthored with my partner, Maiken Derno, and previously published in *Women in Performance* 24, 12:2 (2002): 140–156.

2. "Ese Hombre" was written by Manuel Alejandro and Ana Magdalena, and produced and arranged by Sergio George. Lyric translation by the author.

3. I consulted India while researching and writing this chapter, sharing my observations and discussing her ideas about her performance practice. Her feedback greatly enhanced my work. However, India did not want to be quoted directly concerning issues of sexuality, and I have respected that request in the following pages.

4. Celia Cruz passed away at the age of 77 on July 16, 2003, maintaining an active touring schedule up until her death.

5. One arena where women's voices have been represented in salsa is the all-women bands in Colombia, Puerto Rico, Cuba, the Dominican Republic, and New York City. On the New York salsa scene, however, these bands never obtained major recording deals, received only a modicum of airplay, and rarely performed in the most prominent venues. Works by Lise Waxer (2001) and Umberto Valverde and Raphael Quintero (1995) examine all-women bands in Colombia.

6. Some writers, Aparicio (2002) and Valentín-Escobar (2002) in particular, actually view the stylistic changes from dura to romántica as a "feminization" of the genre. Besides the essentialist perspective of gender construction this perspective purports, it also posits maleness as uniformly "hard" and neglects to acknowledge the multivalence of masculinity, the fluidity involved in gender construction, and the fact that "limp" is just as much a phallic reference that firmly engenders maleness, albeit a softer rendition.

7. There is a small number of female composers, such as Mimi Ibarra, whose compositions have been widely recorded by male salseros. However, as in most popular music styles, the role of composers remains mostly out of the public eye.

8. Whereas physical fights between two men in a salsa club are not an uncommon phenomenon, and fights between two women are rare but do occur, violent encounters between a man and a woman are highly unusual.

9. *Chusma* is a Spanish word denoting scum, rabble, and mob.

10. I chose to use the term "macho" to describe India's role-playing, fully cognizant of the essentialist and racist connotations associated with that term and Latino culture. However, this is the term that members of her band attributed to her staged behavior, and, as such, I believe it best represents how her fellow salseros interpreted this aspect of her performance practice. For further analytical discussions concerning machismo, see Matthew Gutmann (1996), Roger Lancaster (1992), Ilán Stavans (1996), and Evelyn Stevens (1973).

11. Internet interview, http://www.geocities.com/indiasworld/articles.html. (Author's note: At press time, this site was no longer available.)

12. Rivera, George, "Dicen Que Soy . . . All That and More: The India Interview," www.jazzconclave.com/i-room/india.html.

13. RMM Records (RMD-80864).

14. Sony Records (CDZ-81373).

15. Women dancing together in salsa clubs was not an uncommon practice; however, the combination of dancing together on stage and the flirtatious nature of India's performative gestures was quite novel.

16. See Colón's album covers, in Chapter Three.

17. Lupe's recording of "La Tirana" ("The Great Tyrant") provides one of only a few antecedent examples in New York Latin music in which a female singer paints an emboldened feminist perspective of heterosexual relations.

18. For an extensive discussion of these various positions on third gender and transgendering, see Rosalind Morris (1995).

19. See Kath Weston (1993).

CHAPTER 6: "THEY ARE GOING TO HEAR THIS IN PUERTO RICO. IT HAS GOT TO BE GOOD!"

1. Leonardo Padura-Fuentes, *Faces of Salsa: A Spoken History of the Music* (Washington, D.C.: Smithsonian Books, 2003), 59.

2. Sue Steward, *The Rhythm of Latin America, Salsa, Rumba, Merengue, and More* (London: Thames and Hudson Ltd., 1999), 6–7.

3. These bands were not the only influences that the pioneering salsa groups drew upon, simply the most dominant.

4. The mambo emerged as a distinct genre in 1938 when Orestes Lopez's composition "Danzon Mambo" was performed and recorded in Cuba by Antonio Arcaño's orchestra. Lopez claims that he composed this work in 1937; however, the use of the term "mambo" in music performance predates this composition. As such writers as Leonardo Acosta, Max Salazar, and Odilio Urfé have documented, "mambo" also was used as a vocal interjection during performances, especially during an instrumental section featuring solos. According to José Fajardo, Lopez would say "Oye, coge el mambo aquí!" ("Blow your mambo here!") when it was time for him to solo (Salazar 2002b: 28). The mambo, as a genre and dance, was popularized in the United States in the 1940s and 1950s by the bands of Perez Prado, Tito Puente, Tito Rodríguez, and Machito. Throughout his book, David Garcia (2006) argues convincingly that the mambo sections of salsa arrangements also are derived from Arsenio Rodríguez's *diablo* sections, which share many of the same characteristics of salsa mambos.

5. There is considerable disagreement as to the derivation of this musical term and how "hair curl" came to mean an improvised repeating riff figure in salsa.

6. Notating salsa with four beats per measure is the standard practice. However, most musicians actually feel these measures in cut time, often tapping their feet on beats one and three of each bar. See Rebeca Mauleón (1995) for playing techniques and rhythmic variations used in these rhythm section patterns.

7. On occasion, additional conga drums (up to five in total) will be added to the primary two. These extra drums are tuned to both higher and lower pitches and are used more for soloing and to provide a variety in timbre than for basic time-keeping.

8. According to pianist Sonny Bravo, *repicar* or *repiquetear* means "to play on the skins" or "to play 'licks' on the bongos," and this term distinguishes another function of the bongocero, that of keeping time with the martillo pattern. However, Bravo claims that *martilleo* is the proper term for this role rather than the more commonly used

martillo. He states, "This term applies to the *bongos* and not to the *congas* which were originally intended to maintain a '*marcha*' [time-keeping pattern] while the *bongos* supplied the '*floreos*' or embellishments" (S. Bravo, pers. comm.).

9. This mambo montuno ride pattern can also be played on the cymbals, especially during highly energetic and loud moments, such as a trumpet or trombone solo.

10. The cascara pattern played on the timbales can also be played on the guiro.

11. Latin Percussion (LP), founded in 1964 by Martin Cohen, is the instrument-maker of choice for instruments used in salsa. A considerable number of salsa percussionists are sponsored by LP, receiving free or discounted equipment.

12. The Korg M1 and the Yamaha DX7 were popular choices throughout the 1990s.

13. Ampeg makes the most popular baby bass among salsa bassists, preferred for its dry, low frequency and percussive sound.

14. See Peter Manuel (1985) for a historical discussion that explores the roots of this phenomenon. Also see Carlos Borbolla, "Cuban Folk Music," in *The New Grove Dictionary of Music and Musicians,* Vol. 5, ed. Stanley Sadie (London: Macmillan, 1980), 85–89.

15. Charanga bands grew out of colonial and postcolonial string and woodwind salon orchestras in Cuba that featured a more genteel and refined sound. At various periods throughout the twentieth century, their popularity resurged. They were most popular in New York in the 1960s. Larry Harlow, Johnny Pacheco, and many other Fania-associated artists led charanga bands at various points.

16. Originally published in Ramon Brenes, "A Puerto Cerrada con Ismael Rivera," *Centro* 3:2 (1991): 56–61.

17. This is by no means the only rhythmic influence in salsa, just the most prevalent. Other rhythms frequently heard are rumba, bomba, and plena.

18. Often a hollow plastic block, known as a "clave block," is attached to the timbale stand and struck by a drumstick to simulate the sound of clave sticks.

19. Occasionally, salsa arrangements will include short rumba interludes that employ the rumba clave (which differs slightly from the son clave in that the third stroke of the three-stroke measure hits on the "and" of beat four instead of directly on beat four, displaced by one eighth-note), but invariably the arrangements will return to the son clave after such brief sections. One example is Pete "El Conde" Rodríguez's recording of "Tambó" (*A Touch of Class*; Fania 519).

20. In a previously published article, I examine the connection between African rhythmic structures and clave (see Washburne 1995).

21. In my chapter entitled "Salsa Romántica: An Analysis of Style, Sound Structure, and Contemporary Performance Practice" in *Situating Salsa: Global Markets and Local Meanings in Latin Popular Music* (2002), through musical analysis, I explore the particularities of the salsa romántica style.

22. See Peter Manuel (1991b and 1995) for further comment and criticism of the recording techniques used in salsa productions.

23. Paul Théberge (1997) writes about the central role of sound quality of the recorded medium in such processes. And timbre is finally beginning to receive much overdue attention in ethnography. For instance, see Fox (2004), Porcello (1996), Averill (1997), and Willoughby (2002).

24. Ray Barretto, interviewed by Nancy Rodríguez, WBAI 99.5 FM, September 19, 1993.

25. See Peter Manuel (1991b), where he examines the effects of commercialization and other music styles on the popularity of salsa.

26. These descriptive labels have been chosen by the author and do not reflect emic descriptive language.

27. (R. Vega, pers. comm., 1996). Vega performed with Mongo Santamaria throughout the 1980s.

28. This is not to deny that I, too, have had my own share of clave crossings.

29. Perfectionism and refined musicianship long have been associated with Puerto Rican musicians. Attesting to their skills and reputation, James Reese Europe recruited a number of Puerto Rican brass and wind players for his band in the early part of the twentieth century.

30. One of George's first independent productions was for Dark Latin Grooves (DLG), a group that explored the mixing of salsa with hip-hop and rap music.

Bibliographic References

Abrahams, Roger D. 1975. The theoretical boundaries of performance. In *Form in performance, hard-core ethnography,* ed. Marcia Herndon and Roger Brunyate, 18–27. New York: McGraw-Hill.

Abu-Lughod, Lila. 1986. *Veiled sentiments: Honor and poetry in a Bedouin society.* Berkeley: University of California Press.

Acosta, Leonardo. 1983. *Del tambor al sintetizador.* Havana: Editorial Letras Cubanas.

———. 1993. *Elige tu, que canto yo.* Havana: Editorial Letras Cubanas.

Aguirre, Benigno E., and Rogelio Saenz. 1991. A futuristic assessment of Latino ethnic identity. *Latino Studies Journal* 2 (3): 19–32.

Alba, Richard, with John Logan and Paul Bellair. 1994. Living with crime: The implications of racial/ethnic differences in suburban location. *Social Forces* 74 (2): 395–434.

Alén, Olavo. 1992. *De lo Afrocubano a la salsa.* Puerto Rico: Editorial Cubanacán.

———. 1995. Rhythm as duration of sounds in tumba francesa. *Ethnomusicology* 39 (1): 55–72.

Alvarado, Alfredo. 1995. Rey Ruíz finds success in Puerto Rico. *Latino* (Fall): 10–13.

———. 1996. Marc Anthony gets ready for his Broadway debut with Paul Simon and Ruben Blades. *Latino* (Winter): 9–11.

Aparicio, Frances R. 1994. "Así son": Salsa music narrative and gender (de)construction in Puerto Rico. *Poetics Today* 15 (4): 659–684.

———. 1998. *Listening to salsa: Gender, Latin popular music, and Puerto Rican culture.* Hanover, NH: Wesleyan University Press.

———. 2002. La Lupe, La India, and Celia: Toward a feminist genealogy of salsa music. In *Situating salsa: Global markets and local meanings in Latin popular music,* ed. Lise Waxer, 135–160. New York: Routledge.

———. 2004. U.S. Latino expressive cultures. In *The Columbia history of Latinos in the United States since 1960,* ed. David G. Gutiérrez, 355–390. New York: Columbia University Press.

Aparicio, Frances R., and Susana Chavez-Silverman, eds. 1997. *Tropicalizations, transcultural representations of Latinidad.* Hanover, NH: Dartmouth College/University Press of New England.

Appadurai, Arjun. 1991. Global ethnoscapes: Notes and queries for a transnational anthropology. In *Recapturing anthropology,* ed. Richard G. Fox, 191–210. Santa Fe, NM: School of American Research Press.

Araújo, Samuel. 2006. Conflict and violence as theoretical tools in present-day ethnomusicology: Notes on a dialogic ethnography of sound practices in Rio de Janeiro. *Ethnomusicology* 50 (2): 287–313.

Arendt, Hannah. 1969. *On violence.* New York: Harcourt, Brace and World.

Arteaga, José. 2000. *La salsa: Un estado de ánimo.* Madrid: Acento Editorial.

Arteaga-Rodríguez, José. 1988. Salsa y violencia: una aproximacion sonoro-historica. *Revista Musical Puertoriqueño* 4: 20–33.

Attali, Jacques. 1985. *Noise: The political economy of music.* Minneapolis: University of Minnesota Press.

Averill, Gage. 1994. Anraje to Angaje: Carnival politics and music in Haiti. *Ethnomusicology* 38 (2): 217–247.

———. 1997. *A day for the hunter, a day for the prey: Popular music and power in Haiti.* Chicago: University of Chicago Press.

Babín, María Theresa. 1958. *Panorama de la cultura Puertorriqueña.* New York: Las Americas.

Baron, Robert. 1977. Syncretism and ideology: Latin New York salsa musicians. *Western Folklore* 36: 209–225.

Barthes, Roland. 1977. *Roland Barthes.* Trans. Richard Howard. London: Hill and Wang.

Basch, Linda, Nina Glick Schiller, and Cristina Szanton Blanc. 1994. *Nations unbound: Transnational projects, postcolonial predicaments, and deterritorialized nation-states.* New York: Gordon and Breach Science Publishers.

Bar On, Bat-Ami. 2002. *The subject of violence: Arendtean exercises in understanding.* Oxford, UK: Rowman and Littlefield Publishers.

Bauman, Richard. 1975. Verbal art as performance. *American Anthropologist* 77: 290–311.

Becker, Howard. [1963] 1973. *Outsiders: Studies in the sociology of deviance.* 2nd ed. Glencoe, NY: Free Press.

Béhague, Gerard. 1973. Latin American folk music. In *Folk and traditional music of the Western continents,* ed. Bruno Nettl, 179–206. Englewood Cliffs, NJ: Prentice-Hall.

———. 1980. Improvisation in Latin American musics. *Music Educators Journal* 66: 118–125.

———. 1984. *Performance practice: Ethnomusicological perspectives.* Westport, CT: Greenwood Press.

Bell, Catherine. 1992. *Ritual theory, ritual practice.* New York: Oxford University Press.

Bell, Daniel. 1975. Ethnicity and social change. In *Ethnicity: Theory and experience,* ed. Nathan Glazer and Daniel P. Moynihan, 100–117. Cambridge, MA: Harvard University Press.

Benítez-Rojo, Antonio. 1996. *The repeating island: The Caribbean and the postmodern perspective.* Trans. James E. Maraniss. Durham, NC: Duke University Press.

Berliner, Paul F. 1994. *Thinking in jazz: The infinite art of improvisation.* Chicago: University of Chicago Press.

Berrios-Miranda, Marisol. 2000. The significance of salsa music to national and pan-Latino identity. PhD diss., Univ. of California-Berkeley.

Bhabha, Homi K. 1996. Culture's in-between. In *Questions of Cultural Identity,* ed. Stuart Hall and Paul du Gay, 53–60. London: Sage Publications.

Birnbaum, Larry. 1994. Eddie Palmieri heads south. *New York Latino* 1 (Spring): 17–19.

Blacking, John. 1955. Some notes on a theory of African rhythm advanced by Erich von Hornbostel. *African Music* I (2): 12–20.

———. 1973a. Fieldwork in African music. In *Reflections on Afro-American music,* ed. Dominique-René de Lerma, 207–221. Kent, OH: Kent State University Press.

———. 1973b. *How musical is man?* Seattle: University of Washington Press.

———. 1977. The ethnography of musical performance. Background paper for the 12th IMS Conference, Berkeley.

———. 1979. The study of man as music maker. In *The performing arts, music, and dance,* ed. J. Blacking and Joann W. Kealiinohomoku, 3–15. The Hague, the Netherlands: Mouton.

Blum, Joseph. 1978. Problems of salsa research. *Ethnomusicology* 12 (1): 137–149.

Boggs, Vernon W. 1992. *Salsiology: Afro-Cuban music and the evolution of salsa in New York City.* New York: Excelsior Music Publishing Company.

Bourgois, Philippe. 1996. *In search of respect: Selling crack in El Barrio.* Cambridge: Cambridge University Press.

Brown, Robert McAfee. 1987. *Religion and violence.* Philadelphia: Westminster Press.

Buckland, Fiona. 2002. *Club culture and queer world-making.* Middletown, CT: Wesleyan University Press.

Butler, Judith. 1990. *Gender trouble: Feminism and the subversion of identity.* New York: Routledge.

———. 1993. *Bodies that matter.* London: Routledge.

Calvo-Ospina, Hernando. 1995. *Salsa! Havana beat, Bronx beat.* Trans. Mick Caister. London: Latin American Bureau.

Caroll, Charles R. 1985. *Drugs in modern society.* Dubuque, IA: William C. Brown Publishing.

Casey, Edward S. 1996. To get from space to place in a fairly short stretch of time: Phenomenological prolegomena. In *Senses of place,* ed. Steven Feld and Keith Basso, 13–52. Santa Fe, NM: School of American Research Press.

Casteñeda, Omar. 1996. Guatemalan macho oratory. In *Muy macho: Latino men confront their manhood,* ed. Ray González, 35–50. New York: Anchor Books Doubleday.

Chernoff, John. 1979. *African rhythm and African sensibility: Aesthetics and social action in African musical idioms.* Chicago: University of Chicago Press.

Clifford, James. 1988. *The predicament of culture: Twentieth-century ethnography, literature, and art.* Cambridge, MA: Harvard University Press.

———. 1997. *Routes: Travel and translation in the late twentieth century.* Cambridge, MA: Harvard University Press.

Cohen, Sara. 1991. *Rock culture in Liverpool: Popular music in the making*. Oxford, UK: Clarendon Press.

Concepcion, Alma. 2002. Dance in Puerto Rico: Embodied meanings. In *Caribbean dance from Abakua to Zouk: How movement shapes identity,* ed. Susanna Sloat, 165–175. Gainesville: University Press of Florida.

Contreras, Felix. 2006. Interview with Johnny Pacheco. *NPR Morning Edition* (June 1).

Cornelius, Steve, and John Amira. 1992. *The music of Santería: Traditional rhythms of the batá drums.* Crown Point, IN: White Cliffs Media Company.

Coronil, Fernando, and Julie Skurski. 1991. Dismembering and remembering the nation: The semantics of political violence in Venezuela. *Comparative Studies in Society and History* 33 (2): 288–337.

Cortes, Felix, Angel Falcón, and Juan Flores. 1976. The cultural expression of Puerto Ricans in New York: A theoretical perspective and critical review. *Latin American Perspectives* 3 (3): 117–150.

Creed, Gerald, and Barbara Ching, eds. 1997. Recognizing rusticity: Identity and the power of place. In *Knowing your place: Rural identity and cultural hierarchy,* 1–38. New York: Routledge.

Dannen, Fredric. 1991. *Hitmen: Power brokers and fast money inside the music business.* New York: Vintage Books.

Davis, Miles, with Quincy Troupe. 1989. *The autobiography.* New York: Simon and Schuster.

De Genova, Nicholas, and Ana Y. Ramos-Zayas. 2003. *Latino crossings: Mexicans, Puerto Ricans, and the politics of race and citizenship.* New York: Routledge.

Delgado, Celeste Fraser, and José Muñoz. 1997. Rebellions in everynight life. In *Everynight life: Culture and dance in Latin/o America,* ed. Celeste Fraser Delgado and José Muñoz, 9–32. Durham, NC: Duke University Press.

Derrida, Jacques. 1981. *Positions.* Chicago: University of Chicago Press.

Desmond, Jane. 1997. Embodying difference: Issues in dance and cultural studies. In *Everynight life: Culture and dance in Latin/o America,* ed. Celeste Fraser Delgado and José Muñoz, 33–64. Durham, NC: Duke University Press.

Diamond, Stephen. 1996. *Anger, madness, and the daimonic: The psychological genesis of violence, evil, and creativity.* Albany, NY: State University of New York Press.

Doerschuk, Robert, 1992. Secrets of salsa rhythm: Piano with hot sauce. In *Salsiology: Afro Cuban music and the evolution of salsa in New York City,* ed. Vernon Boggs, 312–324. New York: Greenwood Press.

Duany, Jorge. 1984. Popular music in Puerto Rico: Toward an anthropology of salsa. *Latin American Music Review* 5 (2): 186–216.

———. 1988. After the revolution: The search for roots in Afro-Cuban culture. *Latin American Research Review* 23 (1): 244–255.

———. 1990. Salsa, plena, and danza: Recent publications on Puerto Rican popular music. *Latin American Music Review* 11 (2): 286–296.

———. 1996. Rethinking the popular: Recent essays on Caribbean music and identity. *Latin American Music Review* 17 (2): 176–193.

Edberg, Mark Cameron. 2004. *El narcotraficante: Narcocorridos and the construction of a cultural persona on the U.S.-Mexico border.* Austin: University of Texas Press.

Erin, Ronald. 1984. Cuban elements in the music of Aurelio de la Vega. *Latin American Music Review* 5 (1): 1–32.

Ewing, Katherine Pratt. 1997. *Arguing sainthood: Modernity, psychoanalysis, and Islam.* Durham, NC: Duke University Press.

Feijóo, Samuel. 1986. *El son Cubano: Poesia general.* Havana: Editorial Letras Cubanas.

Feld, Steven. 1974. Linguistic models in ethnomusicology. *Ethnomusicology* 18: 197–217.

———. 1982. *Sound and sentiment.* Philadelphia: University of Pennsylvania Press.

———. 1988. Aesthetics as iconicity of style, or "lift-up-over sounding": Getting into the Kaluli groove. *Yearbook for Traditional Music* 20: 74–113.

Feld, Steven and Keith Basso, eds. 1996. *Senses of place.* Santa Fe, NM: School of American Research Press.

Fernandez, Raul. 2005. *From Afro-Cuban rhythms to Latin jazz.* Berkeley: University of California Press.

Figueroa, Frank. 1997. Manny Oquendo up close and personal." *Latin Beat* 7 (9): 20–23.

———. 1998. El Cano Estremera: El dueño del sonero. *Latin Beat* 8 (6): 24–26.

———. 2002. New York's Latin music landmarks. *Latin Beat* 12 (10): 28–31.

Fikentscher, Kai. 2000. *"You better work!": Underground dance music in New York City.* Hanover, NH: University Press of New England.

Finnegan, Ruth. 1989. *Hidden musicians: Music-making in an English town.* Cambridge: Cambridge University Press.

Fitzpatrick, Joseph P. 1990. Drugs and Puerto Ricans in New York City. In *Drugs in Hispanic communities,* ed. Ronald Glick and Joan Moore, 195–202. New Brunswick, NJ: Rutgers University Press.

Flores, A. 1987. Once-hot biz of salsa sound is a cold note. *New York Daily News,* July 14: 1, 6.

Flores, Carlos. 1997. In memory of Ismael Rivera, "el sonero mayor." *Kalinda!* (Fall): 9–11.

Flores, Juan. 1992. Cortijo's revenge: New mappings of Puerto Rican culture. In *On Edge: The crisis of contemporary Latin American culture,* ed. George Yudice, Jean Franco, and Juan Flores, 187–205. Minneapolis: University of Minnesota Press.

———. 1993. *Divided borders: Essays on Puerto Rican identity.* Houston: Arte Público.

———. 1997. Recapturing history: The Puerto Rican roots of hip hop culture. In *Island sounds in the global city,* ed. Ray Allen and Lois Wilken, 61–73. New York: New York Folklore Society.

———. 1999. Rappin', writin', and breakin'. *Centro de Estudios Puertorriqueños Bulletin* 2 (3): 34–41.

———. 2000. *From bomba to hip hop: Puerto Rican culture and Latino identity.* New York: Columbia University Press.

Foster, George McClelland. 1960. *Culture and conquest: America's Spanish heritage.* Chicago: Quadrangle Books.

Fox, Aaron. 1992. The jukebox of history: Narratives of loss and desire in the discourse of country music. *Popular Music* 11 (1): 53–72.

———. 1995. Out the country: Language, music, feeling, and sociability in American rural working class culture. PhD diss., University of Texas at Austin.

———. 2004. *Real country: Music and language in working-class culture.* Durham, NC: Duke University Press.

Freud, Sigmund. 1953. *A general introduction to psychoanalysis.* New York: Simon and Schuster.

Friedman, Robert. 1978. "If you don't play good they take the drum away": Performance, communication and acts in guaguancó. In *Discourse in ethnomusicology: Essays in honor of George List,* ed. Caroline Card, John Hasse, Roberta Singer, and Ruth Stone, 209–224. Bloomington: Indiana University Ethnomusicology Publications Group.

Frith, Simon. 1988. *Music for pleasure: Essays in the sociology of pop.* Cambridge, UK: Polity Press.

———. 1996a. Music and identity. In *Questions of cultural identity,* ed. Stuart Hall and Paul du Gay, 108–127. London: Sage Publications.

———. 1996b. *Performing rites: On the value of popular music.* Oxford: Oxford University Press.

Galán, Natalio. 1983. *Cuba y sus sones.* Valencia, Spain: Pre-textos/Música.

García, David. 2006. *Arsenio Rodríguez and the transnational flows of Latin popular music.* Philadelphia: Temple University Press.

García, Guy. 1997. It's on Broadway, but will it cross over? *New York Times,* November 30: 38, 42.

García-Canclini, Nestor. 1990. *Culturas híbridas: Estrategias para entrar y salir de la modernidad.* Mexico City: Grijalbo.

Gerard, Charley, with Marty Sheller. 1989. *Salsa: The Rhythm of Latin music.* Crown Point, IN: White Cliffs Media Company.

Glasser, Ruth. 1990. Paradoxical ethnicity: Puerto Rican musicians in post–World War I New York City. *Latin American Music Review* 11 (1): 63–72.

———. 1995. *My music is my flag: Puerto Rican musicians and their New York communities, 1917–1940.* Berkeley: University of California Press.

———. 1998. Buscando ambiente: Puerto Rican musicians in New York City, 1917–1940. In *Island sounds in the global city,* ed. Ray Allen and Lois Wilken, 7–22. New York: New York Folklore Society.

Glick, Ronald, and Joan Moore, eds. 1990. *Drugs in Hispanic communities.* New Brunswick, NJ: Rutgers University Press.

Glissant, Edouard. 1976. Free and forced poetics. Ethnopoetics: The first international symposium. *Alcheringa* 2 (2): 95–101.

Goldberg, Norbert, ed. 1991. *Understanding Latin rhythms.* Garfield, NJ: Latin Percussion Inc.

Gómez, José Manuel. 1995. *Guia esencial de la salsa.* Valencia: Editorial La Máscara.

Gómez, Zoila, ed. 1984. *Musicología en Latinoamérica.* Havana: Editorial Arte y Literatura.

González, Elmer. 1999. Tite Curet Alonso: Primoroso cantar. *Latin Beat* 9 (1): 21–23.

Gootenberg, Paul, ed. 1999. *Cocaine: Global histories.* New York: Routledge.

Greene, Paul D., and Thomas Porcello, eds. 2005. *Wired for sound: Engineering and technologies in sonic cultures.* Middletown, CT: Wesleyan University Press.

Grenet, Emilio. 1939. *Popular Cuban music: 80 revised and corrected compositions.* Trans. R. Phillips. Havana: Carasa & Co.

Guarnizo, Luis Eduardo, and Luz Marina Díaz. 1999. Transnational migration: A view from Colombia. *Ethnic and Racial Studies* 22 (2): 397–421.

Guarnizo, Luis Eduardo, Arturo Ignacio Sánchez, and Elizabeth M. Roach. 1999. Mistrust, fragmented solidarity, and transnational migration: Colombians in New York City and Los Angeles. *Ethnic and Racial Studies* 22 (2): 367–396.

Gupta, Akhil, and James Ferguson. 1997. *Anthropological locations: Boundaries and grounds of a field science.* Berkeley: University of California Press.

Gutmann, Matthew. 1996. *The meanings of macho: Being a man in Mexico City.* Berkeley: University of California Press.

Hall, Stuart. 1992. Cultural identity and cinematic representation. In *Ex-Iles: Essays on Caribbean cinema,* ed. Mbye B. Cham, 220–236. Trenton, NJ: Africa World Press Inc.

———. 1996. Who needs "identity"? In *Questions of cultural identity,* ed. Stuart Hall and Paul du Gay, 1–17. London: Sage Publications.

———. 2003a. Créolité and the process of Creolization. In *Créolité and Creolization: Documenta 11,* Platform 3, ed. Okwui Enwezor, Carlos Basualdo, Ute Meta Bauer, Susanne Ghez, Sarat Maharaj, Mark Nash, and Octavio Zaya, 27–41. Ostfildern-Ruit, Germany: Hatje Cantz.

———. 2003b. Creolization, diaspora, and hybridity in the context of globalization. In *Créolité and Creolization: Documenta 11,* Platform 3, ed. Okwui Enwezor, Carlos Basualdo, Ute Meta Bauer, Susanne Ghez, Sarat Maharaj, Mark Nash, and Octavio Zaya, 185–198. Ostfildern-Ruit, Germany: Hatje Cantz.

Handler, Richard. 1988. *Nationalism and the politics of culture in Quebec.* Madison, WI: University of Wisconsin Press.

Handler, Richard, and Jocelyn Linnekin. 1984. Tradition, genuine or spurious. *Journal of American Folklore* 97 (385): 275–290.

Hannerz, Ulf. 1989. Notes on the global ecumene. *Public Culture* 1 (2): 66–76.

———. n.d. The world system of culture: The international flow of meaning and its local management. Manuscript.

Herdt, Gilbert. 1994. *Third sex, third gender: Beyond sexual dimorphism in culture and history.* New York: Zone.

Hobsbawn, Eric, and Terence Ranger, eds. 1983. *The invention of tradition.* New York: Cambridge University Press.

Hochschild, Arlie Russell. 1983. *The managed heart: Commercialization of human feeling.* Berkeley: University of California Press.

Hood, Mantle. 1960. The challenge of "bi-musicality." *Ethnomusicology* 4 (2): 55–59.

Hunt, Alfred. 1988. *Haiti's influence on antebellum America.* Baton Rouge: Louisiana State University Press.

Irvine, Judith T., and J. David Sapir. 1976. Musical style and social change among the Kujamaat Diola. *Ethnomusicology* 20 (1): 67–86.

Jabri, Vivienne. 1996. *Discourses on violence: Conflict analysis reconsidered.* New York: Martin's Press.

Jackman, Mary R. 2002. Violence in social life. *Annual Review of Sociology* 28: 387–416.

Jackson, Irene V., ed. 1985. *More than drumming: Essays on African and Afro-Latin music and musicians.* Westport, CT: Greenwood Press.

Janson-Pérez, Brittmarie. 1987. Political facets of salsa. *Popular Music* 2: 149–159.

Jimenez, R. Emilio. 1929. *Al amor del bohio: Tradiciones y costumbres Dominicanas.* Tomo II. Santiago, Dominican Republic: La Informacion C. por A. Editora.

Kartomi, Margaret. 1981. The processes and results of musical culture contact: A discussion of terminology and concepts. *Ethnomusicology* 25 (2): 227–245.

Keil, Charles. 1966. Motion and feeling through music. *Journal of Aesthetics and Art Criticism* 24 (Spring): 337–349.

———. 1985. People's music comparatively: Style and stereotype, class and hegemony. *Dialectical Anthropology* 10: 119–130.

Kent, Mary. 2005. *Salsa talks: A musical heritage uncovered.* Altamonte Springs, FL: Digital Domain.

Koning, Jos. 1980. The fieldworker as performer: Fieldwork objectives and social roles in County Clare, Ireland. *Ethnomusicology* 24 (3): 417–429.

Kubik, Gerhard. 1996. Emics and etics: Theoretical considerations. *African Music* 7 (3): 3–10.

Laclau, Ernesto. 1990. *New reflections on the revolution of our time.* London: Verso.

Lancaster, Roger. 1992. *Life is hard: Machismo, danger, and the intimacy of power in Nicaragua.* Berkeley: University of California Press.

Lastrucci, Carlo L. 1941. The professional dance musician. *Journal of Musicology* 3 (3): 168–172.

Lawson, Helene. 1991. Learning to suspect and betray: The transformation of car sales women. Paper presented at the annual meeting of the Midwest Sociological Society, Des Moines, Iowa.

Leidner, Robin. 1993. *Fast food, fast talk: Service work and the routinization of everyday life.* Berkeley: University of California Press.

Lenson, David. 1993. *On drugs.* Minneapolis: University of Minnesota Press.

León, Argeliers. 1974. *Del canto y el tiempo.* Havana, Cuba: Instituto Cubana del Libro.

Leymarie, Isabelle. 1985. Salsa and Latin jazz. In *Hot sauces: Latin and Caribbean pop,* ed. Billy Bergman, 99–115. New York: Quill.

Limón, José E. 1994. *Dancing with the devil: Society and cultural poetics in Mexican-American south Texas.* Madison: University of Wisconsin Press.

Linares, Maria Teresa. 1974. *La música y el pueblo.* Havana: Instituto Cubano del Libro.

Lipsitz, George. 1994. *Dangerous crossroads: Popular music, postermodernism, and the poetics of place.* New York: Verso.

———. 1995. The possessive investment in whiteness: Racialized social democracy and the "white" problem in American studies. *American Quarterly* 47 (3): 369–387.

Locke, David. 1987. *Drum gahu: A systematic method for an African percussion piece.* Crown Point, IN: White Cliffs Media.

López, Alfredo. 1973. *The Puerto Rican papers: Notes on the reemergence of a nation.* Indianapolis: Bobbs-Merrill.

Lopez, Alfredo. 1977. It don't mean a thing if it ain't got that clave. *Village Voice,* November 7: 37, 49, 50.

Loza, Steve. 1999. *Tito Puente and the making of Latin music.* Chicago: University of Illinois Press.

Loza, Steve, Milo Alvarez, Josefina Santiago, and Charles Moore. 1994. Los Angeles gangsta rap and the aesthetics of violence. *Selected Reports in Ethnomusicology* 10: 149–161.

Lugo, Elmo. 1993. Sergio George: Identidad de RMM. *Miami Herald Tribune,* October 22: D27.

MacLeod, Bruce A. 1993. *Club date musicians: Playing the New York party circuit.* Chicago: University of Illinois Press.

Maldonado, Lionel A. 1991. Latino ethnicity: Increasing diversity. *Latino Studies Journal* 2 (3): 49–57.

Mangual, Rudy. 1999. La India—red hot diva. *Latin Beat* 9 (9): 20–23.

Manuel, Peter. 1985. The anticipated bass in Cuban popular music. *Latin American Music Review* 6 (2): 249–260.

———, ed. 1991a. *Essays on Cuban music: North American and Cuban perspectives.* New York: University Press of America.

———. 1991b. Latin music in the United States: Salsa and the mass media. *Journal of Communication* 41 (1): 104–116.

———. 1994. Puerto Rican music and cultural identity: Creative appropriation of Cuban sources from danza to salsa. *Ethnomusicology* 38 (2): 249–280.

———. 1995. *Caribbean currents: Caribbean music from rumba to reggae.* Philadelphia: Temple University Press.

Marcuse, Herbert. 1978. *The aesthetic dimension: Toward a critique of Marxist aesthetics.* Boston: Beacon Press.

Marez, Curtis. 2004. *Drug wars: The political economy of narcotics.* Minneapolis: University of Minnesota Press.

Martinez Jr., Ramiro. 1996. Latinos and lethal violence: The impact of poverty and inequality. *Social Problems* 43 (2): 131–146.

Matory, J. Lorand. 1999. Afro-Atlantic culture: On the live dialogue between Africa and the Americas. In *Africana,* ed. Kwane Appiah and Henry Louis Gates, 36–44. New York: Basic Civitas.

Mauleón, Rebeca. 1993. *Salsa guidebook for piano and ensemble.* Petaluma, CA: Sher Music Co.

———. 1996. The heart of salsa: Exploring Afro-Caribbean piano style. *Keyboard* (January): 28–44.

McDowell, John H. 2000. *Poetry and violence: The ballad tradition of Mexico's costa chica.* Urbana: University of Illinois Press.

McLane, Daisann. 1996. Salsa for the high tops generation. *New York Times,* August 11: H26, 29.

McLeod, Norma, and Marcia Herndon. 1980. *The ethnography of performance.* Norwood, PA: Norwood Editions.

Meintjes, Louise. 2003. *Sound of Africa!: Making music Zulu in a South African studio.* Durham: Duke University Press.

Merriam, Alan P. 1964. *The anthropology of music.* Chicago: Northwestern University Press.

———. 1969. Ethnomusicology Revisited. *Ethnomusicology* 12 (2): 213–229.

Meyer, Leonard. 1956. *Emotion and meaning in music.* Chicago: University of Chicago Press.

———. 1979. Toward a theory of style. In *The concept of style,* ed. Berel Lang, 21–71. Philadelphia: University of Pennsylvania.

Milkowsky, Solomon Gadles. 1988. *Ignacio cervantes y la danza.* Havana: Editorial Letras Cubanas.

Moore, Henrietta. 1994. Gendered persons: Dialogues between anthropology and psychoanalysis. In *Anthropology and psychoanalysis: An encounter through culture,* ed. Susette Heald and Ariane Deluz, 131–152. New York: Routledge.

Moreno, Jairo. n.d. Unpublished manuscript.

Morris, Rosalind. 1995. All made up: Performance theory and the new anthropology of sex and gender. *Annual Review of Anthropology* 24: 567–592.

Mulholland, Mary-Lee. 1998. Sensuous politics: Salsa as culture critique. MA thesis, Carleton University.

Muñoz, José. 1999. *Disidentifications: Queers of color and the performance of politics.* Minneapolis: University of Minnesota Press.

Murdock, George Peter. 1956. How culture changes. In *Man, culture, and society,* ed. Harry L. Shapiro, 319–332. New York: Oxford University Press.

Murguia, Edward. 1991. On Latino/Hispanic ethnic identity. *Latino Studies Journal* 2 (3): 8–18.

Murphy, John. 1988. The charanga in New York, 1987–88: Musical style, performance context, and tradition. MA thesis, Columbia University.

———. 1991. The charanga in New York and the persistence of the típico style. In *Essays on Cuban music: North American and Cuban perspectives,* ed. Peter Manuel, 115–136. New York: University Press of America.

Navarro, Mireya. 2001. For sale: A Latin music legacy. NYTimes.com, June 7. http://www.nytimes.com/2001/06/07/arts/07MERC.html?ex=992918359&ei=1&en=8667c55e852d6651.

Nettl, Bruno. 1964. *Theory and method in ethnomusicology.* Glencoe, IL: The Free Press.

Negus, Keith. 1999. *Music genres and corporate cultures.* New York: Routledge Press.

Nodal, Roberto. 1983. The social evolution of the Afro-Cuban drum. *The Black Perspective in Music* XI (2): 157–177.

Oboler, Suzanne. 2005. *Ethnic labels, Latino lives: Identity and the politics of (re)presentation in the United States.* Minneapolis: University of Minnesota Press.

Olmedo, Irma M. 1993. The changing face of the jíbaro and Puerto Rican values. *Latino Studies Journal* IV (1): 41–54.

Omi, Michael, and Howard Winant. 1994. *Racial formation in the United States: From the 1960s to the 1990s.* New York: Routledge.

Ortiz, Fernando. [1935] 1984. *La clave xilofonica de la música Cubana.* Havana, Cuba: Editorial Letras Cubanas.

———. 1965. *La Africanía de la música folklórica de Cuba.* Havana: Editora Universitaria.

Ortner, Sherry. 1984. Theory in anthropology since the sixties. In *Culture/power/history: A reader in contemporary social theory,* ed. Nicholas B. Dirks, Geoff Eley, and Sherry B. Ortner, 372–411. Princeton: Princeton University Press.

Padilla, Felix M. 1985. *Latino ethnic consciousness: The case of Mexican Americans and Puerto Ricans in Chicago.* Notre Dame, IN: University of Notre Dame Press.

———. 1990. Salsa: Puerto Rican and Latino music. *Journal of Popular Culture* 24: 87–104.

———. 1992. Salsa music as a cultural expression of Latino consciousness and unity. In *Race, class, and gender: An anthology,* ed. Margaret L. Andersen and Patricia Hill Collins, 347–358. Belmont, CA: Wadsworth Publishing.

Padura-Fuentes, Leonardo. 2003. *Faces of salsa: A spoken history of the music.* Trans. Stephen J. Clark. Washington, DC: Smithsonian Books.

Palmer, Robert. 1977. Can salsa escape the cultural ghetto? *New York Times,* January 23: B22, 29.

Peña, Manuel. 1980. Ritual structure in Chicano dance. *Latin American Music Review* 1 (1): 47–73.

———. 1985. *The Texas-Mexican conjunto: History of a working class music.* Austin: University of Texas Press.

Pereira-Salas, Eugenio. 1943. *Notas para la historia del intercamio musical entre Las Americas*. Union of American Republics Music Series, no.6.

Pérez-Fernandez, Rolando Antonia. 1986. *La binarización de los ritmos ternarios Africanos en América Latina*. Havana: Ediciones Casa de las Americas.

Pérez, José, and Antonio Mejias. 1997. *The Hector Lavoe story*. New York: Infante Productions, Inc.

Polin, Bruce. 1996. A visit with Ruben Blades. *Descarga Newsletter* 27: 1–19.

Porcello, Thomas. 1996. Sonic artistry: Music, discourse, and technology in the sound recording studio. PhD diss., University of Texas, Austin.

Pratt, Mary Louise. 1992. *Imperial eyes: Travel writing and transculturation*. New York: Routledge.

Quintero-Herencia, Juan Carlos. 1997. Notes toward a reading of salsa. Trans. Celeste Fraser Delgado. In *Everynight Life: Culture and dance in Latin/o America*, ed. Celeste Fraser Delgado and José Muñoz, 189–222. Durham: Duke University Press.

Quintero-Rivera, Angel. 1998. *Salsa sabor y control: Sociología de la música "tropical."* Mexico City, Mexico: Siglo Veintiuno editores.

Quintero-Rivera, Angel, and Luis Manuel Alvarez. 1990. La libre conbinación de las formas musicales en la salsa. *David y Goliath, Revista del Consejo Latinoamericano de Ciencas Sociales* 19 (57): 45–51.

Radano, Ronald. 2003. *Lying up a nation: Race and black music*. Chicago: University of Chicago Press.

Rendon, Victor. 1991. *Rhythms and techniques for Latin timbales*. Published by author.

Reyes Schramm, Adelaida. 1975. The role of music in the interaction of black Americans and Hispanos in New York City's East Harlem. PhD diss., Columbia University.

———. 1979. Ethnic music, the urban area, and ethnomusicology. *Sociologus* 29: 11–21.

Ricoeur, Paul. 1975. *Political and social essays*. Coll. and ed. David Stewart and Joseph Bien. Athens, OH: Ohio University Press.

———. 1988. *Time and narrative*. Vol. 3. Chicago: University of Chicago Press.

Roberts, John Storm. 1979. *The Latin tinge: The impact of Latin American music on the United States*. New York: Oxford University Press.

Rodríguez, Clara E. 1995. Puerto Ricans in historical and social science research. In *Handbook of research on multicultural education*, ed. James A. Banks and Cherry A. McGee Banks, 223–244. New York: Simon and Schuster.

Rodríguez, Nelson, and Patricia Romero. 1998. Gilberto Santarosa . . . a class act! *Latin Beat* 8 (1): 18–19.

Rodríguez-Cortes, Carmen. 1990. Social practices of ethnic identity: A Puerto Rican psycho-cultural event. *Hispanic Journal of Behavioral Sciences* 12 (4): 380–396.

Roldan, Mary. 1999. Colombia: Cocaine and the "miracle" of modernity in Medellín. In *Cocaine: Global histories*, ed. Paul Gootenberg, 165–181. New York: Routledge.

Rollins, Judith. 1985. *Between women: Domestics and their employers*. Philadelphia: Temple University Press.

Roman-Velázquez, Patria. 1999. The embodiment of salsa: Musicians, instruments and the performance of Latin style and identity. *Popular Music* 18 (1): 115–131.

Rondón, Cesar Miguel. 1980. *El libro de la salsa: Crónica de la música del caribe urbano*. Caracas, Venezuela: Editorial Arte.

Rosaldo, Renato. 1989. *Culture and truth: The remaking of social analysis*. Boston: Beacon Press.

Rosario, Edward. 1976. Getting inside the classroom. *Latin New York* (October): 27.

Rotker, Susana, ed. 2002. *Citizens of fear: Urban violence in Latin America.* New Brunswick, NJ: Rutgers University Press.

Rowe, William, and Vivian Schelling. 1991. *Memory and modernity: Popular culture in Latin America.* New York: Verso.

Sabourin, Tony. 1985. Latin international. In *Hot sauces: Latin and Caribbean pop,* ed. Billy Bergman, 118–123. New York: Quill.

Salazar, Max. 1980. Latin music: The perseverance of a culture. In *The Puerto Rican struggle: Essays on survival in the United States,* ed. Oscar Alers, Clara Rodríguez, and Virginia Sánchez-Korrol, 74–81. New York: Puerto Rican Migration Research Consortium.

———. 1998. Ray Ramos: A salsa musician's struggle. *Latin Beat Magazine* 8 (4): 41.

———. 2002a. *Mambo kingdom: Latin music in New York.* New York: Schirmer.

———. 2002b. Orestes López and the mambo. *Latin Beat Magazine* 17 (7): 26–28.

Salazar, Rodrigo, and Jorge Cano-Moreno. 1995. Marc Anthony: Salsa's new flava. *Urban: The Latino Magazine* (Summer): 7.

Sanábria, Izzy. 1976. Editorial. *Latin New York* (May): 6.

Santana, Sergio. 1992. *Que es la salsa? Buscando la melodia.* Medellín: Ediciones Salsa y Cultura.

Santos-Febres, Mayra. 1997. Salsa as translocation. In *Everynight life: Culture and dance in Latin/o America,* ed. Celeste Fraser Delgado and José Muñoz, 175–188. Durham, NC: Duke University Press.

Sassen-Koob, Saskia. 1979. Formal and informal association: Dominicans and Colombians in New York. *International Migration Review* 13 (2): 314–332.

Saumell, Manuel. 1981. *Contradanzas.* Havana: Editorial Letras Cubanas.

Scarry, Elaine. 1985. *The body in pain: The making and unmaking of the world.* Oxford: Oxford University Press.

Schivelbusch, Wolfgang. 1993. *Tastes of paradise: A social history of spices, stimulants, and intoxicants.* New York: Vintage Books.

Schneider, Jo Anne. 1990. Defining boundaries, creating contacts: Puerto Rican and Polish representation of group identity through ethnic parades. *Journal of Ethnic Studies* 18 (1): 33–57.

Schroeder, Pollyanna T. 1978. The growth of Latin American pop music in the United States. *College Music Symposium* 18 (2): 124–129.

Seeger, Anthony. 1987. *Why suya sing: A musical anthropology of an Amazonian people.* Cambridge: University of Cambridge Press.

Seeger, Charles. 1958. Prescriptive and descriptive music writing. *Musical Quarterly* 44: 184–195.

Sephocle, Marie-Line. 1992. Interview with Aimé Césaire. In *Exiles: Essays on Caribbean cinema,* ed. Mbye B. Cham, 359–369. Trenton, NJ: Africa World Press Inc.

Sher, Chuck, ed. 1997. *The Latin real book.* Petaluma, CA: Sher Music Company.

Simonett, Helena. 2001. *Banda: Mexican musical life across borders.* Middletown, CT: Wesleyan University Press.

Simpson, Ian. 1988. Guerra musical en Puerto Rico: Rock vs. salsa. *Noticias del Mundo* (February 12).

Singer, Roberta. 1982. My music is who I am and what I do: Latin popular music and identity in New York City. PhD diss., Indiana University.

———. 1983. Tradition and innovation in contemporary Latin popular music in New York City. *Latin American Music Review* 4 (2): 183–202.

———. 1988. Puerto Rican music in New York City. *New York Folklore* 19 (3–4): 139–150.

Singer, Roberta, and Robert A. Friedman. 1977. Puerto Rican and Cuban musical expression in New York. Album liner notes to *Caliente-Hot: Puerto Rican and Cuban Musical Expressions in New York.* New World Records (NW 244).

Slobin, Mark. 1992. Micromusics of the West: A comparative approach. *Ethnomusicology* 36 (1): 1–88.

Smitherman, Geneva. 1994. *Black talk: Words and phrases from the hood to the amen.* Boston: Houghton Mifflin.

Somers, Margaret. 1994. The narrative constitution of identity: A relational and network approach. *Theory and Society* 23: 605–649.

Sommers, Laurie Kay. 1991. The creation of "Hispanic" pan-ethnicity in the United States. *Journal of American Folklore* 104: 32–53.

Stavans, Ilán. 1996. The Latin phallus. In *Muy macho: Latino men confront their manhood,* ed. Ray González, 143–164. New York: Anchor Books Doubleday.

Stevens, Evelyn. 1973. Marianismo: The other face of machismo in Latin America. In *Male and female in Latin America,* ed. Ann Pescatello, 89–101. Pittsburgh: University of Pittsburgh Press.

Sterns, Marshall. 1956. *The story of jazz.* New York: Oxford University Press.

Steward, Sue. 1999. *The rhythm of Latin America, salsa, rumba, merengue, and more.* London: Thames and Hudson Ltd.

Straw, Will. [1991] 2004. Systems of articulation, logics of change: Communities and scenes in popular music. In *Popular music: Critical concepts in media and cultural studies.* Vol. 4. Ed. Simon Frith, 79–100. New York: Routledge. Originally published in *Cultural Studies* 5 (3): 368–388.

Sturman, Janet. 1984. Advertising and Latin music at a New York City jazz club. *Current Musicology* 37–38: 159–66.

Sublette, Ned. 2004. *Cuba and its music: From the first drums to the mambo.* Chicago: A Cappella.

Szwed, John. 2002. *So what: The life of Miles Davis.* New York: Simon and Schuster.

Tamargo, Luis. 1999. Everything you always wanted to know about the 1990s, but were afraid to ask. *Latin Beat* 9 (9): 30–31.

Taussig, Michael. 1987. *Shamanism, colonialism, and the wild man: A study in terror and healing.* Chicago: University of Chicago Press.

———. 1998. Transgression. In *Critical terms for religious studies,* ed. Mark C. Taylor, 349–364. Chicago: University of Chicago Press.

———. 2004. *My cocaine museum.* Chicago: University of Chicago Press.

Théberge, Paul. 1997. *Any sound you can imagine: Making music/consuming technology.* Middletown, CT: Wesleyan University Press.

Thompson, E. P. 1977. Folklore, anthropology, and social history. *Indian Historical Review* 2 (2): 247–266.

Thompson, Robert Farris. 2002. Teaching the people to triumph over time: Notes from the world of mambo. In *Caribbean dance from Abakua to Zouk: How movement shapes identity,* ed. Susanna Sloat, 336–344. Gainesville: University Press of Florida.

Thoumi, Franscisco. 1994. *Economía política y narcotráfico.* Santafé de Bogotá: TM Editores.

Tinker-Salas, Miguel. 1991. El immigrante Latino: Latin American immigration and pan-ethnicity. *Latino Studies Journal* 2 (3): 58–71.

Torres, J. L. 1976. Santerismo: Interview with Milton Cardona and José Mangual, Jr. *Latin New York* (November): 25.

Trottier, Richard. 1981. Charters of pan-ethnic identity: Indigenous American Indians and immigrant Asian-Americans. In *Ethnic change,* ed. Charles Keyes, 271–305. Seattle: University of Washington Press.

Tsing, Anna. 2005. *Friction: An ethnography of global connection.* Princeton, NJ: Princeton University Press.

Turner, Victor. 1969. *The ritual process: Structure and anti-structure.* Ithaca: Cornell University Press.

Urban, Greg. 1991. *A discourse centered approach to culture: Native South American myths and rituals.* Austin: University of Texas Press.

Valentín-Escobar, Wilson. 2002. El hombre que respira debajo del agua: Trans-boricua memories, identities, and nationalisms performed through the death of Hector Lavoe. In *Situating salsa: Global markets and local meanings in Latin popular music,* ed. Lise Waxer, 161–185. New York: Routledge.

Valle, Maria Eva. 1991. The quest for ethnic solidarity and a new public identity among Chicanos and Latinos. *Latino Studies Journal* 2 (3): 72–83.

Valverde, Umberto, and Raphael Quintero. 1995. *Abran paso: Historia de las orquestas femininas de Cali.* Cali: Ediciones Universidad del Valle.

Vinueza, Maria Elena. 1986. *Presencia arará en la música folclorica de matanzas.* Havana: Casas de las Americas.

von Hornbostel, Erich. 1928. African Negro music. *Africa* I (1): 1–35.

Washburne, Christopher. 1992. Communication as composition: A historical perspective on the music of Gil Evans. MA thesis, Columbia University.

———. 1995. Clave: The African roots of salsa. *Kalinda!: Newsletter for the Center for Black Music Research* (Fall): 7–11. Reprinted in *Clave* 1 (2): 2–3. Also posted on www.chriswashburne.com.

———. 1997. The clave of jazz: A Caribbean contribution to the rhythmic foundation of an African-American music. *Black Music Research Journal* (Spring): 59–80.

———. 2002. Salsa romántica: An analysis of style, sound structure, and contemporary performance practice. In *Situating salsa: Global markets and local meanings in Latin popular music,* ed. Lise Waxer, 101–132. New York: Routledge.

——— and Maiken Derno. 2002. Masquerading machismo: La India transgendering on the salsa scene. *Women in Performance* 12:2 (24): 140–156.

———., eds. 2004. *Bad music: The music you love to hate.* New York: Routledge Press.

Waterman, Christopher Alan. 1990. *Juju: A social history and ethnography of an African popular music.* Chicago: University of Chicago Press.

———. 1991. Juju history: Toward a theory of socio-musical practice. In *Ethnomusicology and modern music history,* ed. Stephen Blum, Philip Bohlman, and Daniel M. Neuman, 49–67. Urbana: University of Illinois Press.

Waterman, Richard. 1952. African influence on the music of Americas. In *Acculturation in the Americas,* ed. Sol Tax, 207–221. Chicago: University of Chicago Press.

Watrous, Peter. 1996. Wooing a new generation of Hispanic audiences. *New York Times,* October 9: C14.

———. 1997. Jerry Masucci, 62, international salsa promoter. http://www.descarga.com/cgi-bin/db/archives/Article8 (December 24).

Waxer, Lise. 2000. En conga, bongo y campana: The rise of Colombian salsa. *Latin American Music Review* 21 (2): 118–168.

———. 2001. Las caleñas son como las flores: The rise of all-women bands in Cali, Colombia. *Ethnomusicology* 45 (2): 228–259.

———, ed. 2002. *Situating salsa: Global markets and local meanings in Latin popular music.* New York: Routledge.

Weston, Kath. 1993. Do clothes make the woman?: Gender, performance theory, and lesbian eroticism. *Genders* 17 (2): 1–21.

Wilcken, Louis, with Frisner Augustin. 1992. *The drums of vodou.* Tempe, AZ: White Cliffs Media Company.

Williams, Raymond. 1976. *Keyword: A vocabulary of culture and society.* New York: Oxford University Press.

———. 1977. *Marxism and literature.* London: Oxford University Press.

Willoughby, Heather. 2002. The sound of han: P'sanori, timbre, and a South Korean discourse of sorrow and lament. PhD diss., Columbia University.

Witmer, Barbara. 1997. *The violence mythos.* Albany: State University of New York Press.

Wolf, Eric. 1956. San José: Subcultures of a "traditional" coffee municipality. In *The people of Puerto Rico,* ed. Julian Steward, 171–264. Chicago: University of Illinois Press.

Yetnikoff, Walter, with David Ritz. 2004. *Howling at the moon.* New York: Broadway Books.

Yúdice, George. 2004. *The expediency of culture: Uses of culture in the global era.* Durham: Duke University Press.

Yúdice, George, and Ana Maria Ochoa. 2002. The Latin American music industry in an era of crisis. Paper prepared for the Global Alliance for Cultural Diversity, Division of Arts and Cultural Enterprise, Paris: UNESCO.

Index

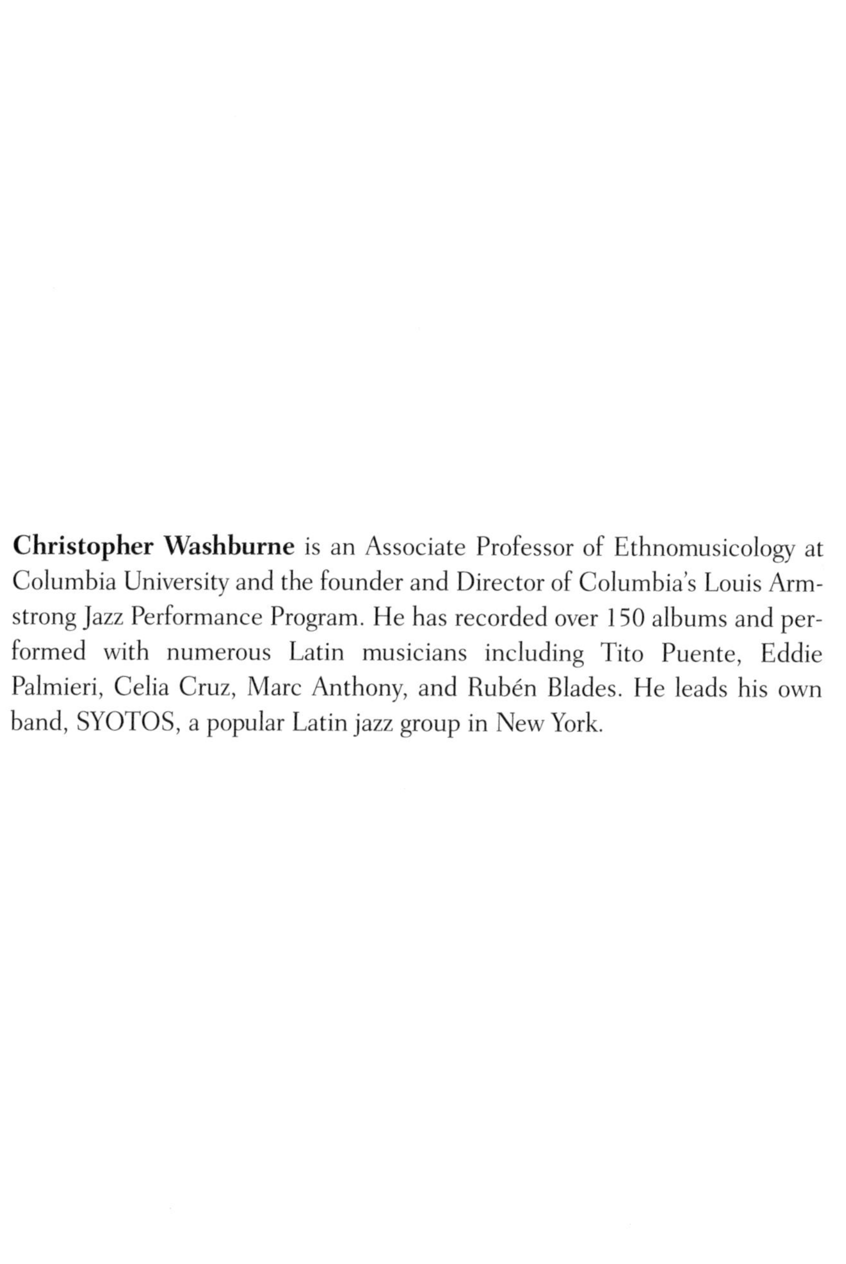

Christopher Washburne is an Associate Professor of Ethnomusicology at Columbia University and the founder and Director of Columbia's Louis Armstrong Jazz Performance Program. He has recorded over 150 albums and performed with numerous Latin musicians including Tito Puente, Eddie Palmieri, Celia Cruz, Marc Anthony, and Rubén Blades. He leads his own band, SYOTOS, a popular Latin jazz group in New York.